Advance Praise for

"Lisa E. Davis has been doggedly tracking the life of FBI informant Angela Calomiris for years. Cold War scholars anxiously anticipate publication of her research on this undercover agent who 'sang' on her 'friends' in the Photo League and beyond, destroying lives in the process under a guise of patriotic duty. In my research of the League, I witnessed aged members weep over its demise; at the heart of its downfall was Calomiris, a spy whose accusations left a long list of casualties. Davis weaves together the messy, often secretive strands of feminist, gay, labor, and political histories into a coherent narrative, a cautionary tale for all ages." —Lili Corbus, author of *Politics and Photography in America: From the New Deal into the Cold War*

"Lisa Davis has unearthed and brought to light what may well have been the most important political trial of the 20th Century, digging it out of the hidden history of J. Edgar Hoover's hateful hysteria where it has been buried for more than half a century. But this is not a story about history. It is about today. In reading this story—the fascinating tale of Hoover's lesbian informer—we not only learn news we desperately need to know—especially in today's Surveillance Society—we enjoy the learning." —Fred Jerome, author of *The Einstein File: J. Edgar Hoover's Secret War Against the World's Most Famous Scientist*

UNDERCOVER GIRL
The Lesbian Informant Who Helped the FBI Bring Down the Communist Party

LISA E. DAVIS

imagine!

For Joan Nestle, author and historian

An Imagine Book
Published by Charlesbridge
85 Main Street
Watertown, MA 02472
(617) 926-0329
www.imaginebooks.net

Library of Congress Cataloging-in-Publication Data
Names: Davis, Lisa E., author.
Title: Undercover girl : the lesbian informant who helped the FBI bring down the
    Communist Party / Lisa E. Davis.
Description: Watertown : Imagine Book, 2017.
Identifiers: LCCN 2016029416 (print) | LCCN 2016045044 (ebook) | ISBN
    9781623545222 (paperback) | ISBN 9781632892089 (ebook) | ISBN
    9781632892096 (ebook pdf)
Subjects: LCSH: Calomiris, Angela, 1916-1995. | Undercover operations--United
    States. | Photo League--History. | United States--History--20th century.
| BISAC: BIOGRAPHY & AUTOBIOGRAPHY / Women. | HISTORY / United
    States / 20th Century. | SOCIAL SCIENCE / Gay Studies.
Classification: LCC HV7911.C355 D38 2017 (print) | LCC HV7911.C355 (ebook) |
    DDC 363.25/931 [B] --dc23
LC record available at https://lccn.loc.gov/2016029416

Production supervision by Brian G. Walker
Cover design concept by Linda Kosarin/The Art Department

Printed in the United States of America
10 9 8 7 6 5 4 3 2 1

"What the Communists had that nobody else had was national and international connections with a point of view. There's nothing more powerful than a point of view."

—Ellenore Hittelman, in *Dorothy Healey Remembers*

"No one becomes an informer at the moment he informs; he's always been an informer, he's just been waiting for the opportunity."

—Arthur Laurents, in *Original Story By*

Contents

Acknowledgments

This type of investigation would not have been possible without the Freedom of Information Act (1967). Angela Calomiris's extensive FBI file tells the long story of a relationship between the Bureau and one of its informants. Other FBI files expose surveillance of individuals, particularly American photographers, and of the New York Photo League (1936-1951), which was early on classified as subversive and denounced publicly at the 1949 Smith Act trial of the National Board of the American Communist Party. The complete transcript of that trial, generously made available to me by the National Archives and Records Administration, Northeast Region, helps to define the painful transition from Franklin Roosevelt's progressive New Deal and the US war on fascism to the reactionary 1950s. We live in the shadow of that policy shift, and must try to understand it in depth.

For assistance with FBI files and material relative to the 1949 Smith Act trial, I am indebted to Veronica A. Wilson, the University of Pittsburgh, Johnstown; Fiona Dejardin of Hartwick College, Oneonta, New York; and Barbara J. Falk, Canadian Forces College, Toronto, Ontario, Canada. It was also my good fortune to know curators of fine photography, like Catherine Evans of the Carnegie Museum, Pittsburgh, and pre-eminent scholars, like Lili Corbus, whose early work on photography and politics in America set the standard for this type of investigation. Survivors of the New York Photo League and their families have kept the memory of the League alive so that future generations can evaluate its importance. Sincere thanks to filmmakers Nina Rosenblum and Daniel Allentuck, to photography historian Naomi Rosenblum, keeper of the Rosenblum Archive Collection, and to Pamela Gilbert-Bugbee for their kindness and support of this project.

But the original source for information about Calomiris—and a hiding place for secrets—remains the Lesbian Herstory Archives, Brooklyn, New York, which provided Melva Wade and her partner Mary Johnston with a home for an entire file cabinet full of papers and photographs left to their care. Discovered after Calomiris's death, this wealth of material ensured the survival of unusual insights and secrets about the McCarthy era. My thanks to Joan Nestle, Deborah Edel, Teddy Minucci, Saskia Scheffer, and other volunteer staff for their unfailing support.

I am also indebted to the precious collections open to scholars in New York City—research branches of the New York Public Library, and especially the Schomberg Center for Research in Black Culture, and the Miriam and Ira D. Wallach Division of Art, Prints and Photographs. The Tamiment Library & Robert F. Wagner Labor Archives at New York University are a unique and vital resource for anyone investigating the development of the America Left. Divisions of the Library of Congress, and especially the Motion Picture, Broadcasting and Recorded Sound Division, Prints and Photographs Division, together with Duplication Services, have all been generous with their time and energies

Without the history and confidences shared in interviews by people who knew Angela Calomiris personally, this book would not have been possible. But I am most indebted to the people who listened to me, sympathized, empathized, and assured me it was a story that needed telling. Thank you to Einstein scholar Fred Jerome, to Virginia Giordano, artist and friend to artists, to my patient and gentle spouse Lisa Tollner, and to my editor Donald Weise at Charlesbridge Publishing. If it becomes apparent to anyone, upon reading this book, that jailing leftists, keeping people from taking photographs, breaking up labor unions, and promoting racial inequality are somehow related, it will have all been worth it.

Introduction: Red Scare, Lavender Scare

The story of FBI informant Angela Calomiris (1915-1995)—sometimes "Angie" to old friends—would never have come to light if she had not testified for the prosecution at the 1949 Smith Act trial of the leaders of the American Communist Party, where she had worked undercover since 1942. The names of others, who had reported on Communist Party activities and collected the same money from the FBI as Angela, were not revealed because they did not take a public stance. In defiance of convention, Angela—whose lesbian identity was no secret to most of the people she came in contact with, including FBI agents—took a chance based on high expectations of even more money, greater fame, and a good job in the photography field through her FBI connections. But as months turned into years, Angela's star dimmed, and her hopes faded. McCarthyism also faded with the Senate censure of Joseph McCarthy, while the witch hunt for Communist sympathizers slowed down. Angela did not talk about her past, and the celebrity that had been hers.

She settled for the small real estate empire she had built in Provincetown, Massachusetts, at Land's End on Cape Cod. Many old-timers remember her as the former proprietor of Angel's Landing at 353 Commercial Street and a pillar of the community. She owned

more properties on Commercial Street—for a while the Firehouse
Leather shop—plus a house on Nickerson Street, a couple of lots
in Wellfleet, and seaside cottages in North Truro. There were people
in New York City who remembered Angela, too, old friends, dating
back forty or fifty years. Some of them respected her ambition,
determination, and what is sometimes called "entrepreneurship."
She was a small woman, a lesbian under five feet tall, but not the
delicate type. On the contrary, she was somewhat masculine, with
rugged features and very short hair. She had been born into a Greek
immigrant family on Manhattan's Lower East Side, but had risen
out of poverty against all odds. She always kept an apartment in
Greenwich Village, first on Jane Street, and then Horatio. At one time,
she owned a brownstone on West 12th Street, just off Greenwich
Avenue, in the Village. Hers was a real American success story.[1]

On the other hand, there were those who disliked her. They
thought her at best ruthless, at worst, conniving. Perhaps some
were envious of her success, and kept their distance. But as the years
turned into decades, rumors began to circulate about Angela's past,
from a time before settling in Provincetown and the real estate she
began to acquire in the 1960s. She had been involved somehow in
government spying during the Red Scare, her critics said. But more
specifically, in Greenwich Village, she had "turned in" lesbians to
the police and the FBI, and ruined lives and careers of people in the
photography business, which had been her first career—people in
the New York Photo League, an organization of professional and
amateur photographers, who had been kind to her. How kind they
had been and how she had betrayed them were not clear at first. The
stories dated back decades to the "McCarthy era," which began with
Senator Joseph McCarthy of Wisconsin waving a piece of paper in
front of the Republican Women's Club of Wheeling, West Virginia,
in 1950. He made headlines by claiming it was a list of 205 names of
known Communists working for the US State Department.

Angela's history with the New York Photo League went back
a lot further. Undoubtedly she came to the League, like so many
individuals with limited income, because of the inexpensive classes
and a real desire to do meaningful work in photography. But she did
not ever share the ideology that had inspired the original Workers

Film and Photo League (1931-1935). That beacon for idealists and leftists had explored innovations in the Soviet film industry, and had called for the production of American films that reflected the reality of the Great Depression. It was the beginning of documentary filmmaking in America.[2]

Born of the split between filmmakers and photographers, the Photo League, which lasted from 1936 to 1951, shared the artistic ideal of documenting reality. Still photography had come into its own by the 1930s, thanks to technical advances in film and the lightweight cameras that made for greater mobility. It was a great age for photojournalism, reflected in the launch of picture magazines like *Life* (1936) and *Look* (1937). But, even before McCarthy, the Photo League was suspect to government agencies like the FBI, because they advertised their classes in *The Daily Worker,* and took pictures of poor people—even poor African Americans. Their "Harlem Document" (1939), which showed the neighborhood in the depths of the Depression, attracted the attention of friends and detractors alike. Angela suggested, years later, that the photos were selected because they showed the worst aspects of the community, and she was sure that "if a picture could incite to riot, these pictures were just the ones to do it." On the other hand, she insisted that she sympathized with the Photo League's ideal of "documenting" contemporary reality. She loved the streets of Manhattan, she said, and wanted to show others "the many human dramas" she witnessed, "with no false props and no sentimental angles."[3]

Angela appears to have started studying at the Photo League in 1941, when they were renting studio and darkroom space on East 21st Street. In fact, that was the story she told the FBI when she presented her qualifications for the post of Confidential National Defense Informant in March 1942. It was a job created in the name of national security when the Bureau was empowered to investigate not just criminals but political subversives. Director J. Edgar Hoover, Washington's longest-serving bureaucrat (1924-1972), hired Angela and hundreds, perhaps thousands of other informants. This domestic undercover operation was financed by big budget increases ($10 million from 1941 to 1942 alone). The Bureau would have been pleased to have someone inside the League, an organization they already considered dangerous, perhaps subversive. By the time of Angela's initiation, it was already the subject of a local New York Office investigative file, and considered a force in the Communist propaganda war.[4]

While Angela was helpful to the Bureau's on-going surveillance of the Photo League, the larger target was the Communist Party of America (CPUSA), which under that name dated back to 1929. Joining the CPUSA and reporting back on names and activities would be Angela's principal job—and source of income—from 1942 to 1949.[5]

The FBI had watched the Party closely since its inception. But an increase in membership during the Depression and later, during World War II, when America was allied with the Soviet Union in the fight against Fascism, made J. Edgar Hoover and the Bureau uneasy. With an estimated 50-80,000 Party members nationwide, Joseph Stalin made the cover of *Time* magazine as Person of the Year (twice, 1940 and 1943), and New York City declared a "Stalingrad Day" to celebrate the Russian victory over the German army, finally accomplished, on February 2, 1943, after more than five months of fighting. As the tide of war turned, two years later, on April 25, 1945, American and Russian troops embraced and celebrated victory on the banks of the Elbe River in eastern Germany. The Russians were our allies and friends.

Hoover, on the other hand, did not expect our alliance with the Soviet Union to survive the war, and treasured memories of the first Red Scare after World War I. Recently appointed to the Justice Department by Attorney General A. Mitchell Palmer, a youthful Hoover (age twenty-four) had helped to organize the Palmer Raids (1919, 1920) on radical foreign-born leftists—especially anarchists—that resulted in numerous deportations. Like many others, Hoover was haunted by the specter of the Russian Revolution of 1917, and feared ideas brought from Europe that he considered alien to the American experience. Communism was one of those.

He intended to reduce the influence of American Communists, and the *annus mirabilis* of 1949 marked a giant step in that direction. While America's new enemies, the Russians, exploded a nuclear device, and Mao Zedong announced the triumph of the People's

Republic of China over America's ally Chiang Kai-shek, Hoover realized his dream of putting the CPUSA on trial for sedition. The trial took place in New York City's Federal Court House at Foley Square. Eleven members of the National Board of the CPUSA, men who had been labor union activists and Party members for years, had been indicted under the 1940 Smith Act (officially the Alien Registration Act) for "conspiracy to advocate the overthrow of the US Government by force and violence"—a bit of a stretch even for Red Scare hysteria. The eleven included Eugene Dennis, general secretary of the Party, whose name identifies the proceedings as *Dennis v. US*; several state chairmen, Robert Thompson for New York, Gus Hall for Ohio, Gilbert Green for Illinois, Carl Winter for Michigan; John Gates, editor of *The Daily Worker*; John B. Williamson, the Party's labor secretary; Jacob Stachel, education director; Irving Potash, vice-president of the Fur and Leather Workers Union, CIO; and the two African-American board members Henry Winston, organizational secretary, and Benjamin J. Davis. The latter was head of the Legislative Committee and a New York City Councilman representing Harlem. They were all accused of stealthily laying the groundwork for a "Soviet America," which would be prefaced, according to one prosecution witness, by a Red Army invasion from Siberia. Sworn testimony from Charles Nicodemus, former CPUSA member and Maryland local official of the Textile Workers Union, CIO, announced that the Russians would "invade Alaska down through Canada and they could even destroy Detroit." The trial had many such dramatic moments.[6]

One was the appearance of surprise witness Angela Calomiris, on April 26, 1949. She achieved instant fame at the 1949 trial with testimony, quoted in all the New York dailies, about the Communist Party's "conspiratorial devices" used "in teaching the need for violent revolution to set up a Soviet dictatorship." The press celebrated her as the all-American girl, certainly an unusual role for a lesbian in the 1940s. One of the period's most powerful journalists expressed gratitude for an Angela Calomiris, at a moment when federal government employees Alger Hiss and Judith Coplon had both been convicted of passing secrets to the Russians. Beautiful and sympathetic, Judith Coplon, formerly with the Justice Department in Washington, would have been, under other circumstances, a more likely candidate for all-American girl. But Angela won out, while ongoing hearings by Congressional committees also helped keep the country in a heightened state of hysteria. As the Korean War raged on, Julius and Ethel Rosenberg would be executed in 1953 for conspiracy to commit espionage.[7]

Angela spent five days on the witness stand, testifying to the dangers that the CPUSA represented to the labor movement, and particularly New York dockworkers. But her first target, and probably the principal reason she had been drafted into the prosecution line-up—the only woman to testify—was the Photo League. Already under attack from the US Attorney General's Office, which had placed the League on a December 1947 list of organizations labeled "totalitarian, fascist, Communist, or subversive," Angela provided additional ammunition. In answer to questions about her profession and associations, she named the Photo League as a place where she had received formal training, and identified Sid Grossman, according to Angela's testimony "director of the Photo League," as the person who had recruited her into the Communist Party. Grossman never worked in photography in New York again, and by 1955, he was dead, age forty-two. The Red Scare killed.[8]

Angela, on the other hand, like other FBI informant/witnesses before and after her, tried to capitalize on the free publicity the trial had brought her. And like so many of them, she published a book—*Red Masquerade: Undercover for the F.B.I.* in 1950—gave interviews and lectures. Her new career was lucrative, and she hoped to sell her story to TV and the movies, the way her fellow informant/witnesses had done. They all published books in the 1950s. Some of the more successful were Herbert Philbrick's *I Led Three Lives: Citizen, "Communist," Counterspy* (1952), which later became a long-running TV series; and Matt Cvetic's *I Was a Communist for the FBI*, originally published as a series of articles in *The Saturday Evening Post,* and made into a very successful feature film (1951) by Warner Brothers. Elizabeth Bentley published *Out of Bondage* (1951), followed up the next year by Whittaker Chamber's *Witness,* and in 1955 by Harvey Matusow's *False Witness.* As a vital component of Red Scare culture and history, the often bizarre lives, careers and media successes of these individuals have become the subjects of recent biographies—including *Whittaker Chambers, A Biography* (1997) by Sam Tanenhaus, and Kathryn S. Olmsted's *Red Spy Queen: A Biography of Elizabeth Bentley* (2002).[9]

Apparently, Angela had found tolerance, perhaps acceptance as a lesbian and fellow outsider, among the artistic types of the Photo League. Even the CPUSA seemed to appreciate her hard work and offered her positions of responsibility. On the other hand, if the FBI agents, or Hoover, knew she was a lesbian, and considering her masculine appearance a rather "obvious" one at that, they did not seem to mind. Reliable informers were not easy to come by, and some did not last long. It was one of those rare moments in American history when there was something worse than being a lesbian, and that was being a Communist.

Of course, the CPUSA had many gay and lesbian members, people of political conscience like Harry Hay, later founder of the Mattachine Society in 1950 on the West Coast, one of the earliest gay rights organizations in the United States, probably second only to Chicago's Society for Human Rights (1924). But Angela preferred the FBI, who told her how much they liked her photographs, and paid her. The issue of compensation is vital because her problems were, from a blighted childhood forward, essentially economic. Her immigrant father had died when she was seven years old, and her mother had sent her along to an orphanage with an older sister. By 1930, according to the US Census, she was at home again with her mother, who had moved from the Lower East Side to Brooklyn, but Angela did not linger. As soon as she was old enough, she left and never looked back, telling people her mother was dead because she wanted to sever all ties with her past. She lived in Greenwich Village from the late 1930s on, back when the Village was the Village—when apartments were cheap, and creative people could afford to live there.

The hardships of the Great Depression, together with being a lesbian in a hostile environment where one could get beaten up or worse, would have taken a toll. But a childhood spent in the Sevilla Home for Children in the Bronx, an institution for destitute girls five to ten years old, would have left an indelible scar. By turns, charming and fair-minded, cold-blooded and a phony, Angela was always intelligent and knew how to please—and to deceive, and to hang tough. With the FBI she was demanding, even defiant. She was a complex, probably troubled person.

Other gay people caught up in the Lavender Scare did not fare as well as Angela. The war had brought young draftees and volunteers in record numbers into training camps, and too many of them (to suit the military) had turned out to be gay. Unable to identify and banish everyone, commanding officers put the more flagrant GIs into drag shows to entertain the troops. Butch women maintained and repaired military vehicles and drove for the motor pool. But with the usual excuse of safeguarding military readiness and cohesion, stricter screening procedures were put into place. As the war dragged on, a variety of tags—*habitual homosexual, sexual pervert, true sodomist, confirmed pervert*—were devised to identify and muster out servicemen and women. Punishment was a dishonorable blue discharge, which made you ineligible for postwar GI benefits—federally subsidized home loans, college loans, job training, hospital care, and cash bonuses. Such a discharge would also jeopardize employment opportunities in civilian life.[10]

After the war, homosexuals were targeted again. An ongoing purge in Washington, DC, decimated the ranks of civil servants who had come to the nation's capital to work in New Deal federal programs, and later for the war effort. Gay people were thought to be weak-willed pawns, seduced and blackmailed into spying for our former allies, now our enemies, the Russians. "Lavender lads" from the State Department (ninety-one of them) were removed as security risks. On Capitol Hill, the witch hunt picked up speed. In defense of Western Christian civilization, a Republican Congressman from Nebraska, Arthur L. Miller, assured the House "that homosexuality goes back to the Orientals, long before the time of Confucius; that the Russians are strong believers in homosexuality." A conservative Senator, Kenneth Wherry, the Republican floor leader, also from Nebraska, followed up with news of "a conspiracy of subversive and moral perverts" and "a world list of gays who could be enlisted for espionage, sabotage, and terrorism." According to Senator Wherry, the list had been compiled by Adolf Hitler, and had fallen into the hands of Joseph Stalin. Fear stalked Washington, DC, whose gay population had increased during the war years.[11]

Other prominent queers, like Angela, took an anti-Communist stand, either because they believed there was some real threat to national security, or because it was a good cover. Nasty rumors suggest the latter. As David Ehrenstein has declared, in his groundbreaking *Open Secret: Gay Hollywood 1928-1998*, so many of the McCarthy era's key figures who were closeted homosexuals— "Roy Cohn, Whittaker Chambers, J. Edgar Hoover, and McCarthy himself"—were spurred on in their anti-Communist zeal by fear of being found out. With a slightly different cast of characters, one of Angela's fellow FBI informants, the notorious and flamboyant Harvey Matusow, who was not gay, assigned queers a leading role in the Red Scare. "See," Matusow explained in a 1990's interview, "Hoover and Cardinal Spellman and Cohn were part of a kind of closet gay group. Cohn's rise to political power came because of his gay relationship with Cardinal Spellman. It was a high-level group of closet gays who kind of kept to themselves. If you look at Nazi Germany, there was a similar group in Germany that built the Nazi Party." While Matusow's comparison of Red Scare gays with the homosexual leadership of Ernst Rohm's SA (*Sturmabteilung*/Storm Battalion), the early paramilitary wing of the Nazi Party, may be a bit exaggerated, both had Communists and Communism as primary targets.[12]

Joseph McCarthy himself, middle-aged and unmarried until 1953, was sometimes the subject of homosexual innuendoes. His association with Roy Cohn, chief counsel to his Permanent Subcommittee on Investigations (of the Senate Committee on Government Operations), did him no good in this regard, particularly as the scandal broke over Cohn's attempts to get his friend, the young, rich, and handsome David Schine, a commission in the US Army and a stateside posting when he was drafted. Lillian Hellman once referred to the bachelor combo of McCarthy, Cohn, and Schine as "Bonnie, Bonnie and Clyde."[13]

Rumors about Roy Cohn's sexual orientation date from the time of the Army-McCarthy hearings in the early 1950s. But because he was a powerful figure in his own right and close friend to men yet more powerful than he, his secret life only came under public scrutiny after his death from AIDS in 1986. Subsequently his biographer Nicholas von Hoffman provided more revelations, and Tony Kushner's *Angels in America* pulled back the curtain for all the world to see. Cohn is a character in *Millennium Approaches*, where in Act 3, Scene 5, Ethel Rosenberg visits him to announce his imminent death. He also stars in the recent film *Ptown Diaries*, which gives ample coverage to sexual escapades on the Cape.[14]

A secret history also lurks behind one of the McCarthy era's most famous episodes, once dubbed the "Trial of the Century." Whittaker Chambers, a former American Communist and courier for Soviet operatives, accused Alger Hiss, a former State Department employee, of being a Communist and passing documents to the Russians in the 1930s. If you were searching for spies in the State Department (left over from FDR's New Deal administrations) or liked publicity (like the Freshman Congressman from California, Richard M. Nixon, a member of the House Un-American Activities Committee), Chambers was a Republican answer to prayer. But he was also the subject of many rumors. These were substantiated in Chambers' secret confession to the FBI that he had struggled with "tendencies" and had a history of one-night stands up and down the East Coast between New York and Washington in the course of his spy missions. But when he broke with Communism in 1938, he swore, he had also given up homosexuality.[15]

Nobody much believed him, especially not Hiss' stepson Timothy Hobson, who, long after the fact, called the whole Chambers/Alger Hiss incident a "closet case." In 2007, in a declaration before a day-long conference at New York University on the Alger Hiss case, Hobson, age eighty and a doctor of medicine, said a short, dumpy Chambers was in love with the refined, good-looking Hiss, the quintessential New Dealer—part of FDR's American Delegation to the Yalta Conference (1945), later secretary-general of the United Nations Charter Conference, then president of the Carnegie Endowment for International Peace. According to Hobson, who is gay and was given a blue discharge from the Navy during the war, Hiss was quite naïve about homosexuality. Never imagining that Chambers was attracted to him, Hiss could not have gauged the sense of rejection that inspired the stories fabricated and told on the witness stand—about visiting the Hiss family, a close friendship, and spying.[16]

Alger Hiss was finally convicted of perjury in 1950, for lying about knowing Chambers and for passing documents, and served forty-four months in Lewisburg (Pennsylvania) Federal Prison. He spent the rest of his long life (1904-1996) trying to exonerate himself. Anti-Communists fared better. Ronald Reagan awarded the Presidential Medal of Freedom posthumously to Whittaker Chambers in 1984.[17]

But perhaps the biggest anti-Communist closet case of them all was J. Edgar Hoover. Since the 1940s, gossip within the gay community had identified Hoover as one of those perverts the Congress railed against. In interviews, Allen Ginsberg recounted beguiling stories of Hoover on the prowl from Washington to New York City, and suspected that the FBI boss' reluctance to acknowledge the existence of organized crime stemmed from the Mafia having some compromising evidence on Hoover. More scandalous stories of dubious authenticity surfaced over the years, like the one repeated by Anthony Summers in his biography of Hoover, *Official and Confidential*, about Hoover in a fluffy black gown at New York's Plaza Hotel. One expert historian of the FBI and certainly no fan of Hoover's, Athan Theoharis, took time out to refute such talk. The Director, who was adept at intimidating those in high places (and low) on whom he had the goods and knew how the system worked, would not have taken chances with his own career. Nowadays, however, more speculation about Hoover—his relationship with FBI second-in-command Clyde Tolson, even his mother—has played out on the big screen in Clint Eastwood's *J. Edgar* (2011), with Leonardo DiCaprio in the title role. Almost everyone seems to suspect that J. Edgar had secrets.[18]

Angela would have done well to stay on Hoover's good side. But that is another story. During the war years, at least, she did well as she rose through local Communist Party ranks to positions, like that of financial secretary of her branch, which gave her access to information—names, addresses, dues paid. She was a good and loyal confidential informant, and safe from recriminations as long as she did not break her cover. But once she took the witness stand at Foley Square, and named names of old friends, she was labeled—the way informers had been labeled from time immemorial—fink, stool pigeon, rat.

No one seems to know if, in the end, Angela had regrets about betraying old comrades. She would have liked the photojournalist job that the FBI had probably promised, or a spot as technical advisor for a movie or TV show about her spy career. And because she had known poverty from childhood and through the Great Depression, she would certainly have liked to make a lot more money off her short-lived celebrity.

The CPUSA, on the other hand, suffered a grave defeat. All eleven defendants in the Foley Square trial were sentenced to five years in federal prison except for Robert Thompson, recipient of his country's second highest military honor, the Distinguished Service Cross for heroism in the Pacific during the war. Thompson got three years. Fifteen more trials of the American Communist leadership followed, with 106 convictions. With its leaders in prison or on trial, the Party, as the song goes, was pretty much over, and the fear of Russian hordes attacking the United States and installing a dictatorship (of the proletariat?) should have subsided. Instead, the panic grew and spread, and would go on to become the Cold War that would last until the dissolution of the Soviet Union in 1991. Even an architect of American policy like George Kennan, one-time US Ambassador to Moscow, finally came to the conclusion that the whole thing had been an "unnecessary, fearfully expensive and disoriented process."[19]

Meanwhile, Angela's was a life touched by historic events, and she came to know many famous and near-famous people, including powerful figures in the anti-Communist network. A closer look at her life and times can teach us many things. It shows clearly how the FBI operated through its corps of informants, how America came to put people on trial for their political beliefs, how perennial issues like labor and race figured into the mix, and how the Red Scare swept all before it. Gay people and survivors of the Lavender Scare may, of course, understand why Angela, as a perennial outsider, made a break for the inside track when she got the chance. But she chose badly, and ended up on the wrong side of history.

1. Village Gossip

Angela Calomiris took her time emerging from the closet as informant/witness. Vague rumors about government connections and stories about famous people she had known made the rounds in the gay community. But no one came forward with significant details until the 1980s, more than thirty years after Angela's appearance on the witness stand. The McCarthy era spawned great controversy—and especially bitterness toward informants—and was generally not a topic for conversation. An older lesbian who had known Angela well in the homosexual underworld of Greenwich Village finally broke the silence, but quite by accident and unintentionally. She was Buddy Kent (aka Bubbles Kent, "exotic dancer," aka Malvina Schwartz of East New York, Brooklyn) who, like Angela, had lived in the Village since the late 1930s. In an interview with gay historians, Buddy touched on a variety of topics about a time when unconventional people—artists, Bohemians, political radicals—flocked to the Village, and lesbians felt safe from catcalls and threats of violence. But it was also a time when identities were closely guarded, when silence and loyalty were community values. Not unlike other secret and semi-secret societies (the Mafia, the American Communist Party), the less outsiders knew about the gay world, the better, particularly sworn enemies like the police. While gays threatened with exposure at mainstream jobs were routinely blackmailed right up until the Stonewall uprising, as an entertainer working in drag shows in downtown nightclubs of the 1940s (the 181 Club, 181 Second Avenue at East 12th Street, and the Moroccan Village, 23 West 8th Street), Buddy Kent had the advantage of the best in protection from the Mafia that owned and ran those establishments.[1]

Buddy did not intend to name names, in fact she never did. Instead, like a mystery writer, she wove a series of clues into her recording with Joan Nestle, co-founder of the Lesbian Herstory Archives, who conducted the interview. Sharing old photo albums (now lost to history), Buddy mentioned several gay friends and acquaintances long dead, which was permitted if they had been dead long enough. She added a few observations about Eleanor Roosevelt in the Village before Joan asked her, "Who else would you see in the street sometime, or hanging around here [the Village]?"

Buddy didn't hesitate. Remembering stage and screen personalities she had known, celebrities whose names still resonated with a contemporary public, she began, "Not too much theatricals, 'cause they were afraid then. But Judy Holliday ..." Buddy paused. She had named one of the brightest screen stars of the 1950s, who had won an Oscar for Best Actress as Billie Dawn in *Born Yesterday,* a role Judy had created on the Broadway stage. Other nominees that year included Bette Davis for *All About Eve* and Gloria Swanson for *Sunset Boulevard.* Judy Holliday (née Judith Tuvim) was a big moneymaker for the irascible President of Columbia Pictures Harry Cohn, and her reputation had to be protected.

The plot thickened when Buddy added, her voice a bit altered, "She was going with a female who was a cop." This was not idle Village gossip. Other sources, Boze Hadleigh's *Hollywood Lesbians* among them, suggest that Judy Holliday went through a lesbian "phase" before she "discovered" men, married David Oppenheim, and gave birth to her son Jonathan. Of course, Judy was no longer a teenager when, according to Buddy, she was "going with a female who was a cop."[2]

This brief foray into Judy's love life was followed up by more sensational gossip about her unnamed girlfriend/lover. The girlfriend had her own story, Buddy explained, because "somebody blew the whistle on her being a Communist. And she had quite a bad time. She couldn't get work for about eight years because of this."

"Was this in the fifties?" Nestle was quick to respond. "During the McCarthy period?" These would have been serious charges at a time when the hunt for Communists, former Communists, and Communist sympathizers ("fellow travelers") was at its height.

Significantly, Buddy pushed the date back a bit, trying to pinpoint the events she had described. "During the war, I think," she replied. "1946, yeah, '46." Then, a little fuzzy on chronology, Buddy jumped ahead to the events that defined the Red Scare for most Americans of her generation—the trial and execution of Julius and Ethel Rosenberg, the "Atomic Spies," convicted of conspiracy to commit espionage.

"Everything was with the Rosenbergs," Buddy said. "What year was it with the Rosenbergs? That was about the era. With the spy case."

While Buddy may not have been political in the larger sense, within the closeted homosexual world of the Village, she did take a stand on principle—the one about not informing on gay people. Returning to the betrayal of Judy Holliday's girlfriend, Buddy struggled to temper her anger with compassion. "And it was a gay girl who blew the whistle," she blurted out. "In fact, I wasn't friendly towards her until quite recently. 'Cause I figure you can't have somebody wear a hair shirt the rest of their lives. 'Cause everybody's allowed one mistake in their life."

Careful not to name anyone still living, neither the informer nor Judy's girlfriend, she added, "In fact she [the informer] is around today and I don't want to mention her name. [...] But it meant some good jobs for her [the girlfriend] and even though she turned, you know, turncoat." It seems significant that Buddy considered the "turncoat" less morally reprehensible than the informer who denounced her. Nobody liked a snitch, as Victor Navasky reminds us in his classic blacklist history *Naming Names*, and the snitches did not seem to like themselves much either.[3]

Listening to Buddy Kent's interview, one has to wonder who the unnamed informant might have been who laid waste a career ("a female who was a cop") with the New York Police Department, which had offered few real opportunities to women before the late 1930s. Buddy described the stoolpigeon in different terms when she summed up: "And there was 'Petite Feminine Girl on Stand Tells Her Undercover Work for the FBI.' And that was this dyke who put the finger on one girl who was on the police force and she was going with Judy Holliday. And she [the girlfriend] never really came out of it well. She was in therapy after that."[4]

By adding newspaper headlines and a courtroom context, Buddy deepened the mystery. When did the FBI hire lesbians to work undercover? And if this one had made headlines when she appeared in court as a witness, what had she been witness to?

Without a name for the informer (or the girlfriend) their secrets were safe. By chance, it was Victor Navasky who provided information that brought everyone out of the closet. Early on in *Naming Names*, he mentions some "confidential informants" who reported on Communist Party activities to the FBI, and cites two who "surfaced to testify in the key 1949 Smith Act trial in Foley Square." One was an Angela Calomiris, whose name Navasky repeated, and quoted extensively from *Red Masquerade,* the book she had published about her undercover work. He listed other informant/witnesses who had written books, too, about their brush with the Red Menace, and sold their scripts to radio, TV, even the movies. "Angela Calomiris," he writes, "a witness in the Dennis trial, won a citation for patriotic assistance to the FBI."[5]

Navasky struck a resonant chord. That name Calomiris, Angela Calomiris. It was that name, and Buddy Kent on tape, out of the blue changing the subject, volunteering:

> You know Angie Calamares [as Buddy pronounced it] has started coming to our socials. [...] Fell in love with SAGE [Senior Action in a Gay Environment]. I kept telling her 'Come, come.' She says, '... That cornball shit.' I said, 'No, no, Angie, you'll like it. It's really not ...' She was there till the last one. She had a ball.

Calamares, Calomiris, Angie, Angela. Maybe Buddy Kent had

revealed the name without meaning to. She would have welcomed a new supporter (Angie "Calamares") to the SAGE socials, but she could not forget that this was also the FBI informer who had made accusations against Judy Holliday's girlfriend.

At that time, in 1983, there were many people around who remembered. Others confessed that they had known "an Angie Calomiris." "Oh, sure, but I didn't like her," said Miriam Wolfson, who once lived on West 4th Street in the Village. "She was very mannish." When Wolfson was confronted with an ancient copy of *Red Masquerade: Undercover for the F.B.I.*, purchased online, she quipped, "Angie wrote a book? You gotta be kiddin'." The masquerade in the title was Angela pretending to be a Communist in order to spy on them. A second masquerade would have been pretending to be straight in order to pull all that off. When Miriam was offered a passage or two to read from *Red Masquerade*, she observed, "She's talking about picking out the right dress for the trial and doing her hair. That would be the only time she ever wore a dress!" In another interview, Morry Baer, who had worked to retirement for the New York Police Department, said she had no idea how or why Angela had gotten involved with the FBI. "She didn't talk about it." Morry paused. "You know she ran Angel's Landing in Ptown for years. We used to go up there." That was prime Provincetown real estate that would have increased exponentially in value over the years.[6]

But of those people with stories to share, nobody remembered anything about a trial—"the key 1949 Smith Act trial in Foley Square […] the Dennis trial" that Navasky identifies with Angela. As luck would have it, a collection of papers left to the Lesbian Herstory Archives in Brooklyn by the executrix of Angela's estate held the key to that and other mysteries. The Special Collections Boxes #99-02, labeled "Angela Calomiris," brought to life in lurid detail the opening salvos of the Red Scare and Angela's role in it. She had made the front pages of all the New York dailies of the era—the *Journal-American*, the *World-Telegram*, the *Herald Tribune*. The *Daily News*, the *Post*, and the *Times* all celebrated her testimony as a witness for the prosecution at the Dennis trial. As evidence of the anti-Communist celebrity she had enjoyed, there were letters from all over the country—from admirers, from self-identified amateur spies, her literary agent,

Diarmuid Russell, of the prestigious Russell & Volkening agency, her lover Myrtis Johnson, aka Marta Robinet, writer of short stories, newspaper, and magazine pieces (and the sister-in-law of her FBI recruiter), and the Freedoms Foundation, Inc. of Valley Forge, Pennsylvania, that wanted to give her an award for patriotism. In addition, universities, churches, and synagogues invited her to speak and sought her advice about the danger Communism represented to the country while she pitched her *Red Masquerade* story to TV and film executives. Maybe Angela had collected all of this material, and kept it for forty-five years, because she recognized its historical importance. Or perhaps, like FBI informant/witness Harvey Matusow, she found it hard to discard anything mentioning her name. It was testimony to a fleeting fame and respect she would never know again. Working for the FBI and the anti-Communist cause was the most important thing that ever happened to her, and she had not wanted to let it go. Acquiring properties and managing real estate, while lucrative, did not compare. The material that had found its way to the Lesbian Herstory Archives was in pristine condition, and told the story of Angela Calomiris, undercover girl, in dramatic detail.[7]

Angela even saved one death threat, mailed to her right after the Communist defendants in the trial were convicted of "conspiracy to advocate the overthrow of the government by force and violence." Since her would-be assassin (who had "no use for a Rat") had obligingly included his name and return address on the envelope, there was probably little to fear. His threats, at any rate, were counterbalanced by a musical composition stored away among her papers. It was dedicated to her by an unsung American patriot, Julius Rutin of New York City, who praised her service in defense of the nation. Dated 1951, the song "Who is Angela Kalamiras [sic]?" says she was someone who, according to Rutin's lyrics, "made us care for our Country" and alerted us to be "on the watch" for "danger, danger in the world." Rutin also composed an "Einsenhower March" and a third piece, "Soldiers in Overalls," which he shared with Angela.[8]

Despite a few sour notes of dissent, the fan mail in her archives was overwhelmingly positive. She had become, like other informant/witnesses during the heyday of the Red Scare, a "folk hero," as Navasky defined it, a sort of "Saint George who could slay the [Red] dragon." No longer an outsider, a "freak," or a "mannish lesbian," for once in her life, Angela Calomiris had gotten herself on the winning team, and she intended to take full advantage.[9]

To judge from the book reviews she preserved from all the New York papers, the publication of *Red Masquerade* in late 1950 had revived interest in her courtroom appearance and catapulted her to minor stardom. Schedules for radio and TV appearances traced her progress toward media celebrity and showed her commentary to be much in demand. Network radio programs like CBS' *You and Communism*, with conservative political analyst Dwight Cooke, and *Inside Communism*, with Bill Slater, who doubled as a popular sportscaster, analyzed evidence of a Red conspiracy that threatened America. NBC's nighttime espionage thriller *David Harding, Counterspy* usually featured fictional heroic Americans fighting subversives who were trying to bring down the government and take away our freedoms. But this time, in a plug for Angela and her book, it was an "average citizen" who had faced danger "so that free men will continue to remain free." Taken as a whole, the press clippings and radio shows were reminders of how fear of Communism—foreign and domestic—had come to dominate the American conscience by the early 1950s.[10]

On *Inside Communism*, Angela was lucky enough to be paired with prominent reporter for the *New York World-Telegram*, Victor Lasky, who had won fame with his coverage of the Alger Hiss trials where Hiss had finally been convicted of perjury, and with a book he had recently co-authored—*Seeds of Treason: The True Story of the Hiss-Chambers Tragedy*. Angela and Lasky were, according to the host, "two noted experts on the mental poisons of Communism." Lasky seemed quite fond of her— "a slight figure of a woman" as he described Angela—and praised "her exciting book, *Red Masquerade*." He would prove a good friend, who would later give her another boost on the road to stardom.[11]

But confirmation of Buddy Kent's story, about Angela's betrayal of "one girl who was on the police force and she was going with Judy Holliday," came from another source. Together with the papers in the Lesbian Herstory Archives, it is the extensive file the FBI kept on Angela over a period of fifteen years that takes the reader deep into that fearful world of the postwar Red Scare. Spies are allegedly everywhere, everyone is spying on everyone else, and leftist sentiment (even dating back twenty years) may merit swift punishment. Angela, with all the pent-up anger of an abandoned child and the driving ambition of an intelligent, disadvantaged, marginalized woman, took to the Red-baiting game with a vengeance.[12]

A series of memos from 1950 that debated whether she should testify at a hearing by the New York City Board of Education, which had just fired eight public school teachers "alleged to be CP members or sympathizers," reveals that Angela had shared a helpful tip with the FBI. "In her opinion one [name blacked out] who has a responsible desk job in the Women's Bureau of the NYCPD was a definite security risk." Reporting on "a social gathering on New Year's Eve about three years ago," Angela said she had "heard [name blacked out] mouth the Party line so effectively that she persuaded the entire gathering to think as she did, that is, sympathetic to Henry Wallace, the Progressive Party, the *Daily Worker* and the CP in general." Here Angela echoed the right-wing line, as she often did, this time identifying Henry Wallace, FDR's Vice-President before Truman, who ran against Truman in 1948 on the Progressive Party ticket, with Communism and Communists. As an official third party, the Progressive Party was committed to preserving the New Deal and to peaceful co-existence with the Soviet Union. If Wallace had been elected, postwar American history might have played out differently.[13]

The story Angela told about a subversive policewoman who was voting for Henry Wallace continued, with more names blacked out in the FBI style, to conceal identities and frustrate scholars and other readers. Sometimes entire paragraphs or pages are blacked out. But near the end of this particular memo, a FBI censor made a rare slip of the black permanent marker and failed to conceal the name "Cohen." Give or take a letter, that slip-up proved Angela's target was, indeed, Yetta Cohn, cited throughout Judy Holliday biographies (and elsewhere) as a one-time lover, and subsequently lifelong friend and confidante. She had been, in fact, a New York City policewoman and editor of the Department's newsletter, *Spring 3100*. In some versions of her story, Yetta quit after she was called in by her superiors for interrogation about her politics. In Buddy Kent's version, she was forced out thanks to Angela.[14]

In between lay Judy Holliday's command performance, in 1952, before the Senate Internal Security Subcommittee (SISS, the Senate equivalent of HUAC) under Senator Pat McCarran (Democrat-Nevada) that investigated "subversive infiltration" of the television, radio, and entertainment industry. Judy was summoned alongside singer Burl Ives, comic Sam Levenson, and actor Philip Loeb. In what is undoubtedly more than a coincidence, the lawyer hired by Columbia Pictures to help clear Judy of all charges of subversive sympathies was Kenneth M. Bierly, Angela's FBI recruiter, with whose sister-in-law, writer Marta Robinet, Angela was having a long-term affair. It is difficult to imagine that Angela did not have Ken Bierly's ear to inform and advise. Judy survived her appearance before the McCarran Committee by playing the role of dumb blonde that had won her the Academy Award. Her ordeal illustrates the savagery of a process that ravaged the lives of many Red Scare victims. She had already been listed in *Red Channels: The Report of Communist Influence in Radio and Television*, compiled and published by Ken Bierly and his partners at American Business Consultants/ *Counterattack* in June 1950. Among the pages and pages of artists and writers—from Leonard Bernstein to Arthur Miller, Dashiell Hammett to Gypsy Rose Lee, Pete Seeger to Orson Welles—*Red Channels* found room for Judy Holliday, just before Lena Horne. She had also been attacked by right-wing groups like the Catholic War Veterans, who had pegged her for a leftie and picketed theaters showing *Born Yesterday*. The McCarran Committee also saw fit to question Judy about Yetta Cohn, who was defended vigorously by her old Village companion as "the most blameless creature, the most patriotic and honest creature." But the hearing and the three-year radio and TV blacklist that followed doubtless took their toll. Perhaps her health was also compromised by the stress of public life and a demanding show business career. A few years later, Judy was diagnosed with breast cancer, to which she succumbed after a long struggle in 1965, age forty-three. The Red Scare and the blacklist could devastate lives.[15]

Buddy Kent did not know about all that and merely passed on

the story the way it had been told to her—blaming Angela. In Village lesbian circles, while identities were closely guarded from outsiders, virtually everybody knew everybody, and there was more than enough gossip to go around. Angela's spying had made her many enemies among lesbians who knew and liked Yetta, and considered Judy, despite her marriage, one of their own. In the Waverly Place apartment that she and David Oppenheim rented, gay people and theater people (especially of a leftist persuasion) mingled freely. According to her biographer Will Holtzman, there were "new faces like Carson McCullers, Jane Bowles, John La Touche, and Arthur Laurents." It would be hard to imagine a gayer gathering.[16]

The first entry in Angela's FBI file located her residence at 9 Jane Street, between Greenwich Avenue and West Fourth Street, only a few blocks away from Judy's apartment. Both lay in the heart of the Village. Long a haven for political radicals and unconventional people of all sorts, it was not somewhere you would have expected to find an FBI informant. It was also not the place you would have expected to find the nation's First Lady. But Eleanor Roosevelt, wife of Franklin Delano Roosevelt, maintained a residence in the Village for more than fifteen years, and had many friends among that generation of strong independent women.[17]

A single sheet from among Angela's papers on file at the Archives established the remarkable connection between her and Mrs. Roosevelt—by that time one of the most respected public figures of her day, the only female member of the US Delegation to the first sessions of the United Nations, and the chairperson of the Drafting Committee that authored the "Universal Declaration of Human Rights." Harry Truman had called her "the First Lady of the World." That piece of paper, a "memo of Network radio dates for Angela Calomiris" as confirmed in mid-November, 1950, announced an "Interview by Mrs. Eleanor Roosevelt, already recorded," to be played over the NBC Network on December 1.[18]

Was it possible that Angela had actually shared a microphone with Eleanor Roosevelt? The former First Lady's media career, independent of her own and her husband's political interests, is well documented. Since the 1930s she had written a daily syndicated newspaper column called "My Day." In 1950, she began broadcasting on her own radio show *Today with Mrs. Roosevelt,* and premiered a half-hour Sunday afternoon TV program called *Mrs. Roosevelt Meets the Public.*

Angela's guest appearance on the radio show—broadcasting from the Park Sheraton Hotel (now the Park Central), on Seventh Avenue between 55th and 56th Streets—represented a high point in her anti-Communist career. But she would always tell everyone that she had known Mrs. Roosevelt back when they both lived in Greenwich Village.

2. Eleanor Roosevelt and Village People

Part of Angela's heterosexual masquerade, as described in *Red Masquerade*, was her contention that she had "naturally drifted into Greenwich Village" because she "enjoyed living in an art center" where she "met a great many friendly people" with whom she "found a lot in common." According to her, one of those people was Eleanor Roosevelt. Prone to the kind of exaggeration that had made her a success on the witness stand, where a grain of truth was enough, Angela repeated that tale for years. A great storyteller, according to old friends, she also relished any connection she had to a prominent person.[1]

Decades after the fact, she shared with skeptical Provincetown acquaintances that she had been "a gofer for Eleanor Roosevelt in New York." Joy McNulty, proprietor of Provincetown's Lobster Pot restaurant on Commercial Street, "wasn't sure this was true," but Angela could make you "laugh so with her stories. She was very funny." Because by that time, memories of the trial and her celebrity had faded, and Angela had chosen not to talk about her FBI career, it was unlikely that anyone had read the original version in *Red Masquerade*. There she stated that she had worked for $18 per week "as a glorified errand girl" for Esther Lape. As Angela points out,

"Miss Lape was close to Eleanor Roosevelt," then added that "the First Lady used to breeze in for surprise visits, Malvina Thompson trailing along with Mrs. Roosevelt's overladen briefcase." Noticing that the worn case was coming unstitched, Ms. Thompson, long-time personal assistant to Mrs. Roosevelt and a character well-known to a contemporary public that took an interest in details of the Roosevelts' lives, chose a star-struck Angela to go "out to have a shoemaker sew the briefcase up." Angela ran all the way "for fear Mrs. Roosevelt would be gone" before she could get back with the repaired briefcase. No one would have remembered a brief moment involving the "gofer," though Angela would have been sure to remind Eleanor Roosevelt when next they met.[2]

According to those who remembered her, Angela was ambitious and determined. But it is anybody's guess how she got the job working for Esther Lape, a journalist, and director of the American Foundation for Social Research, the organization she founded to promote causes she believed in. Pressing for US participation after World War I in the Permanent Court of International Justice, an agency of the League of Nations and predecessor to the International Court of Justice, and the creation of a US national health-care program were two favorites. The US failure to join the League of Nations sealed the fate of the former, and the latter is still a source of hot debate. Lape shared her home in the Village with another strong, capable, independent woman, her partner Elizabeth Read, a graduate of Smith College and the University of Pennsylvania Law School. They were among the "New Women" of the Village—educated professionals, politically astute, deeply involved in the struggles of their times, and often in the public eye.[3]

Some of those New Women were lesbians, but gay or straight, they were generally stalwarts of the National Woman's Party, the League of Women Voters, the Women's Committee of the Democratic Party, and related social and political organizations. The tolerant and ample closet that was Greenwich Village in its heyday had always welcomed new ideas and novel styles, bringing together artists, writers, teachers, and political radicals of all stripes. Feminists advocating for the vote for women (finally conceded in 1920) mingled with pacifists, Socialists, and Anarchists who saw a cooperative commonwealth as the future of America.[4]

Back in New York after FDR's tenure in Washington as Assistant Secretary of the Navy under Woodrow Wilson, the Village became Mrs. Roosevelt's second home. A plaque beside the doorway on 11th Street, just off Fifth Avenue, reads "Eleanor Roosevelt lived at 20 East 11th Street from 1933 to 1942." The brownstone belonged to Esther Lape, and the plaque is mute testimony to a lasting friendship that was neither all business nor casual. Mrs. Roosevelt habitually spent several nights a week with her friends and eventually rented an apartment in their brownstone. Elizabeth Read became her personal attorney and financial advisor. When she moved on to a larger private space, Mrs. Roosevelt stayed in the Village, at the Holly Chambers apartments, 29 Washington Square West, from 1942 to 1949. Other Village friends included Marion Dickerman and Nancy Cook, her partners in the Val-Kill enterprises housed on Roosevelt's Hyde Park estate, who lived for some time in a cooperative apartment building over on 171 West 12th Street. Across the hall from them resided Molly Dewson, a reformer and comrade in Democratic Party politics, with her partner Polly Porter. Mrs. Roosevelt obviously felt at home in the Village with her friends.[5]

Connections between that more discreet, politicized, upscale female presence in the Village and out lesbians, like Angela and Buddy, on the lower rungs of the economic ladder would have been few. But gossip circulated through the grapevine. A great fan of Mrs. Roosevelt, Buddy Kent, in her interview, remembered the First Lady walking through Washington Square Park in the 1940s. She was also spotted by wealthier friends of Buddy at "more elegant" gatherings, "some of [Helen] Tamiris' dance recitals. Or you know, where it was considered artsy. So it wasn't gay-gay. It was artsy, see. [...] That's where she would appear."[6]

Angela sought to bridge the social gap. That she did work for Esther Lape, in the late 1930s, is confirmed by her FBI file. Her position as "a messenger to the Chairman of the American Foundation for Social Research" was part of the work history she gave to agents on her application for confidential informant. Angela would not have lied to the FBI.[7]

By the time of her radio interview with Mrs. Roosevelt, in 1950, it was a very different world. FDR was dead. World War II was over, but the war of nerves between Russia and the United States threatened international stability. Still it seems a bit of a stretch that Eleanor Roosevelt—who had defended the liberal reforms of the New Deal, had opposed the House on Un-American Activities Committee, Joseph McCarthy, and post-war militarism, and was often accused by right-wingers of being a Communist herself— would have Angela, an FBI informer, on her radio show. During her White House years, she was certainly no fan of Bureau Director, J. Edgar Hoover. When Mrs. Roosevelt learned of the intense FBI inquiry into the lives of her staff, Malvina Thompson among them, she expressed her indignation to Hoover. Not one to mince words, the First Lady suggested that "this type of investigation seems to me to smack too much of the Gestapo methods." She did not wonder, she said, that "if you have done this type of investigation of other people, we are beginning to get an extremely jittery population."[8]

With the passing years, however, Mrs. Roosevelt's attitude toward the Bureau seems to have changed. She implied that in the "My Day" column where she first mentioned the saga of Angela Calomiris, and added that "the Secret Service and the FBI in this country do such remarkably good jobs." At least she preferred them to HUAC. When the Alger Hiss-Whittaker Chambers scandal broke, and raised the specter of American officials spying for the Soviets, she suggested that "the FBI [not HUAC] is the proper agency to find that out."[9]

Hoover, on the other hand, was more consistent in his attitude toward Mrs. Roosevelt. He never liked the liberal causes she supported, especially civil rights for African Americans, and he did not like her. He always said that he had never married because "God made a woman like Eleanor Roosevelt," and kept a file on her as a security risk, of which 449 pages survive. At a remove of twenty years, he denounced her again, to young agent G. Gordon Liddy of Watergate fame, as "a most dangerous enemy of the Bureau," someone who "might well have succeeded in interfering with the Bureau's ability to contain the Communist menace in the United States." Such claims are a testament to Hoover's tendency to see Communists everywhere—a tendency ridiculed by even his closest Washington associates. In a brief anecdote shared with journalist and author Ovid

Demaris for a well-known collection of stories about the Director after his death, Tom Clark, Ramsey Clark's father, Truman's Attorney General (1945-49) and an Associate Justice of the Supreme Court (1949-67), recalled a skit in a New York nightclub. Clark himself and someone pretending to be Hoover looked around the club, under the tables "and stuff like that, to see if there were any Communists hiding." Clark went on to say that "it was sort of a reflection of an attitude many people had towards Mr. Hoover's activities in the Communist field." Exaggerated or even comic, Hoover's attitudes prevailed as the Cold War took shape.[10]

By 1950, liberalism was on the ropes, or at best had shifted to the right, away from its New Deal and World War II sympathies for the radical Left. Mrs. Roosevelt had her doubts about Communists—both Russian and American—and, as old alliances dissolved under the weight of new wars, she didn't like the way the world was shaping up. While she did not forget the Russian contribution to the Allied defeat of the Nazis, and she did not equate Soviet Communism with Fascism (as many did), she did not like what she saw as the Russian "policy of world revolution" that threatened peace. With the outbreak of war in Korea in June 1950, Mrs. Roosevelt, like many others, denounced "the aggression," which she attributed to the Soviet Union, the "one truly imperialistic nation [...] which is plotting today to spread communism throughout the world."[11]

On the domestic front, she did not advocate outlawing the CPUSA (as many did) and she did not accept labeling everyone a communist who held different political views. But she did not trust American Communists and did not want to work with them. In 1947, Mrs. Roosevelt expressed her adherence to the principles of the recently organized Americans for Democratic Action (ADA), which preferred to have its staff "and policy-making groups completely free of any American Communist infiltration if we can possibly prevent it." In 1953, she would become honorary chair of the ADA. Following the Foley Square trial where Angela testified, Mrs. Roosevelt agreed with the verdict that the Communist leadership had, in fact, advocated the use of force to overthrow the US government, and predicted that the Party would be outlawed.[12]

Angela came to Eleanor Roosevelt's radio show as the anti-

Communist wave was rising. NBC's *Today with Mrs. Roosevelt* never lacked for celebrities, with reputations much more distinguished than Angela's, from stage and screen personalities like José Ferrer and Tallulah Bankhead, to author John Steinbeck, to Roger Baldwin, founder of the American Civil Liberties Union, to Senator Estes Kefauver, chairman of the Senate Special Committee to investigate organized crime. Angela's name, on the other hand, was not exactly a household word, despite her appearance at the trial and the recent publication of a book. Her recorded interview housed in the Library of Congress is labeled "Angela Callomariss."[13]

From Elliott Roosevelt, his mother's announcer, Angela received a hero's welcome, some indication of the prestige accorded her FBI spy mission. She was introduced as a "courageous young woman" who had served her country bravely at great personal risk. She had "successfully posed as a Communist Party member for seven years" and "faced constant danger of recognition by the very Communists she worked with."

Eleanor Roosevelt also baptized Angela "a young lady of great courage." And when she assured Mrs. Roosevelt that there had been no official promise of protection from the FBI while she was undercover, the former First Lady gave Angela a war-weary nation's highest compliment. "Officially, you were just doing something like being a soldier," Mrs. Roosevelt said. "And if you got shot, you got shot." Angela said she had felt that way about it, and her host agreed that it was "a pretty fine way to think about it."

The interview continued for a half hour in that congenial vein, with Angela explaining in the same detail she had used in *Red Masquerade* (likely fictionalized) her recruitment by the FBI. Two FBI agents had come to her Greenwich Village apartment unannounced, introduced themselves, and asked her to join the war effort—"not pretty jobs" but "work that has to be done, and somebody has to do them." Even back then America's Soviet allies were apparently not to be trusted, so she would "go into the Communist Party and observe it" because they would "have the advance program of the Soviet Union which is always carried out in the Party here." It was "the kind of information [...] not usually printed in the papers."

Throughout, Angela's replies to questions about why she

was chosen, how her photography was an asset, how she kept her undercover work secret, how she maintained contact with the FBI, and more, displayed intelligence, poise, and preparation. For her part, Mrs. Roosevelt showed interest in Angela's individual exploits, but perhaps more concern for the inner workings of the Party, which Angela defined for her as "a conspiracy." "Different than any party we have in America," she said, "it's dedicated to a foreign power and it is controlled by a foreign power."

Mrs. Roosevelt considered that and then asked, "So you just must give up your freedom of thought and action?" Having already talked at great length about her rigorous schedule of meetings and demonstrations, Angela responded with, "You don't even have time to think." And Mrs. Roosevelt echoed her with, "You don't really think."

There is more, of course, some of it related to the trial and the Smith Act, which was not, Angela insisted, "an act to control thought." "The Communist Party leaders were not tried for anything they believed or for their ideals," she continued. "They were tried for their actions, for advocating and teaching the violent overthrow of our country."

"You believe the Communist Party is actually controlled from Russia?" Mrs. Roosevelt asked in conclusion. Implying insider knowledge, and a close relationship with Party heads that she did not have, Angela summed up with, "Well, Mrs. Roosevelt, I was told that by the leaders themselves."

What was obvious in all this was that, after long years of war and sacrifice, there was to be no peace. In the transition from ally to enemy, the Russians had to be contained and domestic Communists purged. Meanwhile, Angela's FBI gig had raised her, in Mrs. Roosevelt's eyes, from Esther Lape's "glorified errand girl," the "gofer," to defender of American freedoms.

It seems likely that another Village connection worth mentioning had given Angela access to Mrs. Roosevelt, plus a boost up the ladder of success with her book and her anti-Communist career. While the former First Lady might have contracted with Angela on her own, the support or intervention of Mary Margaret McBride, America's First Lady of Radio—without exaggeration the Oprah Winfrey of her day, earning a salary rumored to be around $200,000, a small fortune in 1950s currency—should not be discounted.[14]

A former farm girl from Missouri, Mary Margaret, as she was known to everyone, had become a pioneer talk show host back in 1934. By the time she quit the business in 1954, she had interviewed some 30,000 people—everyone from General Omar Bradley to Douglas Fairbanks and Mary Pickford, from Frank Lloyd Wright to Admiral Richard Byrd, polar explorer, and, of course, her friend and favorite guest Eleanor Roosevelt, who appeared on the show many times. The two women had met back in the 1920s when McBride was a freelance journalist, looking to write about how famous men were helped by their wives, and a friendship had developed over the years. It was Mrs. Roosevelt who greeted the 18,000 fans who jammed Madison Square Garden in 1944 to celebrate McBride's tenth anniversary on radio. The fifteenth anniversary gala took place in Yankee Stadium, the only place in town big enough to hold the 45,000 fans who attended. The next celebration, someone suggested, would be held in the Grand Canyon.[15]

An audience of six to eight million (mostly housewives) tuned in every afternoon at 1 PM for twenty years to see who Mary Margaret McBride's guest would be and to absorb a bit of big city culture. She had worked for the New York City stations of every radio network—first the Mutual Broadcasting System, then CBS, then NBC, and finally ABC, where on October 25, 1950, she had hosted Angela Calomiris. *Red Masquerade* was hot off the press; review copies had been mailed out but no one had written about it. Following her own ground rules, McBride would only have individuals promoting their work on the show if she had the first interview. To transgress that requirement would mean cancellation and the loss of a chance at some of the best publicity in the business. The experts said that McBride could sell anything, a fact that stood her in good stead with her sponsors. She only accepted products she believed in (and one must assume that included Angela), then put her considerable energy and enthusiasm into the commercial pitch.[16]

In the relaxed style that was McBride's trademark, her conversation with Angela began as a chat between girlfriends. They talked about Angela losing weight while working for the Party because she "was so busy running around all the time." Before the FBI asked for her cooperation, she had never been particularly political, she said, but had rung doorbells for FDR. As the tone of the interview deepened, she told McBride that she was an artist first, but had found herself "in an organization which [sic] its entire leadership was Communist." That was the Photo League. These and other Communists she met in her spy role she characterized as "misfits," "dishonest," "willing to lie under any circumstances in order to promote the Party program," and always criticizing America. She claimed the Communists fasten on issues like "negro discrimination, […] anti-Semitism," which Angela rather naively insisted "all Americans are against anyway." According to her, those same Communists "pretend that they have originated the idea" of opposing prejudice.

Not only were the Communists flawed and deluded individuals, she insisted, but they were also more numerous and dangerous than McBride and her audience might have imagined. If there were only about 50,000 card-carrying Party members, "for each Party member you have ten people who are willing to do their work and that makes it a very influential group." This meant, said Angela, that "the communist menace is a very big menace," and it was "really a public responsibility for every one of us to fight this communist menace."

As the Cold War shifted into high gear, it is not surprising that by the end of 1950, following the publication of *Red Masquerade,* both Mary Margaret McBride and Mrs. Roosevelt would choose Angela Calomiris, former FBI Confidential Informant, as a radio guest. In that context, it is only fair to note that both radio hosts had already had their uncomfortable brushes with the Red-baiters. The year before, McBride had been accused of advertising Polish hams, which back then amounted to harboring Communist sympathies. She fought back on her radio show with an angry retort, but quickly hired a lawyer, "as staunch a Republican anti-communist" as her business manager, Stella Karn, could find. Because the program could lose sponsors, who were intolerant of "pinko" performers, she acquiesced by agreeing to keep "subversives" off her guest list. "It was that or go off the air," she explained. She was reminded that suspicious characters like actor Fredric March, novelist Howard Fast, and journalist William Shirer, plus prominent African Americans like Langston Hughes and Ethel Waters had appeared on her show. And she had kissed Walter White, head of the NAACP, at the celebration in Yankee Stadium. The Red Scare was beginning to show its true American, and racist, colors.[17]

Mrs. Roosevelt, while perhaps not as vulnerable as McBride, was also subject, as a media personality, to pressures from sponsors and the networks. It was early in 1950, when the first installment aired of her half-hour Sunday afternoon TV program, *Mrs. Roosevelt Meets the Public*. On that occasion, her guest was the distinguished scientist Albert Einstein, who seized the opportunity to denounce the manufacture of a hydrogen bomb, a weapon he said could annihilate mankind. At a time when war fever was rampant, and Truman had authorized continued work on the hydrogen bomb, Einstein's remarks provoked a firestorm of controversy. That was soon followed by an uproar around Mrs. Roosevelt's invitation to Paul Robeson to appear on the TV show to discuss "the role of the Negro in American political life." A barrage of right-wing protest led to Robeson—who, among other transgressions, had appeared as a witness for the defense at the first Smith Act trial in 1949— being canceled, with assurances by a network spokesman that the actor, singer and political activist would *never* appear on NBC. Mrs. Roosevelt could only reply to her critics that these decisions were up to the station.[18]

McBride, as it turned out, had her own secrets and her own masquerade as she faced down the Red-baiters. Despite the enormous popularity of the radio persona that McBride had depended on over the years—that of a heterosexual woman who had chosen an exciting career over marriage and motherhood—and despite the fact that she talked so much on the air and wrote books about her life, her fans did not have the whole story. Her peculiar radio staff included her manager/partner Stella Karn, whose on-air arguments with McBride livened up the broadcasts. Her long-time announcer Vincent Connolly, "a confirmed bachelor" whose failure to marry became a running joke on the show, had a private life— like McBride's own—that was more "a closeted book" than an open book. Connolly, a Princeton graduate with an extensive background in literature, theater, and the arts, who introduced McBride every day and helped sell the sponsors' products, was probably "what would now be referred to as gay," according to Susan Ware's groundbreaking book *It's One O'Clock and Here Is Mary Margaret McBride*. Likewise, her relationship with Stella Karn, which spanned almost four decades until Karn's death in 1957, was more than the loving tumultuous friendship the radio audience was invited to share in.[19]

They had met in 1920 as co-workers at the Interchurch World Movement, where Karn wrote press releases for missionaries. She had originally honed her skills as a press agent on the rough and tumble traveling carnival circuit. At an interfaith convention in Atlantic City, according to McBride, they got to know each other better, and upon their return to New York, moved in together—a third-floor Village walkup on West 4th Street. All masks cast aside, it sounded like a typical Village romance.[20]

It was in the Village, too, that McBride experimented with more radical politics as a member of the Village Heterodoxy club that held bi-weekly luncheon meetings. The membership boasted an eclectic mix of remarkable women committed to enlightenment and social reform. Prominent "Heterodites" included art and literary patron Mabel Dodge Luhan; Elizabeth Irwin, who founded the Little Red Schoolhouse; activist and editor of *The Masses* Crystal Eastman; playwright and co-founder of the Provincetown Playhouse Susan Glaspell; actress, labor activist, and daughter of Senator Robert La Follette, Fola La Follette; members of the CPUSA Elizabeth Gurley Flynn and Rose Pastor Stokes; and Grace Nail Johnson, the only African-American member, a life-long civil rights advocate, active in the NAACP. She was also the wife of Harlem Renaissance author James Weldon Johnson. McBride remained a member of the Heterodoxy club until its demise in 1940, and ten years later, was living uptown with Stella Karn, in a duplex on Central Park South, overlooking the park. Her shows, including her interview with Angela, were broadcast from there.[21]

But McBride was apparently willing to come down to the Village again if the occasion suited her. That occasion would have been a portrait session in the photo studio Angela had set up in a second apartment financed by her FBI earnings, in the back garden of 9 Jane

Street. The First Lady of Radio wanted a new series of photos for ABC, she said, and wanted Angela to tackle the job. Maybe she just wanted to come downtown to that special world she remembered fondly. A postcard from McBride, written right after the show, was followed up by another one a couple of weeks later. "I've tried several times to call," she wrote Angela in November, "but no answer." She then proposed "Tuesday (the 21st isn't it?) for that picture" and gave Angela her "very private number" to call with an admonition not to give it out to anyone.[22]

It's not known if the meeting ever took place, or if Angela ever photographed Mary Margaret McBride. She did save the postcards for forty-five years, perhaps as a reminder that she had once shared some common ground with a celebrity, in a Greenwich Village where there was no need for masquerades. For its part, the FBI requested and archived a copy of the full text of McBride's interview with Angela.[23]

What McBride knew of Mrs. Roosevelt's personal history, of what now seems quite certainly an affair with the Associated Press' top woman political reporter Lorena Hickok in the early 1930s, remains unknown. Of course, back then the Roosevelts' private world was generally off limits to a fairly respectful press corps. There were scandals enough—from FDR's dalliance with his wife's social secretary, Lucy Mercer, to Eleanor's affair with Hickok—but they were reported much later.[24]

Mary Margaret McBride's devotion to Mrs. Roosevelt endured to the end. Too heartbroken to attend the funeral in 1962, she taped a moving tribute with none other than Lorena Hickok that aired on the radio and was subsequently lost to history.[25]

Angela Calomiris, on the other hand, would soon discover that celebrity, if you had something to hide, could be risky outside the safe confines of the Village. She would need a lot of nerve and an identity that played well for the New York press. Fortunately for her, all was forgiven and swept under the rug because she had testified against the leadership of the CPUSA. The anti-Communist cause, in need of informant/witnesses, would protect her and promote her career as long as it suited their purposes.

3. A Red Mata Hari

When Angela left the Village to play a prominent role in the Red Scare—as the only woman to testify for the prosecution at the Foley Square trial of the Party leaders—she could not afford skeletons in the closet (or out of the closet). But if she did not look exactly like the girl next door, only more patriotic, she did not fit the "female spy" bill either. As she later confessed in *Red Masquerade*, she was not a "sloe-eyed, slim blond beauty who wore black nightgowns, looked divine in sables, and wormed state secrets out of Balkan prime ministers."[1]

In spite of those limitations, the New York press gave her its enthusiastic support, and a generous portion of the intense publicity surrounding the trial. With a front-page banner headline that read "Girl Tells of 7-Year Role as FBI's Red 'Mata Hari,'" Howard Rushmore of William Randolph Hearst's *New York Journal-American* made her part of a glamorous legend. As far as the spy business was concerned, Angela came off far better than the Dutch-born Mata Hari, who was executed by the French as a German agent during World War I. But for a short, skinny, boyish Angela, with close-cropped thick, dark hair, and a nose too big for classical beauty, identification with the lithe and beautiful Mata Hari, who had introduced exotic Javanese dance moves to Paris, could only be helpful.[2]

Fortunately, the media did not ask too many questions, and history was on Angela's side for the moment. Harvey Matusow, another informant who made frequent headlines with his testimony at Congressional hearings and court trials, explained that "it was fashionable to be an informer and a witness against Communists when I became one." In fact, a sure path to overnight celebrity when Matusow "climbed on that bandwagon" was to tell stories about American Communists, especially stories of their infiltrating and taking over otherwise democratic organizations, planting division and unrest among peaceable law-abiding citizens (like African Americans), spying on government agencies and passing on classified information to the enemy (the Soviet Union), and finally overthrowing the US government to establish a Soviet America.[3]

Admittedly it was a tall order for the CPUSA, whose membership at its greatest strength during the Depression and World War II (when we were allied with the Russians against the Nazis) numbered around 80,000 in a nation of 120 million. John Steinbeck placed the American population at 165,000,000 people, who shuddered "in terror at a problematic 50,000 Communists." Even more frightened were the old leftists, some of whom had been activists since the 1920s in support of the Russian Revolution, and during the 1930s and 40s in opposition to the rise of Fascism. For them the "Red Scare" could mean ostracism, loss of livelihood by blacklisting, the possibility of deportation, or a stiff prison sentence. Sylvia Thompson, wife of Robert Thompson, New York State Chairman for the CPUSA and one of the 1949 Smith Act trial defendants, explained, "We were Red, and we sure were scared."[4]

The informant/witnesses hired to spy on them by the FBI fared much better. Business, for people like Angela, was booming during the early 1950s, when Harvey Matusow confessed it was "the easy way up—to let the world know that I was not just another guy." As a child of the Great Depression with limited job prospects, Angela could not have been more pleased, especially when the press set about re-packaging her unconventional appearance. *Journal-American* reporter Howard Rushmore (of the Mata Hari banner headline), an ex-Communist turned Red hunter, and later editor of the Hollywood scandal sheet *Confidential,* who had a penchant for the sensational, and ended up making lurid headlines himself, identified Angela as "a trim, brunet photographer" who knew her way around "Communist circles of Greenwich Village." Relying on the kind of coverage women usually got—comments about their clothes and looks—Rushmore observed that she was "dressed in black" but sported a "long green feather on her hat" that "bobbed as she nodded in assent to several questions." The *New York Herald Tribune* had more to say about Angela's "black faille suit, and an off-the-face straw hat trimmed in black velvet and sporting a twelve-inch green feather." On the second day of testifying, Angela's outfit—"a gray double-breasted gabardine suit, a high-necked black blouse and a velvet beret cocked over her right eye"—made news again.[5]

Trying to figure out what to do with Angela, the first female witness and the only one for the prosecution, the press took a harder look. At a time when women favored long tresses swept up into elaborate coiffeurs, a *New York Times* reporter found Angela's "black cropped hair" worth a mention. The *New York Herald Tribune* made the best of a bad job and called her hairdo "the new short look." Angela, who if she understood anything understood advertising, a field where she had enjoyed some success as a photographer, knew, of course, that her hair would arouse suspicion. In *Red Masquerade*, she relates how she had tried "with brush and comb and mirror" to fix it but ended up going back to what she called "the old comfortable slightly waved bob." That sounded respectable, and was "really the best hairdo for a long face on a little person," she explains.[6]

Angela doubtless knew from experience that a masculine look was not good for business, and embraced the re-packaging of herself, if not quite as femme fatale counterspy, at least as fashion-conscious and anxious to look her best. "Just like a woman," she says as she assembled her wardrobe to look her best "come hell or high water" for her first time in the public spotlight. All the outfits that had made the front pages of New York dailies during the trial are described in *Red Masquerade*, showing a kind of couturier fascination with fabrics and styles—"Oxford gray all wool sharkskin," "covert cloth coat cut in pseudo-princess lines." Maybe that insider lingo had something to do with Angela's having attended a vocational high school called Straubenmuller Textile High School, in Manhattan, which trained young people for the textile trades, taught fashion design, and had a textile mill in its basement. Angela aspired to greater things than textiles, but some of her closest friends were part of the industry: Hilda Mayorga, who made wigs for the Metropolitan Opera and dressed Angela for the trial, and another Village lesbian everyone called French Jacky (Jacqueline Moritz) who sewed for Broadway shows.[7]

An undated photograph of Angela in very feminine attire, clipped from the *New York Mirror,* shows how she looked for the trial. "The short white gloves" she liked rest primly on her lap, one hand clutching the shoulder strap of "a new black calfskin purse." The "green Robin Hood feather" that had caught the eye of several reporters—"a long green feather," "a jaunty feather" claimed the *Mirror* and the *New York Herald Tribune*—belonged to one of several hats Angela had chosen and would wear during the proceedings "to bring something springlike into the courtroom." According to an old friend of hers, that masquerade continued for a couple of years while Angela went around the country, under contract to the Lee Keedick Agency, "Manager of the World's Most Celebrated Lecturers," addressing the dangers of communism, a popular topic in those days, at $200 per lecture. On those occasions Angela wore a brown velvet skirt and jacket with a ruffled white shirt. But even in that getup, the old friend confided, she "still didn't look like a woman."[8]

All this raises the difficult question of why and how did the FBI choose to employ a rather obvious, even notorious Village lesbian as a confidential informant in the first place, and how and why did she end up on the witness stand in one of the most highly-publicized trials of the period? It was a question (omitting the reference to sexual orientation) that several interviewers posed to Angela in the months following the publication of *Red Masquerade.* During their interview, Eleanor Roosevelt, for one, wanted to know, "Why did the FBI pick you for this difficult work? What background led them to choose you?" Angela more or less gave Mrs. Roosevelt the runaround by affirming that "the Communist Party always looks for the person who is disgruntled with life in general," and that she (the FBI told her) had just the requisite "background" that "would be considered underprivileged." But on a positive note, she added, the Bureau was looking for "the kind of person [...] above all who was an American citizen and a loyal American."

Not surprisingly, the real story about the choice and employment of informants was a bit different, and would not have fit in with Angela's heroic portrayal of herself. William C. Sullivan, head of FBI intelligence operations and for a time third-ranking Bureau officer after Hoover and his longtime companion Clyde Tolson, offered a more objective analysis. There was no point in hiring Boy Scouts, and presumably Girl Scouts, as informants, remarked Sullivan, because they did not have access to the information needed. Producing the goods mattered more than "moral fiber." Similarly, someone like Angela was ostensibly "unattached." She had no spouse and no family. If problems arose, no one would miss her, no one would ask questions. Angela's FBI recruiter gives us the rose-colored version of those qualifications in *Red Masquerade*. "The ideal plant," he observes, "shouldn't have any family ties," but "his morals must be above reproach." Questions of "morality," a term not casually chosen, would become increasingly important to Angela as doubts about her virtue (more specifically her sexuality) surfaced inside the CPUSA, during the defense team's cross examination at the trial, and finally among FBI officials.[9]

How she initially made contact with the FBI is another subject veiled in mystery, despite the explanation in *Red Masquerade* that was repeated ad infinitum in interviews. As the story went, one early morning, in February of 1942, when Angela was getting ready for work, she received a surprise visit at her Village apartment. Two FBI agents who knew her address and that she was studying photography had come to offer her "secret work [...] essential to the internal security of the United States at war." Despite the US war-time alliance with the Soviet Union, spying on American Communists was important, the visiting agents said, because America had to be on guard against any shifts in Russian policy. If change came, Angela was given to understand, "leading American Communists would be the first people in the United States to know it." After the agents left, Angela wonders how the FBI found her, and speculates that they might have heard of her "through Communists" involved with the Photo League, where she studied photography, or the WPA—

that New Deal job-creation miracle—where she was employed as a Recreation Director for Settlement Houses. Later on, and probably closer to the truth, Angela throws out the hint that she "had been recommended to the FBI by someone who was an FBI undercover agent, too." The identity of that "someone" remains unknown.[10]

It seems the FBI did recruit in the Village, where "unattached" people abounded. A story told by Emma "Jerre" Kalbas, a longtime resident, has an authentic ring. It begins on a night at a time before Pearl Harbor, in one of several bars run by the Mafia, catering to lesbians, on MacDougal between West Third Street and Washington Square Park, where New York University's law school now stands. A man claiming to be from the FBI approached some of the women. The bouncer at the door, hired to keep out troublesome types, assured them that this guy was all right, that he was not a cop. What he needed, the visitor explained, were women to "spy on the Russians," and although some of the lesbians, the children of immigrants, spoke Russian at home, Jerre said, nobody "wanted anything to do with that."[11]

Maybe Angela ran into such a recruiter. Back then the FBI enjoyed tremendous prestige, and would have represented for her a chance at recognition by people who mattered. On the FBI team she would be an insider, with secrets to tell to important officials, and the work was not hard. Basically you had to attend Party meetings and report back to the FBI on what was said, but especially the names of those in attendance. From the beginning her FBI recruiter in *Red Masquerade* urges, "Names, addresses and descriptions we always want." And since the Communists could give false names, definitive identification was often by photos, like the ones Angela's handlers showed her— "photographs, Photostats of newspaper pictures, rogues' gallery pictures with prison identification numbers across them." While matching names to faces of people she had seen at meetings, she claimed, she got the idea to use her photography for the FBI. "Would you like pictures of some of these people I've been telling you about?" she asks in *Red Masquerade*. "You bet we would," replies the agent.[12]

Angela's approval ratings went up another notch and stayed there through seven years of active service. If any of the stories told by former agents about the FBI's uphill struggles to find and keep reliable informants are true, those agents assigned to Angela must have rejoiced at her cunning and loyalty. In the end, the Bureau praised her as "an excellent confidential informant" who "kept the New York Office completely advised of any information coming to her attention relative to activities of the Communist Party, USA," and she was chosen out of about sixty candidates to testify for the prosecution at the 1949 trial—both for the testimony she could offer, and doubtless because other informants would not dare go public.[13]

The trial made Angela famous, an overnight Cold War sensation at a time when informers were heroes. But celebrity was a fragile commodity. The popular memory did not extend back very far, and keeping herself in the spotlight required some maneuvering. As the trial wore on, and the weeks stretched into months, press coverage shifted away from Angela and onto other witnesses and issues. Once the verdicts were in (and even before) it became apparent that Angela, having risked notoriety, was determined to transform her fifteen minutes of fame on the witness stand into something more lasting and profitable. It was a position her former Party comrades often defined as "opportunist"—someone who, according to Angela's version of Party doctrine, turns away "from the cause of the people to pick up crumbs from the capitalist banquet." In that same revealing passage from *Red Masquerade,* she notes "that 'opportunists' seemed to be people" like herself "who wanted to make their own way." It was part of a fairly standard anti-Communist argument that pitted American individualism against an alien (European) collectivism.[14]

But in a typical oversight, Angela forgot to mention how much help she had making "her own way." The FBI, of course, knew and would rebuke her, in a memo from an Assistant Director to J. Edgar Hoover, for "being very ungrateful as well as completely opportunistic." It was the beginning of Angela's difficulties with the Bureau, which had done for her, though it was not apparent at the time to anyone, all it could or would do. But Angela was not the only opportunist, and competition was already heating up among fellow informers for publication rights to their stories of the Communist threat in America. In the lead was Louis Budenz, a former managing editor of the *Daily Worker,* who had returned in 1945 to the Church under the guidance of Monsignor Fulton J. Sheen, and published *This Is My Story* (McGraw-Hill, 1947) dedicated to Mary Immaculate, "Patroness of Our Beloved Land." A prominent witness at the 1949 trial, he would go on to earn, in the course of some ten years of expert testimony on the Red Menace at trials and Congressional hearings, from $70,000 to $100,000.[15]

The money was good, and Angela did not waste time. She moved with deliberate speed into the world of anti-Communist propaganda, offering one of the Red Scare's top journalists the inside scoop on her story, which his paper called "one of the most beguiling masquerades of modern times." To place that in perspective, it was a time when New York journalism enjoyed unparalleled prestige, when television was in its infancy and the Internet decades away. News was communicated to the public through newspapers with morning and evening editions. Journalists made careers and reputations were in several major New York dailies whose names only survive today in landmarks like Herald Square (the *New York Herald,* later the *Herald Tribune*) or in institutions like the Pulitzer Prize (for publisher Joseph Pulitzer, owner of the *New York World*). Also, out of New York's distinguished newspaper heritage come the enduring words of Horace Greeley, editor of the old *Tribune:* "Go West, young man!"[16]

One of those distinguished but now defunct newspapers of yesteryear was the *World-Telegram,* part of the extensive Scripps-Howard chain that had turned anti-New Deal and anti-Democrat in the 1930s. Following the death of FDR and the end of the war, a favorite tactic of the *World-Telegram* was tying the Communist threat to Democratic Party coattails. The paper's chief Red-baiter was prestigious columnist Frederick Woltman, recipient of a Pulitzer Prize for reporting (1947) on Communism's infiltration of the US. While his name may not resonate with a contemporary public, back then he commanded an audience as large as any present-day right-wing pundit in the style of Glenn Beck, Bill O'Reilly, or Sean Hannity. Woltman kept mammoth files on everyone with leftist leanings, and had a reputation as an authoritative source on the Red Menace. The *Daily Worker* baptized him "Freddie the Fink," but Gus Hall, Chairman of the Ohio State Communist Party and a defendant in the Foley Square trial, wanted the *World-Telegram* delivered to him in the Federal House of Detention so he could follow Frederick Woltman's column and evaluate the opposition's latest attacks.[17]

Given his reputation back then, good fortune smiled on Angela when, early on, Woltman took up her cause and brought her to the public's attention. His nose for news recognized the sensational appeal of a female spy. In fact, the *World-Telegram* had experience with that kind of reporting because just the year before it had broken the story of another informer—Elizabeth Bentley, an ex-Communist who had worked as a courier during the war, ferrying secrets in her knitting bag from a spy ring in Washington, DC to her Soviet handler (and lover) in New York City. After his death, she turned herself in to the FBI and became one of the most prominent of the informant/witnesses to occupy center stage, from HUAC hearings to the trial of Julius and Ethel Rosenberg. Harvey Matusow, a fellow informant, later claimed Bentley told him that she had given false testimony as a government witness because she needed money.[18]

Woltman met with Bentley in the spring of 1948, when she was testifying before the grand jury that ultimately indicted the Communist Party leadership, but left the publicizing of her story to his *World-Telegram* colleague Nelson Frank, a former Communist. Bentley, intelligent but homely, neurotic and a heavy drinker at forty, also got the Mata Hari treatment. Without publishing her picture, the *World-Telegram* billed her as a "beautiful young blonde," "svelte and striking."[19]

Nelson Frank promised the FBI to hold off publishing Bentley's story until the grand jury proceedings were over. Fred Woltman and Angela, both of whom knew how to sell a story, were in more of a hurry. They sandwiched in two articles about Angela between the guilty verdicts handed down to the Communist leaders (October 14, 1949) and their sentencing (October 21). While public interest in the trial was high, Woltman's front-page "Girl Photog Cut Career to Expose Reds' Plot" appeared on October 17. It hit the newsstands with a two-column photo of Angela sporting a turtleneck and tweed jacket, looking tough, and dangling a cigarette from one hand. A headline above her picture read "Undercover Agent," a blooper that Hoover probably did not appreciate since no women were employed as FBI agents during his lifetime. Just having to face the idea that hiring women at the Bureau was imminent, according to a latter-day female agent, probably helped to finish off the Director in 1972. In Woltman's second article, published October 18, about Angela— "Leading Double Life No Picnic, FBI Girl Found. Communists Demand Everything of Party Members, She Learned"—she was demoted to "undercover girl." [20]

Taken together, both articles highlight essential points in the spy story that would become *Red Masquerade*. First and foremost, Angela's mission was more or less fraught with danger—a "real war of nerves," she told Woltman. The danger lay in the possibility of discovery by the Party comrades, who could never be trusted and were laying plans for a secret "nationwide underground set-up." If her FBI connection was revealed, the Party would, at the very least, brand her a "stoolpigeon." While the comrades did not seem to have anything more drastic in mind, danger also lurked back in Angela's Village neighborhood, presumably full of Communist sympathizers or people who just did not like snitches. Someone called her "a dirty rat," and a family across the street watched her apartment, she claimed, through binoculars. As brave as any spy hero, Angela did not scare easily but "was assigned a 24-hour policewoman bodyguard" anyway. Subsequent re-hashings of her story would serve up ample helpings of danger and intrigue. [21]

According to Woltman, everything hinged on Angela concealing her "dual identity," from both Communists and friends who knew nothing of her commitment to the FBI. If that had been true, it would have been a lonely stance indeed. But boundaries were not so rigid, secrecy not so strict as Angela said. An old friend of hers, someone she had known since about 1940, certainly knew what Angela was up to, and remembered her dressing up and "putting on earrings" to go to Party meetings. Like many aspects of Angela's story, her claims that everything was cloaked in mystery do not stand up well under scrutiny. [22]

Even stranger would have been Woltman's failure, as a fellow Villager, to recognize Angela's other dual identity—the lesbian masquerading as straight (not very successfully) as opposed to her more adroit impersonation of a bona fide Communist. At the time of the trial, he had lived for many years on Barrow Street, and in his own words, thought of himself as "a Bohemian who seldom wandered far from the precincts of Greenwich Village, a man who married a painter, liked a bottle and a cold bird." It is safe to assume he knew the score. He stuck by Angela into the following year when he wrote about the publication of *Red Masquerade* for the November 13, 1950, edition of the *World-Telegram*. By that time, FBI officials, who did not want Angela to publish her book until after the Supreme Court had heard the appeal of the convicted Communist leaders, were not pleased to hear that Woltman had dropped by to visit at her apartment on Jane Street, not far from his place at 27 Barrow.[23]

If Fred Woltman had been an invaluable help in launching Angela's anti-Communist celebrity, she had also provided him with some good copy. What was unprecedented about Angela's story, from Woltman's perspective, was its focus not on the leaders but on the bottom tier of Party operations, on the little guy who was an ordinary branch member, on the organization's "inner workings from the ground level up." This new material, hyped with a dose of fanciful intrigue, provided another example of Communists "undermining our society from within."[24]

According to Woltman's fellow reporter Fred Cook, it was the kind of scoop that fed the "Communist-menace hysteria" that the *World-Telegram* promoted. He gave the bosses what they wanted, Woltman confessed to Cook in private moments when he was "dead on the level," admitting some of his stories were exaggerated. Nevertheless, he enjoyed the confidence of FBI officials in New York and Washington, to whom he passed tidbits of news and received in return notes from Hoover and from his propaganda chief, Assistant Director Louis B. Nichols, whose ranch-style home Woltman had visited with his wife.[25]

But his brush with Angela Calomiris proved unlucky for Fred Woltman. "The articles on the Calomiris girl" caused a commotion in the top ranks of the FBI, from the Director right on down. Lies had been told by Calomiris, and printed by Woltman, and they had done great harm to the FBI's reputation. Parroting Hoover's orders, Lou Nichols reported to second-in-command Clyde Tolson that he had advised the New York Office to be "circumspect in any future dealings with Woltman." Since Woltman had been one of the Bureau's most favored anti-Communist writers, those "who have proved themselves to us," this rebuke constituted a serious change in attitude. As the Bureau struggled to free itself from a web of intrigue spun by Angela, some secrets were revealed, others swept under the rug.[26]

Angela's début as an anti-Communist celebrity was off to a rocky start.

4. The Big Lie

According to Eleanor Roosevelt, the worst thing about the Communists was that they lied. In her "My Day" column for June 22, 1945, she stated her position that "anyone has a right to be a Communist, to advocate his beliefs peacefully," but that she did not and would not trust them, because for years "they taught the philosophy of the lie." In her essay "Liberals in This Year of Decision," originally published in *The Christian Register*, a leading Unitarian weekly, in June 1948, she recalled bitter experiences trying to work, in 1934, with youth groups, "led by the Communist element." Her disillusionment came, she said, "when I found they wouldn't tell me the truth." Because they offered support for the war effort only after Russia was invaded by the Germans, she sent back to say, "I am sorry but you lied to me and I can't work with anyone who lies."[1]

It did not seem to occur to Mrs. Roosevelt that anti-Communist crusaders—like Angela Calomiris, "the young lady of great courage" she introduced to her NBC radio audience, the one who was "just doing something like being a soldier" by spying—might tell bigger lies. Perhaps Angela was not as "charming" as she pretended to be on radio. The FBI knew about Angela's fibbing but kept the former First Lady in the dark.[2]

Not surprisingly, it was all about the money. The first to introduce the theme was Fred Woltman in the two articles about Angela that he published in the *World-Telegram* mid-October 1949—"Girl Photog Cut Career to Expose Reds' Plot" (October 17) and "Leading Double Life No Picnic; FBI Girl Found" (October 18). They told a story that fed popular fears of Communism while making Angela look glamorous as a female spy. But what made her really big news, that resounded in press circles and reached the highest levels of FBI leadership, was that she had given seven years of loyal service to the FBI and braved untold dangers all for free—as Woltman wrote, "many hours of working overtime, none for pay." In a society where memories of war-time sacrifices were still fresh, such an unselfish gesture and "honorable contribution of the first order" to the country commanded respect. In addition, not only had she not been paid, her patriotic service had "left her broke." Woltman's first article ("Girl Photog") reported that Angela's professional life had been disrupted by her commitment to spying and her appearance on the witness stand. Five months after her testimony, as the trial came to an end, he said, she was "still looking for a job." Readers like Stuart Vandervort, in Summit, New Jersey, believed the tale of "this brave, young and self-sacrificing young woman" who was "in financial straits," and wanted to start a fund to help her out. In response to the articles, some, like Isidor Prussack, in Brooklyn, New York, sent in small checks to the *World-Telegram* office with letters of praise for all that Angela had done for "freedom loving and Commie hating Americans."[3]

To anyone with access to FBI records, Angela's claims of destitution are ridiculous. Since the Bureau kept such a meticulous accounting of expenditures (for one reason, because Hoover had to make application to Congress for budget allocations) the truth is apparent. Angela had a lengthy salary history, with periodic renewals as required for good service. Beginning in 1942, she collected $25 per week at a time when rents on Christopher Street in the Village were $60 per month. The FBI paid almost as much as her WPA recreation job ($27 per week), doubling her income. The amount authorized to be paid to her was, in fact, "relatively large" for an informant, according to the Bureau, probably because of her photography skills.

The stipend she received rose by small increments from renewal to renewal—to $30, $40 per week, then $180, $190, and finally $225 per month, which was the amount she was being paid even as she sat testifying in the witness chair. It was the best job she ever had. Her appearance at the trial, which blew her cover and meant that she would have no more information to pass on to the FBI, did not mean the end of the FBI payoffs. On the contrary, payments were scheduled to continue through the appeal of the verdict, which in this case went all the way to the Supreme Court and would not be decided until 1951. It was one way the Bureau hoped to maintain some control over its informant. Despite her diminutive size—"a witty, intelligent girl, slight of build, weighing 100 pounds," as Woltman described her in the *World-Telegram*—she was beginning to prove hard to handle.[4]

Because there was a great deal at stake, the FBI was instantly up in arms over Angela's lie. Together with the US Attorney, they had gone to a lot of trouble to secure the convictions of the Communist leadership, which had been accomplished largely on the basis of informant testimony (like Angela's) and reading long inflammatory passages from the literature they said was taught in Party schools. Lenin, Stalin, Marx, and Engels were favorite sources. Since the verdict in the Communist case was sure to be appealed, US Attorney John Francis X. McGohey (promoted to a federal judgeship at the trial's conclusion) wanted his witnesses, still under subpoena, to avoid commenting for the press. Nothing should jeopardize upholding the constitutionality of the Smith Act of 1940 that made it an offense to conspire to advocate, or belong to a group that advocated, the violent overthrow of the US government. If the appeal of the 1949 convictions failed, the Smith Act could then be used to indict other CPUSA officials. As Assistant Director D. M. Ladd reported in a lengthy memo to his boss J. Edgar Hoover, on the heels of Woltman's articles in the *World-Telegram*, McGohey had early on advised Angela that she was to "make no statements or contribute any articles to the press relative to her testimony," and she had promised him that she "had no intention of making any statement for publication."[5]

But she did talk to the press, defying the admonitions of the US Attorney. It was not a wise move, but Angela's ambition got the better of her. The Bureau was not pleased. A memo to the Director from Special Agent in Charge Edward Scheidt in New York added details. The memo duly noted that McGohey had appealed to her patriotism not to do anything that could hurt the prosecution of the case, or give grounds for appeal. But in reply, Angela had accused FBI agents, including Scheidt, of having no interest in "the witnesses who helped win the case," and confronted him with "McGohey got a judgeship out of this; what's happening to me?" She wanted to know what had been done to find her a job "with a large industrialist." She was getting impatient, she said, and it had been a long time since she testified.[6]

The FBI did not back down. More memos about Angela circulated briskly among Bureau heads, from New York to Washington and around Headquarters, suggesting that she had been, according to their records, a very good informant—"cooperative, dependable, and loyal." But lately, they cautiously observed, she had been considered "temperamental," and "a few incidents" in recent months indicated that "possibly" Angela had not been "forthright with the New York Office." Stories that dated back a few weeks substantiated those suspicions, and suggested that her relationship with Fred Woltman had been more than casual. In early October she had been spotted "in the courtroom of the trial" still in progress, using a press pass that came from Woltman. When the news was whispered to the attorneys for the prosecution, they called her aside and told her that the defense could make an issue of her presence. She left the courtroom peaceably, and later assured the FBI that there was no collaboration "between her and any newspapermen to write a story on her attendance at the trial." Top aides in New York and Washington accepted her story, but insisted that she seek "appropriate clearance" from the US Attorney and advise the Bureau before granting interviews. This, as they later noted, she did not do. Woltman had also made promises to clear any articles he wrote with the US Attorney prior to publication, which he did not do.[7]

But bigger storms were brewing that would shatter the FBI's composure and occasion another flurry of memos. As luck would have it, one of Fred Woltman's readers was Eleanor Roosevelt, whose own syndicated column appeared in the *Washington Daily News*, another Scripps-Howard paper. Without mentioning any names, on October 19, 1949, Mrs. Roosevelt published what was in effect a response to Woltman, written in a rather naïve tone and convoluted style, that sent the Bureau into a minor tailspin. She was "a little bit surprised," she wrote, "if our Government accepts the help of someone who undertakes a considerably risky job and then it does not make some kind of decent financial arrangements to compensate not only for the risk that was run but for the difficulties that the individual, on returning to normal living, finds in getting employment!" Entitling her article "Story of Girl FBI Undercover Agent Is Odd," she noted that regular FBI agents got decent pay on similar jobs, and that civilians should get no less. She found Woltman's story (and Angela's) "a very strange procedure [...] if it is correct." It was a classic example of Eleanor Roosevelt springing to the defense of the underdog, and a lone, single woman at that.[8]

Because a figure of Mrs. Roosevelt's stature had spoken out publicly, calling attention to Woltman's story and suggesting something was amiss, the FBI immediately went into damage control mode. More memos came and went until Hoover's top aides agreed that the whole thing made them look bad because they had not taken care of their informant. Always concerned for the Bureau's image, Hoover was livid. No fan of Mrs. Roosevelt (to whom he referred as the "old hoot owl") his anger spilled over in various handwritten notes, calling the situation "grossly unfair to the Bureau." One reaction from his inner circle was to write "a letter to Mrs. Franklin D. Roosevelt advising her [...] of the true facts"—that Angela had been paid all along and was lying about it. On second thought, another memo suggested that, if there was to be a letter, it "should be a very short one [...] personal and confidential" and "not for publication." Finally, it was decided that it would be far better to say nothing at all, as no "good purpose could be served in writing Mrs. Roosevelt." The Director wrote "I agree" to that conclusion, and Eleanor Roosevelt was left out of the FBI's confidence.[9]

Angela's antics continued to worry the Bureau. She was becoming more belligerent, her arguments more distorted. Hoover wanted to stop all payments if she kept on talking and misrepresenting the FBI's attitude toward her. He feared that her claims of poverty and abandonment might "deter others from assisting us," and he was probably right about that. Memos recorded Angela's defense of her complaints, accusing Woltman of misquoting her and, at the same time, unveiling a new angle to justify her lying. She said the payments to her over the years had always been considered "loans," and assumed they were being continued after the trial "in lieu of obtaining for her a position of employment." The Bureau replied that it was not authorized to make loans of government funds to informants but would continue payments "for the protection of the Government's interest in the case." Angela then had a histrionic moment, accusing the US Attorney of trying to "gag" her, and announced that she would accept no further payments from the FBI. The New York Office knew she was bluffing, and noted that she had "never indicated how and when the 'loans' would be repaid." They did not confront her on that issue, but gallantly promised "to intensify its efforts to find suitable employment" for her. With that assurance, she quickly recovered her equilibrium and continued to collect $225 per month.[10]

For the time being, the FBI called on one of its loyal friends to soothe ruffled feathers—Angela's and Eleanor Roosevelt's. Walter Winchell, a trusted crony of Hoover, with whom he delighted to share gossip, was recruited. Into his widely-syndicated "In New York" column, Winchell dropped a tidbit intended to clarify and comfort without disclosing anything much. "The story by Fred Woltman about Angela Calomiris having been of great help to the gov't in the prosecution of the 11 Communist leaders and that she is no longer employed and is worried about her career, was not fully told," wrote Winchell, then continued in telegraphic style. "Mrs. Roosevelt's column commented on it. The facts are these: She had nothing to worry about and will be rewarded with a job." Confirming what Mrs. Roosevelt had suspected, that Woltman had somehow gotten it wrong, and raising Angela's hopes of future employment, Winchell gave Hoover a way out of a tight spot. His promise was also doubtless intended to silence the buzz current among other New York newspapermen, according to Edward Scheidt, head of the local office, that "the Bureau let Calomiris down very badly." Ever alert to criticism of the FBI, Hoover had, once again, come out ahead, but would not forget that Angela had sown discord in his kingdom.[11]

This revealing glimpse of the FBI's relationship with one of its informants would lead one to wonder why the Bureau would have put up with so much foolishness, particularly from someone they were practically supporting. To be sure, Angela was not unique among FBI informants, former Communists, and non-Communists undercover, most of whom talked, drank, or demanded too much. The FBI tried to keep them all in line for as long as they were useful to testify at trials and Congressional committee hearings. On such occasions, despite the sometimes controversial image they projected, they were universally believed, and contributed generously to the success of the Red Scare.

It seems strange that accepted Red Scare lore identified Communists as mentally ill, certifiably mad, while at the same time there is evidence that most of the informers against them were crazier. Angela, for one—no paragon of emotional stability—was invited to consult with the Yale University Institute of International Studies on its project "The Appeals of Communism." Intensive interviews had already been conducted with ex-Communists and with psychoanalysts who had treated Communist patients. Like other such projects, the research team wanted to know if people joined the Party because they were unbalanced. Research Associate Herbert E. Krugman assured Angela that those working on the project were all familiar with *Red Masquerade*, where Angela had variously depicted Party members as "thin, humorless [...] pathologically fat, and not very bright [...] self-confessed neurotics," and "in touch with a psychiatrist." "At one time," she writes, "four members of my branch were undergoing psychiatric treatment."[12]

Informers, on the other hand, were not a generally stable lot. The writer Howard Fast, probably best known today for his historical novel and later film *Spartacus* (1951), described prosecution witness Louis Budenz at the Foley Square trial as a "little nervous rabbit-faced creature who whispered his lies so fervently." A recent study of Budenz's career reported that the informer/author had surgery for a sinus condition and took cocaine for the pain, but did not indicate whether Budenz became addicted or not. The notorious Matt Cvetic, who worked undercover in the Pittsburgh Communist Party and testified before HUAC, caused the FBI no end of trouble as a heavy drinker (and wife-beater) who always wanted more money until they finally fired him.[13]

Other informants had tried the Bureau's patience. In Angela's case, Fred Woltman's articles about her dire financial situation angered Hoover to the point that he would have happily stopped payments to her. But the New York Office suggested that Angela be allowed to linger on so that they, through payments and frequent contacts, could keep tabs on her and "ascertain, if possible, her activities." Also, high-ranking aides in Washington defined the thorny legal problems to be considered. Not only had Angela lied for publication about not getting paid, but she had also lied about it on the witness stand, which constituted perjury. That was the real reason the FBI had not wanted to get into some explanation with Mrs. Roosevelt, and it accounted for the US Attorney's repeated admonitions to Angela to keep quiet, lest she give "the defense the opportunity to ask for a new trial." Likewise, the FBI could not publicly deny Fred Woltman's articles, and if they told him the truth off the record, they feared he might print it. The Bureau preferred silence.[14]

While prosecution attorneys at the trial never touched on the question of remuneration, on cross-examination, defense lawyer Louis McCabe, later Vice-President of the National Lawyers Guild and an Assistant District Attorney for Philadelphia, was curious. He had asked Angela, "What financial arrangements did you have with the FBI?" and she had answered that they paid all the expenses stemming from her Party membership (dues, books, literature, and contributions). But there was no mention of the regular stipend she had received for years. The defense pursued the issue. Angela was asked again, this time by Richard Gladstein of San Francisco, a labor lawyer who had defended Harry Bridges, President of the International Longshoremen's and Warehousemen's Union (ILWU), and she repeated that only expense money had been paid. Gladstein suggested that the FBI would have arranged for her to suffer no financial sacrifice as a result of her work in the Communist Party, and Angela protested, "There was no arrangement of that kind." She followed up with the now familiar portrayal of herself as patriot and martyr: "As a matter of fact, I suffered great financial sacrifice, and it is unimportant to me."[15]

Whether out of pride or delusion, Angela stuck to her story over the years, and there was no one to argue otherwise. One of her oldest friends, who had known her since the early 1950s, confirmed that Angela always told everybody that she had taken no money working for the FBI. "It was a patriotic thing," Melva Wade, who had been Dean of Studies at Brooklyn Tech before retiring to upstate New York, insisted, "and she was very proud of that." Another lesbian who had known Angela for years in the Village, and had not liked her at all, was not so charitable. When asked why she thought Angela had taken the job with the FBI, Jerre Kalbas had a quick and sharp response. "For the money," she replied. "For the money."[16]

But that bit of reliable Village gossip did not reach the ears of the judge, Harold R. Medina, a former Columbia law professor named to the federal bench in 1947 by President Harry Truman. He was sitting as judge in his first big trial. Medina had suggested during the cross-examination of a previous prosecution witness Herbert Philbrick, who had worked undercover in the CPUSA in the Boston area, that "if this man has been receiving large sums of money from the FBI or from the government I think it is perfectly proper to bring that out." The same Louis F. McCabe who would later question Angela had asked Philbrick, "You received no remuneration outside of your actual expenses?" Philbrick had replied that he was a "volunteer worker." Quoting his testimony, the *New York Times* affirmed he had sworn he had never received any money from any source for his work in the service of his country. Philbrick stuck to the story that he was only reimbursed for expenses in the book-length version of his FBI adventures *I Led Three Lives* (1952). While all that sounded good and had a patriotic ring to it, their FBI files proved that both Philbrick and Angela had perjured themselves on the witness stand in order to disguise their indebtedness to the Bureau.[17]

It was lucky for Angela that defense attorneys did not have access to those files that recorded exactly when and how much the FBI had spent on its confidential informant over the years. About a week after her appearance on the stand, the defense came up with another strategy to challenge the notion that informants had not been paid, and paid well. The target was prosecution witness William Cummings, an African American born in rural South Carolina, who, like so many, had made the trek from the Jim Crow South to the industrialized North looking for work and a better life. He had settled in Toledo, Ohio, and joined the United Automobile Workers (UAW), which had a policy of encouraging racial integration in the union. To his chagrin, under cross-examination by defense attorney George Crockett of Detroit, also African-American, a member of the National Lawyers Guild, later a judge and US Congressional Representative from Michigan, Cummings had confessed that he had not reported moneys received from the FBI on his income tax returns. But since he had also claimed they were just reimbursements for expenses incurred in the completion of his spy assignments, Judge Medina broke in to comment that, as he understood the income tax law, "you do not put in your return when you are reimbursed for expenses, you put down your earnings, your income." When Gladstein for the defense offered to correct the judge concerning what he thought was "a misstatement of law on income tax returns," Medina declared an end to the morning session and the court in recess until the afternoon. Debate ended, and Cummings was safe.[18]

While defense attorneys had not questioned Angela about her income tax (the way they had Cummings) later her dealings with the Internal Revenue Service became a matter of some concern to J. Edgar Hoover. Angela's yen for celebrity, giving interviews and publishing her book while *Dennis v. US* was still being appealed, did not endear her to the Bureau. But the matter of her income tax payments made Hoover increasingly nervous. On the eve of *Red Masquerade*'s publication, it was the US Attorney General J. Howard McGrath who requested from the Secretary of the Treasury "copies of the income tax returns filed by Angela Jean Calomiris for the ten year period 1940 to 1950." Those documents revealed, according to the New York FBI Office, that Angela had, in fact, paid no income tax at all for the years 1940 to 1944, and very little thereafter. A follow-up FBI memo advised "all informants of this office including Calomiris [...] that they must consider their salaries as informants as income for income tax purposes." If it had been made public, this admission would have suggested that salaries, not reimbursement for expenses, had purchased the loyalty and the testimony of countless government informants in trials and committee hearings. It would have made less reliable the testimony of others, like prosecution witness Garfield Herron, another African American and UAW man who came to the stand right before Angela. Called up from Arkansas to testify, where he was living after working during the war in Chicago for Douglas Aircraft, and afterwards for Stewart Warner (a company that made instruments for the automotive industry)—"since Douglas Aircraft stopped building planes"—Herron was the only one to admit he had been paid by the FBI, "as high as $60 a month." But, lest that arouse suspicion, he hastened to reassure Gladstein for the defense that "nobody told me what to testify here."[19]

Angela consistently portrayed herself as patriotic and self-sacrificing, but she had gotten a lot more in payoffs than her fellow informant/witness Herbert Philbrick, a neat young advertising executive from Boston. She had gotten "so much more than the other informants who were used as witnesses" (including Philbrick) FBI Assistant Director D. M. Ladd reported to Hoover, because she was not making enough as a photographer to support herself and devote "as much time to Communist activity as she did." Philbrick got praise for "a patriotic motive," while Angela was "active in securing information partly for financial reasons." Or, to put it succinctly—the way Village denizen Jerre Kalbas did—"for the money."[20]

Angela would not have relished the distinction between herself and Philbrick. But the differences between them mounted up, and probably cost her more than she had counted on. The Bureau did not forgive and forget. If she had not been in such a hurry to get her name in the papers, she could have avoided Hoover's wrath. If she had behaved like the more discreet Philbrick, and waited to tell her story until the Supreme Court had upheld the convictions of the Communist leaders, she might have gotten a better deal. Instead, Philbrick "who was so valuable and maintained such a decent attitude since the trial," got the nod.[21]

Ogden Reid, son of the *New York Herald Tribune*'s owner and a devout anti-Communist at the time, had wanted to serialize Angela's spy story, and offer her a job. But the FBI directed Reid to Philbrick because he "had been exceedingly decent" and had not accepted media offers after the trial. His story appeared in 1952, serialized on the front pages of the *Herald Tribune*, at the same time he joined the paper's retail advertising staff. Philbrick's book *I Led Three Lives* came out soon after, and became the basis for a successful TV series that was Lee Harvey Oswald's favorite as a teenager. Richard Carlson starred in 117 episodes from 1953-1956, and earned a star on the Hollywood Walk of Fame. Philbrick profited greatly, and remained committed to anti-Communism far beyond the turbulent years of the Red Scare.[22]

Angela was not so clean-cut as Philbrick, and had taken considerable risks by going public on the witness stand and with her story. While indignation over her betrayal and Woltman's articles seethed through the FBI's ranks, another voice was raised against her. In one of those enticing memos where sentences are deleted, blackened beyond recovery with permanent marker, a Bureau agent reported, in early November of 1949—soon after Fred Woltman's articles claiming that Angela was penniless and in need of a job, after Mrs. Roosevelt's response, and finally Walter Winchell's clarification—that Angela had been asked to drop out of the Party the year before, back in the fall of 1948. The agent said he thought he should let somebody know since the FBI had been trying to get her a job, and because she had been the subject of so much publicity. Why she was asked to drop out would have been explained by the large block of text blacked out, under the heading of "Communist Party, USA; Security Measures"—presumably measures taken by the Party to protect itself. The FBI agent went on to defend Angela against undefined charges, explaining that she was likely being accused because of her cooperation with the Bureau. It was, he wrote, "possible that the Communist Party" is trying to "smear Calomiris since she testified at the trial of the Communist leadership." On the other hand the timing was off, and the Bureau had to be careful, the agent reported, because Angela was asked to drop out of the Party ("brought up on charges") before the trial. The specific nature of those charges would have been contained in the blacked out section, under "Security Measures." In fact, the news that gay people were a security threat had reached Party officials thanks to the "Lavender Scare" that was sweeping Washington, and Angela's homosexuality had to be the secret issue of the memo.[23]

It was the worst accusation—a "morals" charge—leveled at her to date, and a real threat to the prestige she had enjoyed working for the FBI. Not surprisingly, Angela chose to fight rumors with a classic gay defense: deny everything. Ambitious, sometimes ruthless, she also had a lot of nerve.

5. Gay in the CPUSA: Angela and Harry Hay

Despite the best efforts of the Freedom of Information Act censors, black markers always at the ready, it is clear (and at least some FBI agents must have known) that Angela was asked to leave the Party because she was a lesbian. They knew because by that time, thanks to a saturation of paid informants, the Bureau had access to any and all Party communiqués, including the one that announced new "Security Measures." As J. Edgar Hoover always claimed, through the Party dues paid by his spies, he "financed the Communist Party in order to know what they are doing."[1]

Angela "was advised to quietly drop out of the Party," according to the internal FBI memo, in the fall of 1948 for lesbianism, because she was not the only one. In the following accounts, the dates and circumstances coincide with Angela's experience. The difference is that these women had a social conscience that set them apart from the general population, both gay and straight. They were members of the Communist Party out of political conviction, not as undercover informers.[2]

The story of "Janny," interviewed for Marcy Adelman's collection *Long Time Passing: Lives of Older Lesbians*, contains a wealth of emotional detail. There Janny related how she had been a loyal Communist in California, writing songs in the 1940s for the Party, performing at the San Francisco Labor Theatre. She and her partner "Edie" were not out in Party circles; in fact, they denied that they were lesbians when male comrades wanted to know how two women managed on their own. (According to Janny, Edie still [in 1986] "denies her homosexuality.") But hiding did not deceive anyone. In 1948, a prying comrade said he or she had seen Janny "at some gay place." She had never been there, she said, but "somebody testified they saw me in there. [...] I got thrown out of the Party for it anyway."[3]

What happened to Angela was also prompted by tales told by comrades, who demanded through "telephone calls, letters, and verbal statements," according to the FBI memo, that the Party investigate her. Because Angela did not intend to tell the whole truth about the investigation, she did not shy away from it in *Red Masquerade*. Several pages bubbling with righteous indignation are dedicated to describing her initial confrontation with female comrades who announce, "We would like you to drop out of the Party." While Angela shakes "with fear and anger" because she is afraid they may have discovered that she is working undercover for the FBI, they go on to explain: "It has come to our attention [...] that you are anti-Party, that you have been associating with anti-Party people, and that you've been heard making anti-Party remarks." Angela protests, says she will fight any attempt to expel her, and demands they present their evidence at a formal hearing. In conclusion, she notes that her "private life is an open book."[4]

Unlike Janny in San Francisco, Angela did not go quietly and refused to resign. Indicative of the Party's rather feeble resolve, there was no more talk of expulsion, and no action was taken. On the contrary, in what she describes in *Red Masquerade* as a "frenzied shakeup" after the 1948 presidential election, Angela was assigned to a new branch of the West Midtown Section and made "financial secretary." It was "a very busy post at the time," because the Party was in the process of raising "a quarter of a million dollars to finance the trial." Such a massive undertaking, Angela explains, "came on the heels of several others that year, and it was hard to get the money out of comrades who had already been bled white." Nevertheless, without arousing suspicion, she fulfilled her Party duties faithfully to the end, and was still a member in good standing when she took the stand at the trial of the CPUSA leadership in April, 1949. After the publication of *Red Masquerade*, the story of Angela's near-expulsion from the CPUSA would become part of her myth—a remarkable, not atypical example of her mastery of the half-truth. Eleanor Roosevelt and Mary Margaret McBride would want to know all about it.[5]

While the Party's action merely annoyed Angela, who had already been approached by federal prosecutors about appearing as a witness in *Dennis v. US*, Janny's expulsion—because she was sincere in her political convictions—seems to have precipitated a life-altering crisis. "That's when I started drinking," she said. "I stopped writing music, and I started drinking." Years later, when she "came out of the alcohol fog," Janny was able to re-connect politically with new movements more open to homosexuals (the women's movement, the peace movement) because she had always been a person who was "politically aware." The idealistic part of herself, which had attracted her to the Communist Party in the first place, remained intact, and she began to write songs again. Through the lean years, many lesbian friendships had failed her because they were people who "didn't want to identify themselves with anything political," Janny said. "I thought they were reactionary."[6]

In all likelihood, hers is the only story told in print by a lesbian asked to resign from the CPUSA as the Red Scare and Lavender Scare merged into one threat. Straight comrades have recounted, however, how they were told in the late 1940s and the 1950s during the McCarthy and HUAC hearings to request the resignations of "several known lesbians" or women who "had had a lesbian liaison." If the straight Party organizer assigned the task considered these lesbians her friends, it was on the old familiar "don't ask, don't tell" basis. She had "never discussed their sexual preference" with them. Bitter tears were shed, the organizer reported, but "the lesbians 'obeyed' and resigned."[7]

Under ordinary circumstances the membership of the CPUSA included many closeted lesbians and gay men. A small organization even at the height of its influence, the Party did not reject dues-paying recruits who were committed to leftist economic and social policies.

Likewise, no one seems to have been fooled, and straight comrades on the local level often knew who was lesbian or gay without any voluntary disclosures. A long-time activist, the late Dr. Annette Rubinstein said she had known Angela from Party gatherings, some in her own Upper West Side apartment, and had never doubted that she was a lesbian. People from the New York Photo League, where Angela took photography courses in the early 1940s, also remembered her in no uncertain terms. "She was obviously a lesbian," Sol Libsohn, one of the original Photo Leaguers, said matter-of-factly to an interviewer many years later, "and if you think that homosexuals are not popular now, at that time they were terribly unpopular and we knew she was a homosexual but we made nothing of it. We tried to make her feel comfortable."[8]

Other references highlight the presence of homosexuals, whether they announced themselves as such or not, who had thrown in their lot with the most radical movement of their times, an organization that was the conscience of the American Left for at least two decades. According to novelist Howard Fast, the FBI could pick out queers in a crowd. When "dealing with left-wing homosexuals," Fast recalled from his days in the CPUSA, the FBI "turned vicious, frequently beating the homosexuals savagely." More important for the modern gay movement, both Bob Hull and Chuck Rowland had been in the Party back in Minnesota before moving West to Los Angeles, where they became founding members of the Mattachine Society (1950), an early US gay rights group. Rowland had been head of American Youth for Democracy (AYD), which, in the late 1940s, was really a re-christened version of the Young Communist League (YCL), not "officially Communist, but it was," he said. Even though "it was not an issue you discussed," Rowland continued, "all the kids I worked with in AYD knew I was gay. […] Leaders of the Party in Minnesota knew."[9]

Closeted lesbians were also apparently abundant on different levels of Party organization. Based on his Party experience, Jim Kepner—a principal writer for *ONE Magazine*, the first widely distributed US publication for homosexuals, from 1953 to 1967, and avid collector of documents, from newspaper clippings to journal and magazine articles, to correspondence, brochures, and other printed materials that became the ONE National Gay and Lesbian Archives—shared an observation. Amongst the Party rank and file, Kepner saw lesbians everywhere. In fact, said Kepner, "a predominance of lesbians existed in the Party, as they did in the U.S. military." A few notches up in the Party structure was Betty Millard, writer and one-time editor of the radical leftist literary journal *New Masses*, and activist for the Congress of American Women, an affiliate of the postwar Women's International Democratic Federation (WIDF). Hauled before HUAC in 1959 to be questioned about the WIDF, Millard remained in the closet until her 80s, when she became a vocal advocate of LGBTQ causes.[10]

At least one other high-profile female member of the Party during its most influential years has been accused of wandering from the straight and narrow. The suspect is Elizabeth Gurley Flynn, born in 1890, originally an organizer for the Industrial Workers of the World (IWW), who from 1905 advocated for a united working class—One Big Union—to supplant capitalism. Gurley Flynn joined the Communist Party in 1936, rose to membership on the National Board, and co-founded the American Civil Liberties Union (ACLU). Flynn was convicted under the Smith Act at the Second New York trial of the Party leadership and sentenced in 1953 to two years in Alderson Federal Penitentiary in West Virginia. The ten years (1926-1936) that she spent in Portland, Oregon, with Dr. Marie Equi, a very out lesbian for that era, have aroused speculation about the erotic nature of their relationship. Certainly they seemed emotionally bound to each other and shared a common radical ideology. Most recently, Michael Helquist, in *Marie Equi. Radical Politics and Outlaw Passions*, insists that Flynn was a patient of Dr. Equi, recuperating from the severe stress of political activism, and not a lover.[11]

The example most often cited of lesbians in the Party remains that of Grace Hutchins, labor reformer and author, and in her early years a missionary to China, and her long-time companion and comrade Anna Rochester, social worker and child labor activist. Two maiden ladies in the classic American tradition of romantic friendships between women, they would not have embraced the term "lesbian," and we do not know what their reaction would have been to a gay liberation movement. A remark attributed to Grace hints at ambiguity. She and Anna were the witnesses, in 1931, at fellow Communist Whittaker Chambers' marriage, and later on Grace was pleased to assure Alger Hiss' lawyer it was "common knowledge that Chambers had been a sex pervert when he was employed by the *Daily Worker*."[12]

Of course, marriages of convenience were not unusual among the mid-century generation of gay men and lesbians, who often banded together to avoid gossip, please anxious parents, improve their business or political fortunes, or have children. The co-founder of Mattachine and the modern gay movement, Harry Hay, married a straight woman, on a therapist's advice, adopted children, and became an important part of a close-knit heterosexual circle of friends and comrades during the seventeen years he was a member of the CPUSA. It was the San Francisco longshoremen's strike, which turned into a four-day General Strike in July, 1934, that brought Hay to the Party. As he told historian John D'Emilio many years later, "You couldn't have been a part of that and not have your life completely changed." In 1951, he left, taking with him organizing skills and a belief in revolutionary change that shaped and made Mattachine possible.[13]

Because rumors of Party homophobia and stories about Harry Hay's "expulsion" from the Party have circulated widely, it seems worthwhile to insist that the truth is somewhat more complex and closely tied to the same historical moment that prompted the attempt to remove Angela. Explaining himself as a political activist and lifelong radical, Hay talked a lot about his Communist experience to biographers. He regretted the Party's "official attitude" as stated in its "own constitution" of 1938, which classifies "degenerates" (code for homosexuals) alongside a fascinating mix of reactionaries, addicts and informers—"strikebreakers, habitual drunkards, betrayers of Party confidence." Whether the policy echoed Stalinist re-criminalization of male homosexuality (and abortion and divorce) in the USSR during the 1930s, or owed its genesis to homegrown bias and fear, homosexuals should simply not have been in the Party. But they were.[14]

Harry Hay addressed that contradiction, suggesting "that the

Party officially knew of homosexuals only if they were arrested and exposed—in which case they would invariably leave the Party." That kind of talk recalls a time, as one of Hay's biographers writes, when "homosexuality in America was illegal, homosexuals were dangerous perverts, and every move a homosexual made was fraught with the danger of self-disclosure and subsequent persecution." Specifically, police routinely raided bars and arrested patrons, whose names and addresses were then published in the local press. Another common practice was entrapment, when officers—generally young and beguiling—testified in court that a gay man had made a sexual advance. Lives were decimated by these "vagrancy and lewdness" charges.[15]

A less-explored aspect of the problem was that police often turned gay people (under threat of fine, imprisonment, or just exposure as homosexuals) into spies, and one of their targets was the radical Left, and specifically the CPUSA. Harry Hay met one early on in LA, a police (or FBI) informant, who kissed first, then confessed that he was an informant—someone "who got caught once" and "had to pay ever since." It was the first of many times, Hay said, that he saw gay men "blackmailed again and again." Years later, in 1951, he left the Communist Party, because he had started working with Mattachine, which meant coming out of the closet. In a document composed by him and in conversation with Miriam Sherman, his district section organizer—who was later fired from UCLA for being a Communist—Harry recommended his own expulsion as a security risk. His affiliation with Mattachine could invite intimidation, even blackmail, by local and federal authorities, and he declined to endanger the Party. Too many comrades known to both Harry and Miriam, "*best* friends who turned out to be FBI spies," had been forced into compliance with authorities. Hay's decision was a difficult one, and a painful parting.[16]

Though the conclusion may seem unfair—and there might be more than a hint of homophobia—it is not hard to understand how gay people might be considered "automatic security risks" by that other persecuted group of outsiders, the American Communist Party. In fact, some members believed that Angela's sexual orientation played a part in her collaboration with the FBI. Dr. Annette Rubinstein, former New York City educator and author, immediately assumed that Angela had been blackmailed, forced to spy on the Party and to testify at the trial. Likewise, the wife of Angela's photography instructor, Sid Grossman—whose name Angela had offered up from the witness stand as a Communist and her Party recruiter—did not doubt that Angela had been blackmailed. Years ago, Miriam Grossman Cohen explained apologetically in an interview, gay people had been treated very badly. While they were both wrong about Angela, who went willingly into the service of the FBI, their conclusions show just how prevalent was the idea of gay men and lesbians as potential spies and informers. But there was worse to come.[17]

What sealed the fate of homosexuals in the CPUSA was the postwar Lavender Scare, rumors of which reached Harry Hay early on in Los Angeles. A friend of a friend at Hay's work, a young man working as a secretary in the State Department, came home to LA on vacation with the news that gay men were being fired from government jobs in Washington as "bad security risks" under the new Loyalty/Security program instituted by President Truman. Seldom remembered today, it was Executive Order 9835, in 1947, that established the Employee Loyalty Program in the Executive Branch of Government and its Loyalty Review Boards, launching the deadly 1950s witch hunt that cost many people jobs and reputations. Leftists, and especially American Communists, were accused of disloyalty, while homosexuals of all political stripes seemed to Herbert Brownell Jr., Eisenhower's Attorney General, in 1953, "security risks" because "of "personal habits" that might make them "subject to blackmail by people who seek to destroy the safety of our country."[18]

The young man just in from Washington who warned Harry Hay reported that all the guys he knew who had been fired from the State Department had slept with the same "dream-boat" named "Andrew." The implication was that Andrew was being blackmailed by police, threatened with exposure if he did not entrap and rat out other gay men. It was the summer of 1948, and the Party would soon begin the process of divesting itself of its gay and lesbian members. They went after Angela in mid-September.[19]

As the Red Scare and the Lavender Scare lurched into high

gear, homosexuals were at the center of things because of their presumed vulnerability to blackmail. All sides seemed to want to enlist them as spies. The police could blackmail those who feared exposure and possible loss of livelihood, and plant them among American Communists, who also feared exposure and probable loss of livelihood. On the other hand, reports out of Washington insisted that weak, "degenerate" homosexuals were being recruited by that same International Communism to betray the homeland. As Senator Kenneth Wherry (R-Nebraska) suggested in 1950, "You can't hardly separate homosexuals from subversives. Mind you, I don't say every homosexual is a subversive, and I don't say every subversive is a homosexual. But a man of low morality is a menace in the government, whatever he is, and they are all tied up together." To sum up, Nicholas Von Hoffman, Roy Cohn's biographer, observed, that "the only thing the State Department and the Communist Party agreed on was that homosexuals were security risks."[20]

While the Left traditionally held that homosexuality was just another "degenerate phase of a decadent system," which would presumably disappear under socialism, the anti-gay rhetoric on the Right reached dizzying heights, both on the floor of the US Congress and in a book called *Washington Confidential* (1951) by Jack Lait and Lee Mortimer, both journalists from the *New York Daily Mirror* and the authors of other very popular volumes—*New York Confidential, Chicago Confidential, U.S.A. Confidential.* Their Washington story sold 150,000 copies in hardcover in the first three weeks after its publication, and was number one on the *New York Times* bestseller list. In the chapter on "Garden of Pansies," Lait and Mortimer reported that gay bars were attracting foreign agents, who had been "indoctrinated and given a course in homosexuality [in Moscow], then taught to infiltrate in perverted circles in other countries" to "gather secret information." *Washington Confidential* was not alone in these accusations. The front page of the *Washington Times-Herald,* for March 19, 1950, suggested that Soviet agents were targeting heterosexual female civil servants, controlling them by "enticing them into a life of Lesbianism." Exactly how this was accomplished was not explained.[21]

In Los Angeles, Harry Hay saw happening just what he had

feared. As he later set down in notes on what ideas had gone into the organization of Mattachine, he recalled that "the post-war reaction, the shutting down of open communication, was already of concern to many of us progressives. I knew the government was going to look for a new enemy, a new scapegoat." Hay saw African Americans already beginning to organize, and the horror of the holocaust "was too recent to put the Jews in this position. [...] The natural scapegoat would be us, the Queers." They "were the one group of disenfranchised people who did not even know they were a group because they had never formed as a group. They—we—had to get started. It was high time." Believing that the best hope for survival was organization, a concept he had mastered during his years in the CPUSA, Hay turned his considerable energies exclusively to Mattachine, and left the Party (and his straight life) behind.[22]

Because he had been a model comrade who had taught in Party schools, and chosen to withdraw from the Party for his own reasons, Hay's "expulsion" was certainly not typical, though he was certainly aware that being out in the Party was not a likely option. As his friend and local Party executive Miriam Sherman, who was fired from UCLA for being a Communist, recalled, "nobody knew how to handle" the announcement that Harry Hay, "a respected, valued Party member," was openly gay. For her it was an "eye-opener because it was the first time that she had thought of the issue in political terms." In recognition of his years of service as a Marxist teacher, at the People's Educational Center in LA, and at its successor, the Southern California Labor School, the Party officially offered him the equivalent of "an honorable discharge." He was designated "a lifelong friend of the people."[23]

Ironically, Hay was not so lucky with the organization he had founded alongside fellow ex-Communists Chuck Rowland and Bob Hull. In 1953, during the heyday of Joseph McCarthy's influence in Washington, Mattachine held a series of conventions that replaced Hay and other "radical elements." In the spirit of the times, conservative leaders at a November gathering in Los Angeles threatened to "turn over to the FBI the names of everyone in attendance if the convention failed to reject the 'communistic' principles imposed by the old leadership."[24]

The new leadership of Mattachine had rejected Hay's call for "a highly ethical homosexual culture," and for the next couple of years seemed to shy away from any homosexual label. Statements by former Mattachine members suggest that they were coming close, according to John D'Emilio, author of *Sexual Politics, Sexual Communities,* to denying that it was an organization of homosexuals. One of those who resigned his Southern California post in Mattachine in protest, Ben Tabor, said the new leadership had denied both that they were an organization of homosexuals, and that they were interested in demanding their civil rights. Chuck Rowland surmised that "they wanted a gay organization but they didn't want to be hurt. They didn't want to be secret, but they also didn't want to be open. It was a ridiculous contradiction."[25]

Angela Calomiris would have certainly sympathized with their dilemma, since such a label would have put an end to her budding career as all-American anti-Communist heroine. She intended to steer clear of an unpleasant topic by concocting a novel version of the Party's attempt to expel her. She had tried it out in *Red Masquerade,* where Comrade Dora, with the "mousy brown hair," had suggested she leave the Party. Angela, perpetually on stage, had responded with what she hoped sounded like genuine alarm, "exactly what Dora would have expected of a good comrade." Angela continued to fume, refused to leave the Party and threatened to go over Dora's head to demand a hearing.[26]

Because Angela's interviews with both Eleanor Roosevelt and Mary Margaret McBride presumed some knowledge of the book, this whole saga of the Party's attempt to expel her received a considerable amount of air time. Angela's "expulsion" story fastened on the risks run and dangers confronted (real or imagined) as an undercover informant. It became another of those narrow escapes that moved the spy narrative along.

McBride, who had probably actually read Angela's book, commented in her sweet homespun way that Angela had experienced "several narrow squeaks." "There was one time," McBride continued, "when they asked her to resign from the party and to this day you don't know why, do you?"

Angela had her story ready, and it was ingenious. "I don't know exactly," she began, excusing herself, "and so I really can't say." But she had "an opinion," based on what she knew about "so much jealousy in the Party." "I was getting a little too popular," she confided to McBride, "I was the only one who had a little sense of humor [...] and I got work done, and that's how I got a reputation of being a good functionary."

She gave Mrs. Roosevelt a slightly retooled version when the former First Lady asked, "Did you have any narrow escapes? And did they suspect you at any time in the Party?"

"Yes," replied Angela, stating that about nine months before her trial appearance, "there was an attempt to drop me from the Party." She explained that she "was becoming a little too popular with the members." "I really can't say what they had against me," she continued. "There is an awful lot of jealousy in the Party. You have no idea."

McBride went along with Angela's story, confirming that "you don't think they suspected that you were an undercover agent. You think it was just jealousy. Somebody wanted to get you out because you could never find out about it."

It was a good story, designed to deceive and to please. But Angela, of course, knew the truth about what had gone on during the summer of 1948. Without mentioning gay people, *Red Masquerade* outlined the panic that had gripped the Party with the indictment of the National Board members who would stand trial before Judge Harold Medina. More signs of impending disaster included the dismissal "for disloyalty" of government officials, and informant/ witness Elizabeth Bentley's testimony naming more federal employees. Perhaps Angela even knew about discussions in Party circles around banishing gay people as security risks, a threat which she, in fact, personified.[27]

But it was safer to attribute her problems to a clash of personalities, as described in *Red Masquerade,* between herself and a New York County Party executive named Rena Klein, who had, according to Angela, "a long, thin, concave face with a jutting, pointed jaw and near-sighted eyes that squinted." Klein was just one of many American Communists, all of them well-known to the FBI but not to the general public, named in *Red Masquerade.* Another unidentified informant found Klein more attractive than Angela chose to portray her. At "5'5", 125 lbs., good looking, black hair, dark brown eyes, olive complexion," the Rena Klein in the second undercover file radiated much more charm than the "pinched, ambitious girl" of Angela's story. Perhaps a hint of envy, a touch of personal malice accompanied the "scraps of information" about Klein that Angela relayed back to the FBI: "on intimate terms with leaders of the Italian Communist Party [...] married to a Tass press representative at the United Nations." Meanwhile, Klein liked Angela less, and got her removed as section organizer. Their frequent tiffs indicated that Angela was not popular with everyone. But the whole story was probably nothing more or less than an elaborate smokescreen to conceal a potentially harmful truth—that Angela had been asked to leave the CPUSA because she was a lesbian.[28]

To make sure that the attempt to expel her was not about her FBI work, she told Eleanor Roosevelt that she had demanded a trial, with witnesses. She took her demands "from one person to another" and "threatened to take it to the [Party] convention." "If they knew that I was an agent," Angela explained her plan to Mrs. Roosevelt, "find out how they had investigated, who had told them, so that I could prevent other undercover agents from being exposed."

Mary Margaret admired Angela's "courage," going "straight to as many heads as she could get to and she said I want to know what's back of this?"

One of those heads, Angela revealed in *Red Masquerade*, was John Lautner of the Party's State Security Commission who seemed sympathetic, and suggested that she was a valuable Party member who could work with the "Greek comrades" or "in the photographers' section." That reprieve kept her in the Party. Rena Klein would next greet her old nemesis with a sneer at the Foley Square courthouse when Angela took the stand for the prosecution.[29]

Angela was pleased to have put one over on John Lautner, a twenty-year Party veteran responsible for security who had been born in Hungary, and had served with US military intelligence during World War II. Lautner's failure to follow through on Angela's expulsion ("preventing the expulsion of the spy, Calomiris") contributed in part to his own removal from the Party some months later as a "traitor and enemy of the working class." Justifiably or not, as more FBI informers came forward with testimony at trials and hearings, Lautner was blamed for not having detected their infiltration, and suspected of being an informer himself.[30]

His was a very high-profile expulsion that he resented deeply. It drove him into the FBI's embrace, and he became the prosecution's most valuable witness in Smith Act trials of Party leaders from New York to Hawaii, and also at Subversive Activities Control Board (SACB) hearings. From 1952 to 1956, Lautner testified at fifteen Smith Act prosecutions, and nine SACB hearings. The SACB had been set up in November, 1950, under the Internal Security Act (or Subversive Activities Control Act, or McCarran Act, 1950) to oversee the registration of Communist "front" organizations with the US Attorney General. Because of his position in the Party, his expulsion attracted press coverage, something Angela usually reveled in. But this time, in the "National Affairs" section of *Newsweek*, filled with details of the Judith Coplon espionage trials and Lautner's expulsion, new evidence about the Party's attempt to purge Angela from its ranks emerged. She had been accused, said *Newsweek*, not only of "making statements critical of the party" but also "of not being quite as fiercely puritanical in her private life as party rules demand."[31]

Angela did not care what the Communist press said about her, and they said quite a lot. In *Red Masquerade* she cites a pamphlet that Elizabeth Gurley Flynn wrote entitled "Stoolpigeon" that denounced those who joined the Party just to report back on its activities to the FBI. An editorial in *Masses and Mainstream*, an American Marxist monthly publication from 1948 to 1963, also caught Angela's attention, because it referred to prosecution witnesses in the Smith Act trial as "disease-bearing vermin," and the FBI informer program "germ warfare."[32]

But she certainly understood the threat that insinuations of "immorality"—straight or gay—in a prestigious mainstream magazine represented. Talk like that could nip a profitable career in the bud, especially if anyone chose to dig deeper into Angela's love life. But she had answered such threats to her reputation before, on the witness stand with Judge Medina's help, and she was not about to be outed now by *Newsweek*.

6. Angela Takes the Stand

Angela did not like the idea that someone was on to her, since masquerading as straight was essential to the New York press portrayal of her as the "typical American girl." While she usually welcomed publicity, the *Newsweek* inference that her life was less than "puritanical" opened a crack in her armor. And the timing was bad.

Only weeks before, she had unveiled for the first time her plans to publish her story in book form. It was a surprise announcement that erased any doubt as to whether or not Angela intended to capitalize on her FBI connection and the publicity surrounding the trial. Under the headline "Books—Authors," the *New York Times* carried the news in October 1949 that Angela was "at work on a book dealing with her seven years as an undercover agent for the 'Subversive Squad' of the Federal Bureau of Investigation." The New York FBI Office found out that Calomiris was in the process of writing a book by reading the *Times,* and let Hoover know that they had certainly not been consulted. Publication, by the Philadelphia publishing house of J. B. Lippincott—which had recently hired new editorial staff and was in the market for potential best-sellers—was scheduled for "early next year." That would correspond to January

1950, and the issue of *Newsweek* that was full of Red Scare goings-on, including Angela.[1]

But she was by no means the headliner in the "National Affairs" section. That distinction belonged to Judith Coplon, a Barnard College graduate who, like so many others, had taken a job in Washington during World War II. Her position in the Justice Department, Foreign Agents Registration section, had given her access to information of interest to America's war-time Soviet allies. By 1949, when she was arrested, Coplon's Soviet sympathies had fallen out of fashion. She was convicted of espionage at her first trial in Washington, and, as *Newsweek* went to press, her second trial for conspiracy, as co-defendant with her Soviet handler Valentin Gubitchev, was just getting underway in New York. Within a few days, a federal court also found Alger Hiss guilty of perjury. In fact, for a while in 1949, the Foley Square trial of the Party leaders, the first Alger Hiss trial, from May to July, and the first Judith Coplon trial, from April to June, were in session simultaneously. A contemporary commentator, George Marion, in *The Communist Trial: An American Crossroads*, called it "a three-ring circus or a witches' Sabbath." The only possible and alarming conclusion for a frightened public was that the US Government was riddled with spies.[2]

These recent "heresy" trials and the convictions revived for *Newsweek* memories of the previous year's "conspiracy trial of the eleven Communist leaders in New York"—and recollections of "a thin, dark, angular girl," with a "sharp tongue and ready wit," named Angela Calomiris. But alas, the focus again was not on Angela *per se* but on John Lautner, former head of Party security, whose expulsion from the Party had been announced in the *Daily Worker* the week before, on January 17, 1950. There he had been accused of endangering comrades by "preventing the expulsion of the spy, Calomiris." "Unofficial party sources" had let *Newsweek* in on the gossip about Angela's private life, and revealed that Lautner had "refused to put Miss Calomiris on trial, dismissing the charges as preposterous." Angela, on the other hand, was quoted as defending Lautner's loyalty to the Party.[3]

By the time she got to the New York FBI Office presided over by SAC Edward Scheidt, she was livid, her anger doubtless masking the real fear of being found out. Always prone to histrionics, Angela was claiming that *Newsweek* had never interviewed her, had invented comments attributed to her, and "slurred her by inferring her private life was slightly less than puritanical." She told SAC Scheidt that she was writing a letter of protest to *Newsweek*, a course of action that he—in keeping with the Bureau's policy of avoiding adverse publicity—hastened to discourage. He had argued, Scheidt reported back to FBI Headquarters, that it had been a Communist attempt to vilify her, and not *Newsweek*'s fault.[4]

What SAC Scheidt really thought at this point about his former confidential informant and key prosecution witness, who was still on the FBI payroll at $225.00 per month, is not recorded. Regarding her character or the defamation of it, he had certainly had enough clues that she was difficult. Facing her down in his office, he could have only hoped to avoid further scandal, and perhaps hasten her departure. Always determined to have the last word, Angela as a parting shot added that the Party had, in fact, tried to vilify her in the past "by bribing former Party acquaintances to defame her character."[5]

At first glance this might seem a routine off-the-cuff denunciation of Communist guile, an accusation like many others that Angela made from the witness stand and in *Red Masquerade*. But a story told by one of her friends from the old Village days suggests there was more to Angela's remark than anti-Communist rhetoric. It also reveals who the "former Party acquaintances" bribed to defame her might have been, and the relation of the whole to her testimony from the witness stand at the trial of the eleven Communist leaders.

Morry Baer was a lesbian who took the Civil Service exam for the New York Police Department at the height of the Great Depression, in the late 1930s, placed among the top twenty women to qualify, and after graduating from the Police Academy, served her twenty years on the force. During World War II, she worked Special Squads One and Two, monitoring blackouts and countering espionage in the Brooklyn Navy Yard, and later patrolled with the Midtown Youth Division, shepherding stray youth out of harm's way. On assignment at the 10th Precinct on West 20th Street, she took an apartment in Chelsea, and became friends with Angela Calomiris and a group of Village lesbians, among them a seamstress who sewed for Broadway shows named French Jacky (Jacqueline Moritz). Of course, Jacky and Angela had been close for years, and had teamed up to open a second-floor Village club that featured local art. The police closed them down, probably for operating without a liquor license.[6]

One of Morry's favorite stories involving her friend Angela, who taught Morry photography skills in the Jane Street apartment, began with a phone call from French Jacky, who lived back then on Christopher Street. The Communists—that is, comrades from the local branch plus a couple of higher ups—wanted to see Jacky, wanted to come over to her apartment. They wanted her to take the stand as a witness for the defense, said Morry, and give evidence against Angela Calomiris, who had testified for the prosecution beginning on April 26, 1949. Apparently, French Jacky did not welcome the Party's attentions and certainly not the visit. She asked Morry to come over before the delegation's arrival and hide in the hall closet, .32 caliber service revolver at the ready, in case things got out of hand. While there seems to have been no real threat of violence, Morry, who was a crack shot and a member of the NYPD women's pistol team, took up the challenge and concealed herself in French Jacky's hall closet amidst a vast stockpile of sex toys. That collection, for the octogenarian Morry, was the most memorable aspect of the tale, trumping any political or historical significance. She could not say why the Party would have targeted French Jacky, nor why they would have expected her to cooperate.[7]

In hindsight, it is apparent the Party knew French Jacky, knew that she knew Angela, and assumed (or hoped) that Jacky would want to help them out. All that implies that Jacky had been either a Party member or a fellow traveler, and likely the former, which would explain why her long-time companion, Ruth Parish, did not want to talk about it, even years later. Ruth did say that Morry's story was not true, and that Jacky would have never appeared in court to denounce her friend Angela. It is also possible that Jacky might have been approached earlier on by the FBI to collect insider information on the CPUSA. As a lesbian, she would have been vulnerable to such overtures. Could Jacky have been that "someone who was an F.B.I. undercover agent, too"? The someone Angela speculates about in *Red Masquerade* who recommended her to the Bureau. While this is not idle speculation, it leaves many questions unanswered.[8]

But Morry was very specific. The evidence the Party wanted French Jacky to give, she said, would have taken the suggestion that Angela's private life was slightly less than puritanical a step further. They wanted Jacky, who was a rather "obvious" lesbian herself, to say on the stand that Angela was a lesbian, in order to convey to judge and jury that this was a marginal person whose habitual behavior was just a shade above criminal. It was one way, they hoped, to discredit her testimony and get it stricken from the court record. French Jacky, however, would not budge, and apparently reported back to Angela. Without naming names, the story found its way into *Red Masquerade,* where one of her female friends "was offered a bribe if she could produce any discreditable information" about Angela's "moral character."[9]

Since French Jacky declined, the defense was determined to force the issue in other ways. This was obviously their plan when, after some questions about her reports to the FBI, especially since the beginning of the trial on January 17 (a topic to which counsel returned), Louis McCabe for the defense remarked, "You were living down in Greenwich Village at that time?" Following an inquiry into her photography training, he returned again to where and how Angela lived. "You have lived with one or another roommate, is that correct?" asked McCabe.[10]

Despite objections by the prosecution to this line of questioning, all of them sustained by presiding Judge Medina, McCabe persisted. "With whom do you live? Do you have any family?" He later zeroed in on her unmarried status, in an age long before "Ms." became a possibility, with, "Now I believe it is *Miss* Calomiris? I have not heard that. Is it *Miss* Calomiris?" McCabe finally took his cross-examination a step further with "Have any children? [...] Have you ever had any children?"[11]

At that point, Attorneys for the State rose to her defense with objections, while Angela replied, "I do not have any children." Judge Medina offered her his protection. "It is a kind of thing I don't like to see," he interjected, then added, "I certainly would never have asked such a question [about children] when I was a lawyer." After McCabe made another reference to Angela's unmarried state, Medina snapped at him with undisguised hostility, "We have had enough of that."[12]

Since defense counsel had determined to discredit Angela and her testimony, she was lucky to find the cards stacked in her favor. The prosecution rallied around with objections to anything that might have exposed her recollection of events as generally faulty if not downright dishonest. But it was Judge Medina who saved the day. Whether he championed her out of gallantry, or more likely out of hostility for defense counsel and Communists, Medina intervened repeatedly to take the pressure off the witness. "Why don't you let her [answer]? You keep talking," he told Richard Gladstein, a lawyer from San Francisco, who took over the interrogation from McCabe.[13]

Medina had earlier on taken it upon himself to guide Angela smoothly through the judicial process. While she was being questioned by the US Attorney, Harry Sacher of New York for the defense, who had represented left-leaning labor unions, like Mike Quill's Transport Workers (TWU) and the militant Furriers Union, moved to strike one of her answers. "Don't let Mr. Sacher get you excited," Medina comforted Angela. "You just take it easy." He then explained to her that "in the law, you cannot give conclusions, you cannot say people agreed and you cannot say people were confused, [...] but you have to describe in some way what you saw. It sounds silly but that is the way you have to do it."[14]

He was equally patient, considerate, and trusting of other prosecution witnesses and their testimony. Defense witnesses did not fare so well, perhaps most prestigious among them Paul Robeson, at the time one of America's top-flight entertainers, who had starred in stage and movie versions of *Showboat*, and as Othello on Broadway opposite Uta Hagen. His testimony in support of the defendants' contention that they had never taught or advocated "the duty or the necessity of overthrowing the Government of the United States by force or violence" was overwhelmed by prosecution objections, sustained by Medina. Other defense efforts were mounted to refute prosecution witnesses who had made Marxist theory sound like an armed uprising, and reduced "Communism to tales of sabotage and plots to bring the Red Army down through Canada to Detroit."[15]

This was a reference to testimony, cited here previously, by one Charles Nicodemus, former local official of the Textile Workers Union, CIO, and now prosecution witness. He contributed as much as anyone to the common notion, kept alive throughout the trial, that a violent revolution was at hand, aided and abetted by a Red Army invasion. While the defendants smiled and shook their heads in disbelief, Judge Medina treated Nicodemus' remarks with high seriousness. "They could even destroy Detroit, as I understood it," Medina repeated helpfully. For him, as for much of the fearful, war-weary country, the warning rang true, while also highlighting the importance of Detroit—"the Arsenal of Democracy" during the war, and a symbol of American industrial might. For its industries and key role in the labor movement, Detroit would figure in much of the testimony to come. Meanwhile, the press responded hysterically to Nicodemus' revelations, with headlines proclaiming "Red Invasion Plan Reported at Trial" and "Plans to Invade U.S. via Alaska Told at Red Trial."[16]

A second attempt by the defense to diffuse the notion that Marxist theory promoted "armed forays by cutthroat bands" brought to the witness stand Herbert Aptheker, historian and author of classic texts on African-American history. Aptheker was called to rebut the prosecution's lead-off witness Louis Budenz, former Managing Editor of the *Daily Worker* and now a confirmed anti-Communist for hire. In his testimony he had introduced the concept of an "Aesopian language," invented by Lenin to disguise political observations and elude Czarist censors. This language was still in use, he claimed, by the Party. For the prosecution's purposes, this meant that if Communists talked about a peaceful transition to socialism, for example, they really meant violent revolution. In fact, they never said what they meant, Budenz argued, or, simply put, Communists lied. His testimony was solemnly accepted by the court.[17]

On the other hand, Aptheker's attempts to define Marxism as an economic and social theory came a bit late for Medina, who by then was in a rush. He argued that, by August, the trial "had become an endurance contest." In the face of objections sustained by Medina, Harry Sacher ended his examination of Aptheker because he found it "utterly impossible [...] in view of your Honor's rulings, to lay before the jury the teachings of the Communist Party [...] concerning which the witness Budenz was interrogated and was permitted to testify." Aptheker was excused, but Gladstein remarked that "your Honor applied one rule to the prosecution and a different one to us."[18]

Medina made defense counsel pay. As the trial progressed, Harry Sacher, along with Gladstein, became prime targets for his caustic remarks. With ever-increasing animosity, he accused Sacher of "tittering and laughing and giggling." He then charged Gladstein with "digging" at him, "a cruel thing to do," "starting to shout," and speaking to him "in that rough way." Besides taxing his nerves, the defense team also sapped his energies, the sixty-one-year-old judge claimed, by dragging out their interrogations and arguing against his orders. Early on he had decided that lawyers would be limited to objections without discussion, because he had found in this case that such "discussion" had become "absolutely intolerable and such a burden" that he would not be able to "physically continue through to the end of the trial" if he permitted it. Perhaps he feared he would end up like the judge in the war-time 1944 Smith Act trial, in Washington, DC, of suspected Axis conspirators and sympathizers. After eight months of that trial, the presiding judge Edward C. Eicher died, succumbing at age sixty-five to illness and fatigue, and the case ended in a mistrial. For his part, and as the weeks stretched into months at Foley Square, Medina lamented that "we will just never be through that way." To bolster his argument, he complained that the defense's cross-examination of Angela had lasted five days. The prosecuting attorney assured him it had only been four.[19]

Defense lawyers responded to the judge's attitude by assigning numerous remarks of his "as prejudicial misconduct," and with repeated calls for a mistrial—perhaps the loudest concerning charges of bias against one juror, Russell Janney, who had been heard out of court denouncing, among other things, "those God Damn Communists." Historian David Caute's monumental *The Great Fear*, which analyzes the Red Scare in infinite detail, cites other quotes from Janney, asserting he would "fight Communism to the death" and "hang those Commies." Complaints about Janney went unanswered, and Medina denied the motion for a mistrial.[20]

Janney, the last juror picked, had originally gotten on the case after weeks spent on a defense challenge to the jury pool on the basis of discrimination in favor of the "rich, propertied and well-to-do."

It was a challenge that had infuriated Medina. Not one to forgive and forget, later in the trial he remarked to defense counsel, "Every time I think of those jury challenges I just get sick." Meanwhile, Russell Janney, outspoken and opinionated, and a successful author, ended up sharing the jury box with three African Americans, several housewives, and at least one unemployed person. The foreman of the jury was Thelma Dial, a part-time dressmaker from Harlem.[21]

Remarks by Janney had been offered to the defense in support of its motion for a mistrial. A sworn statement from Carol Nathanson, whose stage name was Carol Nason, a singer-actress who had a professional acquaintance with Russell Janney, quoted him as declaring, "I'm so tired of Marxism-Leninism" and "They preach hate." Her gesture of assistance to the defense was a brave one, and not to be underestimated at the height of the anti-Communist hysteria. As a successful theatrical producer, and author of the novel *The Miracle of the Bells*—made into a major motion picture in 1948—Janney had considerable power. In the course of her affidavit, Nathanson cited an occasion when Janney had called her a Communist, which could have easily earned her a spot on the entertainment blacklist.[22]

From long experience in show business, Russell Janney was likely more savvy about some things than most of his fellow jurors. According to Nathanson's account, he was not fooled by the feminine outfits Angela wore to court. "She looked more like a lesbian to me, if anything," he had been heard to declare. What others in the courtroom thought is unknown.[23]

The press, on the other hand, seldom faltered in its praise of Angela, that "slight young woman with black cropped hair and an air of quiet composure." Reporters outdid themselves in creating a complex identity for her. She was brave and defiant, and, according to Russell Porter of the *New York Times*, "answered back with flashing eyes when defense lawyers tried to heckle her." To the *Herald Tribune*, she was charming and feminine, a "pert young brunette" whose "manner was casual, and her voice was soft. She smiled readily." The *Post* let its readers know that Judge Medina had protected "Miss Angela Calomiris" from the "insinuating questions" posed by defense counsel. Other observers of the trial were less generous. At least one supporter of the Communist defendants saw through

Angela's decorous masquerade. In agreement with juror Russell Janney, she remarked to her family that "the government had dressed up that lesbian to put her on the witness stand."[24]

The defense made one more stab at exposing Angela, letting her know that they, at least, knew she had been identified by the Party as a lesbian. Along the way, they hoped to prove her a liar, making all her testimony suspect. When asked if she had ever stated in writing that she was "a loyal and conscientious Communist," she suddenly couldn't recall. In fact, Angela's responses during her cross-examination are filled with a lot of vague replies ("I don't remember," "I don't recall," and "I may have or I may not have"). Even regarding her day job as recreation worker for the WPA—"Senior" worker, she reminded the defense—she could neither recall on which playground she had worked nor when. So much side-stepping may have been obvious to the court, but helped to avoid straight answers whose truthfulness might be questioned.[25]

This time Gladstein for the defense thought he had Angela cornered. The letter he handed her—where she insisted she was "a loyal and conscientious Communist"—was an appeal that harkened back to the Party's attempt to expel her, as it had expelled others for homosexuality. It was addressed to her Party Section leaders, reminding them of the posts that she had held "faithfully and honorably," and asking for a hearing on charges against her. To hold that letter in her hand must have been a bit disturbing, even for the unflappable Angela. There was some back and forth between her and Gladstein about whether the signature was hers, whether she had written the letter herself, but she knew that he knew what the letter meant.[26]

Gladstein insisted on reminding Angela of that moment when "certain persons in the Communist Party were about to make charges against you," charges "of a personal character and had to do with your character." Angela denied all references to her "character" and answered that she had been accused "of being anti-Party, of making anti-Party statements and of associating with anti-Party people." It sounded better than being called a lesbian. Gladstein did not accept her story and did not back down. "Those accusations had to do with your moral character, did they not?" he asked. Angela stood by her "anti-Party" story.[27]

But in that battle of nerves, she must have suffered twinges of anxiety before the government, once again, rose to her defense. The prosecuting attorney was on his feet protesting the "insinuation" and recalling earlier "insinuating questions" without specifying what was being insinuated. Medina, in turn, acknowledged that the defense, in introducing "these matters," was questioning the credibility of the witness.[28]

Faced with thirteen witnesses, most of them in the pay of the FBI, all willing to swear that the CPUSA had been preparing the overthrow of the US government, the defense had hoped to bring down at least one. From what they knew about Angela, they thought they had a good chance. But the government, which probably had no doubts either about who their star witness was, chose to stand behind her one hundred percent. It was, after all, a trial that made for strange bedfellows, and the important issue was to convict the Communists.

Medina sealed the bargain. "What you might think is a matter of moral character," he instructed Gladstein, referring to the sexual innuendoes that had swirled around Angela's testimony, "and what the law regards as matters affecting credibility may be two entirely different things." That, on a positive note, could be interpreted to mean that Angela being a lesbian did not necessarily make her a liar. And besides, lying all along to the Party about being "a loyal and conscientious Communist" had been a basic function of her spy mission. Writing it down in a letter meant nothing, and during this trial (and elsewhere) informers received considerable leeway. A brief re-direct by the US Attorney affirmed the credibility of the witness, that she was "to be believed in what she testified."[29]

For now, Angela had dodged the issue that would have disqualified her for celebrity and curtailed her chances for a book contract and photography jobs she hoped to get through FBI connections. Soon after the next witness for the prosecution, Thomas Aaron Younglove, of St. Louis, Missouri, took the stand, Harry Sacher for the defense moved that Angela's testimony be stricken from the record. Judge Medina denied the motion, and Younglove would go on to prove his worth by testifying for the prosecution at subsequent Smith Act trials—the Second New York trial of 1951, and the 1952 Baltimore trial.[30]

Angela does not talk much in *Red Masquerade* about her experience on the witness stand except to say that "it was long, grueling work." While she does recall being asked by McCabe if she had a child—"desperate, open insinuations which disgusted the judge"—she discreetly left out Gladstein and the letter protesting her expulsion from the Party. It's likely that such a hostile cross-examination, by a defense team who knew about the Party's attempt to expel her and was determined to use it against her, must have left her feeling vulnerable. She survived thanks to support from both prosecution and Judge Medina. Likewise, in an unusual move, the FBI also offered its whole-hearted support. "Soon after she took the stand," the *New York Times* reported, "the FBI issued a public statement lauding her for 'patriotic assistance to the United States Government.'" It was additional proof that it was better to be a lesbian (or almost anything else) than an American Communist as the Cold War began in earnest.[31]

The defense attorneys were not as lucky as Angela. At the conclusion of this rather unconventional exercise in American justice, after the convictions of the eleven Communist leaders were announced, Medina found their lawyers in contempt of court and sentenced each one to from four- to six-month jail terms. One, Louis McCabe, got off with thirty days. Not surprisingly, Communists had a hard time finding someone to defend them in future Smith Act trials. Judge Medina, by contrast, became a national hero for facing down the Communists and their lawyers. Robert Ruark, later known for his novel *Something of Value* (1955) about the Mau Mau uprising in Kenya, published an editorial in the *Washington Daily News*, a Scripps-Howard paper, as the verdicts were announced. It celebrated "Judge Medina for Governor—or President," and insisted that defense counsel had "tried their level best to drive him nuts" and to "knock him loose from his dignity and authority."[32]

Angela, for one, had had enough of the American judicial system, and never took the witness stand again in support of the anti-Communist cause. Her FBI file, in memos dating from 1951 to 1958, indicates that she was much in demand and being pressured to testify. But she declined over and over, remarking that she did not "wish to make a career of testifying." More to the point, she added that she did not "wish to expose herself needlessly to continued harassment from Party sympathizers by projecting herself before the public again." In fact, she declared to FBI agents, anxious to enlist her aid in other Smith Act trials, that she would not testify again under any circumstances—not even, she said, "if the Attorney General should pass a law requiring her to do so."[33]

The only time she considered a second court appearance was in 1950, to aid the New York City Board of Education in the prosecution of eight New York City school teachers, members of the left-leaning Teachers Union and "alleged CP members or sympathizers." In a conversation with US Attorney Irving H. Saypol, who had prosecuted Alger Hiss and would go on to serve as Chief Prosecutor in the case of Julius and Ethel Rosenberg, Angela said she felt obliged to testify. She wanted to assist in establishing a precedent that disqualified from teaching anyone professing an adherence to Communist doctrine. For Angela, as she explained to Saypol, the case against the teachers was as important to the City of New York and the school system as the trial of the Party leaders had been for the country. But US Attorney Irving Saypol admonished her to keep quiet until the appeal of *Dennis v. US* was over. After that, he told her, "he did not care what she did." Angela reported to her FBI handlers that she did not appreciate Saypol's attitude. Without Angela's assistance, the eight teachers were fired in February 1951, on charges of insubordination and conduct unbecoming a teacher.[34]

While the FBI still kept in touch, Angela's Bureau connections were beginning to fray. She would not, as she had declared, become a professional witness or "make a career of testifying" as many of her male counterparts (Louis Budenz, Herbert Philbrick, Matt Cvetic, Harvey Matusow) had done. Again, it was not for lack of invitations, including unanswered subpoenas from HUAC to appear April 1951, and from the Subversive Activities Control Board (SACB) to appear November 1953. SACB's mandate was to combat "Communist infiltration of American society" by insuring the registration of organizations that it found to be "Communist fronts," "Communist action" groups, or "Communist infiltrated" groups.[35]

Why Angela turned down these and other opportunities to make some money (witnesses were paid) and garner more publicity boils down to the simple fact that it was no longer worth the risk. It appears that she had miscalculated both the FBI's ability (or inclination) to protect her following her appearance on the witness stand, and the anger of her betrayed comrades. After the Foley Square trial, she acknowledged to the New York Office that she had "found testifying too harrowing an experience because of harassment to her in subsequent months." And a year later, she complained to Special Agent in Charge Edward Scheidt, when government attorneys wanted her to testify at the prosecution of the International Workers Order (IWO), about mysterious phone calls she received, and strange men hanging around her apartment building. She feared, she said, "rough house tactics from them" since she had photographed IWO members on several occasions. *Red Masquerade* confirms that, through Party comrades, she had gotten "jobs of photographing I.W.O. meetings and officers" and that the FBI "received a duplicate of every print."[36]

Using photography skills that she had honed in classes with the Photo League and on the job, Angela helped to hasten the demise of that unique insurance, mutual benefit, and fraternal organization called the IWO—not to be confused with the earlier IWW, Industrial Workers of the World. The IWO's major appeal lay in its low-cost health and life insurance plans, whose rates discriminated neither against workers in dangerous or high-risk employment (such as coal miners) nor against African Americans, who otherwise could not get insurance at reasonable rates. Friends and members of the IWO included Paul Robeson, Langston Hughes, Rockwell Kent, Jimmy Durante, and Zero Mostel. But because the founders of the IWO had been Communists, the Red Scare sealed its fate, and because it was licensed as an insurance company, the State of New York's Insurance Commission brought the legal action. Its liquidation was ordered on the grounds that its political leanings constituted a hazard for the policyholders, and by 1954, the IWO, founded in 1930, had ceased to exist. An Appeals Court upheld the decision, and the Supreme Court refused to hear the case.[37]

Years later Angela told the harrowing story, whether true or exaggerated, of being beaten up coming off the Seventh Avenue IRT subway, at the 14th Street stop, by three men (presumably

Communists, possibly members of the IWO) who pulled out a handful of her hair that never grew back, leaving a bald spot. And even J. Edgar Hoover had to admit, in a hand-written note, that it was "outrageous the way this woman is being hounded." One wonders what Hoover, and Angela, had expected.[38]

To put a woman, and a lesbian no less, on the stand in such a high-profile trial, the prosecution must have considered her testimony vital to their case. Angela, on the other hand, must have thought going public as an informer was worth it. Out of fear of reprisal, or possibly because they would have been ashamed to betray the trust of comrades, many individuals who had worked undercover did not want their identities divulged, and would not testify at trials and hearings. Angela was an exception. What did she have to say that was so important? And, perhaps more enticing, what did she stand to gain?[39]

7. Books on Trial

From the prosecution's point of view, Angela Calomiris made a good witness for a couple of reasons. While she repeated many of the basic arguments voiced by other witnesses in support of the charges of "conspiracy to advocate...," she had a few original angles. For one thing, she had been working undercover in the Party for a long time—seven years—longer than most of the witnesses, and longer than many informants, who for their own reasons, had broken under the strain or chosen not to continue. In fact, the drop-out rate was high because of the stress involved and fear of discovery. But, as noted previously, Angela had strong economic motives for continuing.[1]

Likewise, the FBI connection made her feel important, as did her position in the Party, even if it was all a subterfuge. The highest rank she held was "branch organizer," which she described for the court as "equivalent to the president of an organization"—something of an exaggeration. That was, of course, before her 1948 demotion (instead of expulsion) to "financial secretary," which still allowed her access to names. In fact, it was an important position, as Angela had pointed out back in 1944 to her FBI handlers. In a memo from the New York Office to Bureau Headquarters, they quoted her promise of "names and addresses of all the members of the club together with their trade union affiliations and important background information concerning them." Party members knew she had that information, which explained one distressed reaction to Angela's appearance on the witness stand as chronicled in *Red Masquerade*. "Good Lord," a former comrade reportedly groans, "that means she has the membership lists!" Angela would have used these to good advantage, alongside "Party cards that should have been destroyed, carbon copies of receipts for dues—the kind of irrefutable evidence of Party membership for which the Bureau was looking."[2]

Besides identifying numerous Party rank and file throughout her FBI career, and also from the witness stand, Angela was able to identify five of the eleven defendants. In that regard she had the advantage over out-of-towners. She was a native New Yorker who had spent her spying career in the city where the Party's national offices were located, at 35 East 12th Street, just below Union Square. She could provide first-hand identification because she had seen them and heard them speak in assemblies. The first person she named was Gil Green, Chicago district chairman, who had welcomed new members in 1942, Angela among them. According to Medina's instructions—the usual procedure "in criminal cases," he said— she left the witness stand and placed her hand on Green's shoulder. Gladstein for the defense objected to the method of identifying the defendants, reminding Medina that he was not "dealing here with people who are accused of robbing a bank" but with "leaders of a political party of national scope [...] whose faces are known generally." Medina overruled the objection. Green responded by shrinking away from Angela's touch and brushing his shoulder. After that, she did not touch any more shoulders, but merely pointed at the defendant she was identifying. Because Angela's activities had been restricted to her local Party branch, none of the defendants would have had any idea who she was.[3]

Angela also identified Robert Thompson, New York state Party chairman; John Williamson, national labor secretary; Ben Davis, New York City Councilman from Harlem; and John Gates, editor of the *Daily Worker*. Another tense moment arose later in the trial when informant/witness Balmes Hidalgo, Jr., came down from the stand and placed his hand on Robert Thompson's shoulder, calling him

"Comrade Thompson." The trial transcript recorded Thompson's reply as "You're no comrade of mine I assure you, you little rat."[4]

Green's contempt for Angela was only one hint of the tension that had been mounting over the past month as the prosecution called to the stand witness after witness who had worked undercover in the Party. Herbert Philbrick from Boston was the first, and his appearance shocked the defense and Party officials, who had not realized how thoroughly the FBI had penetrated their organization. Nobody seemed to know much about Philbrick, and he had not seemed much of a threat, to judge from Gil Green's own recollection years later. "We called Boston," Green said, "to ask if they knew Philbrick, and they said sure, he was a nice guy. He was always inviting us to use his office mimeograph machine."[5]

Angela had aroused more suspicion in her day, but she, too, had slipped through Party defenses. Especially, she had evaded expulsion through the good graces or naiveté of soon-to-be former head of Party security, John Lautner. In *Red Masquerade*, Angela reports that Lautner "didn't seem to get the hang of the case" and seemed only interested in getting her out of his office. Since nothing was done about her, she was left free to collect more information for the FBI, right up until her appearance on the witness stand. As in the case of Philbrick, Angela reminded the defendants how vulnerable they had been to infiltration, how slipshod their security was. These revelations, and more to come, undermined mutual trust among comrades, because almost anyone could or should be considered a spy. It all made penetrating and subverting the Party structure look too easy.[6]

Some of the Party's anger, embarrassment, even despair, spilled over onto the pages of the *Daily Worker*. The day after Angela's initial appearance, the *Worker* accused the chief prosecutor, US Attorney John Francis X. McGohey of fishing "in a cesspool for stool pigeons" and bringing "up the vilest of slime to put upon the stand." Informers in general were despised, but Angela seems to have been the target that time, her lesbianism inspiring more than the usual animosity. A few days later, the *Daily Worker* would portray her as "Mme. Jekyll and Miss Hyde"—"appearing before her neighbors and friends during part of the day as the good Madame Jekyll, the scientific socialist seeking a better world, then prowling secretly in the police underworld as the misanthropic Miss Hyde, betraying the good fight and the hopes of her friends." That portrayal also identified Angela as a "lady police informer who also dabbles in photography and other less popular pursuits"—another hint that the Party knew, to their chagrin, that they had been harboring a lesbian.[7]

Presiding Judge Medina had already been quoted in *Time* magazine (April 11, 1949), declaring that this was "the doggoned-est trial" he had ever seen, and the latest controversy tended to verify his conclusions. In a lengthy and emotionally-charged clash between prosecution and defense, without jury and witnesses present, US Attorney McGohey fought back against the cesspool fishing accusation. The brouhaha had begun over the FBI's public statement, published in the *New York Times* the morning after Angela first took the witness stand, lauding her "for patriotic assistance to the United States Government." Perhaps suspecting that she would be a hard sell as a witness, and most likely because she was such an "obvious" lesbian, the FBI had gone out of its way to throw all its support behind her. The defense was up in arms, with Gladstein declaring that the two men he represented at trial—Gus Hall (Ohio Party Chairman) and Robert Thompson—unlike Angela, had served their country honorably and had "honorable discharges from the United States Navy and the Army for their patriotic assistance to the United States Government." The prosecution was guilty, he said, of "trying this case in the newspapers" to turn public opinion against the defendants. Harry Sacher for the defense took up the argument on behalf of his client John Gates, who had "served his country loyally, and who was ready to make the supreme sacrifice." Angela, on the other hand, Sacher said, had served "in the capacity of a lowly spy and stool pigeon." None of this gained them any ground with Judge Medina, who cut them off and recalled a vindicated Angela to the stand. In this heated debate, which established that spying and testifying against the Communists were patriotic acts, she enjoyed the unequivocal support of the Bureau. At that point in time, she was still useful as a witness, and had not formulated any notion of making her FBI experience a stepping-stone to celebrity.[8]

For now, Angela had more work to do to bolster the prosecution's case. Again, her long years of service to the FBI stood her in good stead, because she could testify first-hand to the Party's ups and downs—which were many as the world war wound down. A major step was taken in 1944, when the Party's National Chairman from 1934 to 1945, Earl Browder, originally from Kansas, promoted the CPUSA's re-organization as the more moderate Communist Political Association (CPA). Based on the optimistic assumption that, in the exceptional case of the US, communists and capitalists could work together, or continue to work together as they had during the war, this short-lived experiment came to an end in June 1945. This latter shift was triggered, from all reports, by a dramatic letter from abroad that denounced Browder's downplaying the class struggle while preaching harmony between labor and capital, and his dissolution of the American Party.

The letter, authored by Party secretary Jacques Duclos, had appeared in France in April's *Cahiers du Communisme,* an official publication. It made its way to America and first appeared in English translation on the front page of the *New York World-Telegram,* the newspaper where, coincidentally, Fred Woltman, Angela's old friend from the Village, was chief Red baiter. The *World-Telegram* article, written by former Communist and Woltman cohort Nelson Frank, called the Duclos letter "an unprecedented public rebuke from the head of one national Communist group to another," and speculated (according to "persons familiar with international Communist protocol") that the whole affair signaled a return to a Moscow-dominated "position of open hostility toward national governments." In other words, the Russians told Duclos to write the letter to bring the Americans back into line. True or false, the Party faithful rose to Duclos' challenge, the CPUSA was re-constituted, and Browder removed. William Z. Foster took over as National Chairman, and Eugene Dennis as General Secretary. Both were defendants at the Foley Square trial.[9]

Party-watchers in the US government, and especially the FBI, were quick to interpret the Duclos affair and the re-birth of the CPUSA as clear signs that the comrades had swung dangerously to the left, and at the behest of an alien enemy force. Better still, fixing the re-organization of the Party in July 1945 provided a handy point from which to date the conspiracy of which the defendants were accused under the Smith Act: "Whoever organizes or helps or attempts to organize any society, group, or assembly of persons who teach, advocate, or encourage the overthrow or destruction of any such government by force or violence."

Angela had been there through it all, and could testify to changes that sounded fundamental. In the transition from Communist Party to a bourgeois Communist Political Association, she said, the members "called each other brother and sister or friends" instead of comrades. The meetings "were no longer secret and only for Communist Party members. [...] In fact, the general neighborhood was invited." Also, Angela, who had held so many positions in her local unit, took on the new job of "recording secretary" during the CPA period, transcribing "complete minutes," she said, and reading them at the next meeting. In line with the return to secrecy, the re-establishment of the CPUSA put an end to that record keeping and the "office of recording secretary." The implication throughout was, of course, that the old organization made new again was up to something they did not want anybody to know about. The contemporary spy trials of Judith Coplon and Alger Hiss fed the popular fear that what American Communists were up to was selling out the country to the enemy. Hoover, of course, two years before, in 1947, during a well-publicized HUAC appearance, had branded the Communist Party a "Fifth Column" in support of an anticipated foreign attack. Such accusations reminded a popular audience of war-time "Fifth Column" threats, for one reason because it was sincerely believed that only some internal force or sabotage could have caused the collapse of France after only a month of opposing the Nazi invasion of 1940. And for New York City, memories of the fire and scuttling of the French liner Normandie, in 1942, while it was being converted to a troop ship, kept alive real fears of sabotage. Hoover's "Fifth Column" declarations could only imply the potential downfall of the Republic, and that the Communists deserved the punishment that was coming to them.[10]

But the biggest change from Communist Political Association back to Communist Party, and the one the prosecution was waiting to hear about, concerned not secrecy, spying, or sabotage, but books—the ones Angela called the Marxist-Leninist classics: Stalin's *Foundations of Leninism*, Lenin's *State and Revolution*, *The History of the Communist Party of the Soviet Union (Bolsheviks)*, and the *Communist Manifesto*. All of these books—and a few other texts like A. Leontiev's *Political Economy*, Marx's *Value, Price and Profit*, Georgi Dimitroff's "Closing Remarks" at the 7th Congress of the Communist International (1935) advocating for the Popular Front—had been cited by other prosecution witnesses, and would be cited again as texts they had been assigned in Party classes and discussion groups.[11]

These were considered by anti-Communists to be the dangerous books, the ones that told tales from the Russian Revolution about uprisings, insurrections, strikes, training of cadres, and arming of the masses. During the short-lived CPA, they were "no longer used," had been "taken from our shelves," Angela said, and new books, less volatile reading, had taken their places—"[Earl] Browder's books, leaflets and pamphlets on current issues." But change was in the air with the re-constitution of the Communist Party "along Marxist-Leninist lines." "All the Browder books went out," Angela said, "off the shelves" and those same "classics" from before, the ones that preached revolt, re-appeared.[12]

As lengthy passages from one or more of them were read (actually read aloud) by prosecution attorneys into the trial transcript, the strategy of showing that the books preached violence and overthrowing the government (at least in Russia) took shape. With faith in the power of the word, the conclusion was that reading assignments like these would bring on the revolution. Or as African American William Cummings, one of the trial's more excitable prosecution witnesses, explained to judge and jury, Communists in Ohio had taught "that in Russia during the revolution they had streets of blood, and [...] in America we would also, before we achieved the peace for the working class, the streets in America would run red with blood." Cummings, who had settled in Toledo, Ohio, had another related threat to recall for the court when he announced that he was presently employed by Electric Auto-Lite, scene of one of the most violent strikes of the Great Depression—referred to by contemporaries, in 1934, as the "Battle of Toledo," between strikers and the Ohio National Guard. 1934 also recalled the San Francisco

General Strike and the Minneapolis Teamsters Strike, major catalysts for the rise of industrial unionism. Obviously, trouble was brewing.[13]

During Angela's testimony, a lengthy passage from *The History of the Communist Party of the Soviet Union* she said she had been assigned threw more light on how the revolution would be accomplished. The Bolsheviks had established a model by working in the army and navy during World War I to turn the weapons of war against the bourgeoisie and the government, converting "the imperialist war into a civil war" that led to revolution. Despite the historical context (1914-1917), which the defense hastened to point out, the prosecution maintained that the important thing about this book, and the others, was that they were being studied in the 1940s in the USA. And if they had inspired one revolution, they might (or might not) inspire another closer to home. In fact, *The History of the Communist Party of the Soviet Union* was so influential, Angela claimed, that "amongst the students we would practically call it a Bible." Harry Sacher for the defense responded, protesting that this juicy selection about fomenting civil war was being read to the jury for the third time.[14]

It was important that Angela and the prosecution portray all American Communist recruits, herself included, as devout readers of dangerous theoretical texts. Throughout *Red Masquerade*, however, and elsewhere she declares that she is not and never was a "genuine Communist" and presumably did not take her studies seriously. Because former Communists—who had once been true believers and later became informants—were often considered suspect, Angela repeats that she has "never, at any time, […] believed in Communism." It is curious that others, who did believe, contradict her testimony about the Party faithful reading their assignments and taking it all to heart. A significant case was Ted (Theodore Alvin) Hall (née Holtzberg), the youngest scientist to be employed at Los Alamos, New Mexico, on the Manhattan Project for the development of the atomic bomb, and later accused of spying for the Russians. In the late 1940s, Ted Hall and his wife, Joan, joined the Party, and for their political education "were told to read *The History of the Communist Party of the Soviet Union.*" Unlike Angela and her comrades, Joan Hall didn't recall "being involved in any discussions of it," and far from considering it a "Bible" found it "awful, heavy, badly written, badly translated, and incredibly doctrinaire. It was a description of all the various wrong tendencies that Lenin and Stalin had triumphantly opposed." Closer to home, John Victor Blanc of Cleveland, Ohio, witness for the prosecution at Foley Square, another union man (UAW), undercover for the FBI since 1944, testified that he had not read all of the *Communist Manifesto*, none of the assigned sections of Leontiev's *Political Economy*, and had never heard of Marx's *Capital*, much less read it.[15]

But according to Angela, hers was an exceptional group, composed of dedicated scholars. The next classic, *Foundations of Leninism*, she insisted they had studied "from cover to cover, chapter by chapter, page by page, paragraph by paragraph." To illustrate the ideas propagated by the book, Special Assistant US Attorney Edward C. Wallace for the prosecution, then plunged into the reading of a lengthy selection, which concerned, coincidentally, the impossibility of a peaceful evolution to proletarian democracy in England and America. Sacher objected again that this passage had been previously read, but to no avail. Wallace read on, page after page, concluding with a quote from Lenin, who declared that "the proletarian revolution is impossible without the forcible destruction of the bourgeois state machine and the substitution for it of a new one." The book was obviously a primer for the violent overthrow of governments.[16]

Once again, there were those who disagreed with Angela. When the defense brought in its rebuttal witness, he addressed the "classics" part of Angela's testimony. A young African American, and former Cotton Club dancer, Howard "Stretch" Johnson for the defense was a Party organizer from 1938 to 1956, and later a sociology professor. When he took the stand to refute Angela, he spoke as the New York County Communist Party educational director during the period in question (January 1948), and insisted that she had, first and foremost, named the wrong person to the office—the unfortunate Rebecca Gretche, whose name was not only pronounced in court but spelled into the record by Wallace for the prosecution. Johnson also denied that anyone had ever ordered a "page by page" study of *Foundations of Leninism*, or any other "classic" text (all of them available in the New York Public Library anyway), and rejected any claims about a campaign "to teach or advocate the overthrow of the United States Government by force or violence."[17]

Nevertheless, even longer readings would occupy much of Angela's five-day stint on the witness stand, and it seems not unlikely that, as attorneys for the prosecution droned on, the eyes of jury, attorneys, spectators, and Angela herself in the witness box, glazed over with boredom. A few minutes after *Foundations of Leninism*, Wallace launched into nine turgid pages (in the trial transcript) of Georgi Dimitroff's speech at the 7th Congress of the Communist International (1935). The passage detailed the importance of training cadres for "a militant movement which is constantly in the firing line," and drew particular attention to the "work of our Party schools" in training "front-rank fighters."[18]

Ironically, almost from the beginning of her spy career to the day she took the witness stand, it was Angela who had been in training as a Party leader, one who had taken "many courses." In fact, in the middle of her testimony, US Attorney Wallace asked her, "And I think you told us you are presently attending the Marxist Institute, is that right?" To which Angela replied with her special brand of humor and a grin. "I have a class tonight," she said. "I don't think I'll go." A grateful press dubbed it "one of the trial's few laughs."[19]

Angela always said that she did so well in the Party because of that sense of humor, something she said most Communists did not have, and because she could make people laugh. Admittedly during the war, women had enjoyed greater opportunities for advancement in the Party because so many men were in military service. Still, Angela's rise through the ranks indicates there must have been a leadership vacuum at the local level, and that hostility toward lesbians was at that time not widespread.[20]

There is speculation, on the other hand, that Angela's Party success might owe something to the zealous sponsorship of one Leona Saron, a name that was read—and spelled—into the record at the Foley Square trial. She was identified as the person who had initially recruited Angela into the Party, and, in *Red Masquerade*, is described simply as "a tall, thin, humorless girl with glasses." But Saron was prominent enough in Party circles to have her name broadcast again to the world a few weeks later at the Judith Coplon trial, in the midst of a legal tug of war between Coplon's attorney and the judge.[21]

It was a moment that illustrates how disclosure issues regarding FBI materials were handled in the sedition and spy trials—the CPUSA National Board, Alger Hiss, and Judith Coplon—that were underway simultaneously in June 1949. Down in Washington, DC, some of the data slips that Coplon was accused of passing to her Russian handler were not introduced into evidence by the prosecution, in the interest of "national security." Coplon's attorney immediately began pushing for release of the documents. His request was miraculously granted by Judge Albert L. Reeves, described by observers as "elderly, crotchety, tired," who found in them no danger to national security. It was a significant ruling, very different from Medina's attitude in the Foley Square trial. In that case, repeated demands to see prosecution witnesses' FBI reports, including Angela's, to substantiate or disprove their testimony, were rebuffed by an angry Medina. Unlike the cooperative Judge Reeves, he scolded defense attorneys for repeatedly asking "to see the files of the FBI," and trying "to put the Government on trial, and to put the FBI on trial."[22]

What happened at the Coplon trial goes a long way toward explaining Medina's hostility. Judge Reeves' historic ruling allowed for the reading in open court of raw FBI files that exposed Bureau spying on a star-studded cast of Hollywood notables, from Frederic March and his wife, Florence Eldridge, to Edward G. Robinson and Paul Robeson, from Helen Hayes to Danny Kaye, from Dorothy Parker to Canada Lee, an African-American actor well-known at the time whose career never recovered. Dozens of others were revealed to be under government surveillance for Communist sympathies. Bernard DeVoto, a liberal Pulitzer-winning journalist of the period, is quoted by Hoover historian Anthony Summers, in *Official and Confidential,* where DeVoto describes the FBI reports uncovered by the Coplon case "as irresponsible as the chatter of somewhat retarded children." J. Edgar Hoover was livid, and it was rumored he would resign from embarrassment. Unfortunately those rumors proved untrue.[23]

Though not a celebrity in the Hollywood style, it was Leona

Saron's misfortune to find her way into FBI reports released at the Coplon trial. She had applied for employment at the Soviet Embassy in Washington, an informant disclosed. It was a tidbit of insider information that an FBI plant inside the Embassy might have supplied, but "the report did not say specifically." It was certain, however, according to *The Chicago Tribune*, that "the employment application was filed by a woman, Leona Saron, who obtained employment last year on the soviet information bulletin, published here." The application included "her scholastic background" at Hunter College, CUNY, Columbia and Cornell, and "her service with the Council of Soviet-American Friendship." Such publicity would have left Saron with few job prospects, and most likely placed her on Red Scare subversive lists. In the 1950s, she worked for the leftist independent weekly newspaper *The National Guardian*.[24]

Angela resurrected Leona Saron for her own purposes almost two years later, as part of the publicity campaign for *Red Masquerade*. Saron's photograph was published in one episode of the book's serialization in the *New York Daily News* (February 1951). *The Daily News* ran eight installments of *Red Masquerade*, from February 18 to 25, with Saron's photo featured in "FBI Girl on the Job in Communist Party," for Monday, February 19. The caption read: "Ardent Communist, who unwittingly sowed the seeds of her party leaders' downfall when she recruited Angela Calomiris." It was a photograph that Angela herself had taken, probably back in 1944, when the FBI was pleased to have a good likeness of "Leona Saron, Director of the Speakers Bureau of National Council of American Soviet Friendship."[25]

At the outset of Angela's spy career, Saron had been helpful, and had shown an interest in her raw recruit receiving a thorough political re-education. As the story goes in *Red Masquerade*, only six weeks after Angela was initiated into the Party, "Leona arranged" for her to attend "the Marxist Summer Day School for 'cadre' training." When Angela told her FBI handlers, they were impressed, praised her for being "a fast worker," and provided her extra cash so she could, in effect, give up her day job. She would attend classes to know what the Communists were reading, and what they were saying about it. That was Angela's first course in Marxism, she announced from the witness stand. It was held at the Workers School, in the same building as National Party Headquarters on East 12th Street. A second course at the Workers School was on trade unionism, in January 1944, and, because by then she had risen to the position of branch organizer, in the summer of 1947 she was selected to attend "a county training class for leaders." The six-day course, Angela proclaimed, included a study of the usual "classics" and more: *"History of the CPSU, Foundations of Leninism, State and Revolution, Communist Manifesto, Socialism— Scientific and Utopian."* The prosecution went a step further when US Attorney Wallace read Angela's invitation to the county training school, clarifying that it would be held at the Jefferson School of Social Science, or the Jefferson School, as it was commonly known, which occupied an entire nine-story building at 575 Sixth Avenue, at the corner of 16th Street in Manhattan. It was the flagship school of a far-flung pedagogical network that included the Abraham Lincoln School in Chicago, the Samuel Adams School in Boston, the Tom Paine School in Philadelphia, and the California Labor School in San Francisco. The Jefferson School had a library of 30,000 volumes, and its courses ranged from a year-long Institute of Marxist Studies to cultural and self-improvement offerings that enrolled as many as 5,000 Communist and non-Communist students alike each term. From 1943 to 1956, the Jefferson School pioneered in "continuing education," but was forced to close its doors after the Subversive Activities Control Board (SACB) designated it a Communist-controlled organization.[26]

Since threats to the Jefferson School and other affiliated schools were already in the air, Harry Sacher for the defense understood what Angela's naming it meant, and rose to challenge the prosecution "which puts schools on trial now," in addition to the "submission of books by the dozen in support of this indictment." He further objected to the implication that "entering a school […] can possibly be a criminal act." But Medina overruled his objection, with a word about "evidence to support the charge that the teachings in these schools and these places had to do with the overthrow of the Government by force and violence."[27]

Clearly there was something suspicious about reading this kind of material, and maybe something suspicious about studying (or thought) in general. That was what Dorothy Healey, a leader in the Southern California District of the Communist Party for many years, observed. During her trial as a defendant in the California Smith Act trial (1951), the prosecutor took exception to the notion of continuing one's education. "Imagine," Healey recalled his remarks to the jury, "these people in their middle ages! They're talking like you still have to study!" She added that "clearly to him, there could be no greater proof of conspiracy than if middle-aged people would continue to study."[28]

In her radio interview with Angela, Eleanor Roosevelt also expressed concern about the long hours her guest had been required to give to study and Party work. "Did you have to attend meetings regularly and to study?" the former First Lady asked Angela, who replied that yes she did. Ever a trifle extravagant in the depiction of her patriotic sacrifice, Angela went on to insist that she had attended meetings almost every night, sometimes "three and four meetings in one night." According to her, there were "study groups at all times," and especially for those with leadership potential. "When the Party decided that you were leadership material, such as they did in my instance," Angela reported with a sort of perverse pride, "they sent me to training school."

Mrs. Roosevelt, much like the prosecutor at the trial of the California Party leaders, seemed to find that excessive. "Heavens!" she exclaimed to the radio audience, perhaps recalling fears she had expressed before about the vocal Communist minority. "The number of Communists in this country is not very large," she had written in 1946, in her "My Day" column. But, she added, "They are very well organized […] and they work so hard."[29]

While Angela may have attended more meetings and participated in more study groups than most, all the prosecution witnesses had attended classes of some sort. It was a prerequisite to their selection for the trial, because proving the treachery contained in the Marxist-Leninist literature was vital to the prosecution's case. Informants had over the years faithfully delivered to their FBI handlers course outlines and literature distributed in conjunction with their study. One of those, a lengthy, detailed "Outline of Marxist-Leninist Fundamentals for Class Use and Self Study," distributed by the

Illinois Party, was the basis for the prosecution's interrogation of Garfield Herron—that African-American prosecution witness who had been paid "as high as $60 a month" as an FBI informant.[30]

A "big grinning character from Little Rock," the Communist press called Herron, and insisted his one big accomplishment in the Party was to have passed that study outline to the FBI. To demonstrate how World War I had been converted in Russia to a civil war that had toppled the Czar, the witness sat through almost twenty pages in the trial transcript of long passages read from the usual books (*History of the Communist Party of the Soviet Union [Bolsheviks], Foundations of Leninism,* for example). While the implication, of course, was that an American conspiracy could overthrow the government, defense attorney George Crockett of Detroit, also African-American, protested that this reading recalled a remote historical period, 1914-1917, and was not relevant to the present. The prosecution thought it was important to show that these things were being taught in 1946. Harry Sacher reminded Judge Medina "that these passages have been read once before."[31]

Despite all that reading and studying of fairly complex material, taken individually or as a group, Foley Square prosecution witnesses were not particularly bookish types. In fact, the closest thing would have been the first witness, Louis Budenz, former Managing Editor of the *Daily Worker* and now a confirmed anti-Communist. He was the one who had testified about the "Aesopian" language invented by Lenin to elude Czarist censors, still in use by the Party, he said, which proved that Communists never said what they really meant. Likewise, because he was a white-collar worker and undercover informer for the FBI in the Boston Party, Herbert Philbrick might have read any number of the classic texts.

Almost half the prosecution witnesses, however, were blue-collar workers, as their testimony indicates, employed in light and heavy industry mostly in the American Midwest, and probably not big readers. In order of their appearance they were: William Odell Nowell, who had worked for Ford in Detroit; Charles Nicodemus of the United Textile Workers, who had worked in a Celanese plant in Maryland; Garfield Herron, who had worked in the aircraft industry in Chicago during the war; Thomas Aaron Younglove, of St.

Louis, who, while undercover for the FBI, had worked for Laclede Gas Company, still the largest natural gas distribution utility in Missouri; William Cummings, who had worked in Toledo, Ohio, for Archer Daniels Midland Company (ADMC), producers of food and animal feed products, and for Electric Auto-Lite, which produced lighting and starting units for several different makes of car; and John Victor Blanc, of Cleveland, Ohio, employed by Park Drop Forge Company, which produced parts for the assembly lines of major automakers. They were also union men, the majority of them members of the UAW, whose principal function on the stand was to tell their insider stories of organized labor's ties to the Party. Angela, who demonstrates little enthusiasm in *Red Masquerade* for the labor movement, as witness number nine in a line-up of thirteen, fell squarely in the middle of this string of six.

Perhaps prosecution attorneys had positioned her there as a change of pace. But to find herself grouped with these working-class individuals cannot have been to Angela's liking. Certainly to judge from everything known about her, she had only hoped to distance herself from a family history of hard times and tragedy. She did not want to be poor, and did not believe that getting poor people together would serve any purpose. The trick was to get in good with the people who had money and power, and make yourself useful. Anybody who did anything else, and that included the American Communist Party, was a fool.

8. Unions on Trial

At the height of the labor movement's union organizing in the 1930s and 40s, Woody Guthrie sang about the union maid who couldn't be scared off by "goons and ginks and company finks," the one who was "sticking to the union." He was not singing about Angela Calomiris. In fact, her testimony on the witness stand, and many passages from *Red Masquerade*, demonstrate that Angela was anti-union and pro-that rugged individualist tradition Americans are supposed to personify. It was not an uncommon sentiment for the period, one espoused by those who insisted that hard work and thrift (those prototypical American values) would enable everyone to climb out of the economic collapse of the Great Depression. Likewise, in the spirit of the Red Scare, unions came to look dangerous because, it was said, they were dominated by Communists who wanted to use them to undermine national security, and finally to deliver the country to the Soviet Union. In support of the indictment on charges of conspiracy to advocate the overthrow of the US government, all this became a major theme of the Foley Square trial.[1]

Early in *Red Masquerade*, on her first job clipping newspaper articles at the Burrelle Press Clipping Bureau, Angela paints a dismal picture of labor organizing. Thanks to what she defines as her natural sympathies "for the working man—the underdog," she was duped, in the parlance of the times, by "a Communist organizer" who came to the shop and told them they ought to form a union. Not surprisingly, "the boss was dead set against" it, "the ringleaders were fired," and Angela did not get the promotion she had expected. So much for unions.[2]

Other organizers had been more successful. In the wake of the Depression, rising desperation among workers had triggered aggressive labor organizing, general strikes—such as the 1934 San Francisco strike that brought Harry Hay into the CPUSA—and factory takeovers. Then, as now, big industrialists opposed unions. Spies on the production line reported organizers, who could then be attacked, dismissed, and blacklisted. To curb strikes and violence, FDR's New Deal government had finally, in 1935, thrown its weight behind labor's right to organize without fear of reprisal in the National Labor Relations Act (Wagner Act) and the National Labor Relations Board (NLRB) created to oversee it. Dubbed the Magna Carta of American labor, it was an unstable arrangement at best. By 1947, it had been seriously undermined by the Taft-Hartley Act, which, among other things, restricted strikes and effectively banished Communists from union leadership. The labor movement referred to Taft-Hartley as the "slave-labor" act.[3]

A few months after Angela's brush with labor organizing at her clipping service job, *Red Masquerade* traces her progress into other areas, and up the ladder of success. While she was only "a glorified errand girl" at Esther Lape's American Foundation for Social Research, she was earning four dollars a week more than at the clipping job. And thanks to Lape's friendship with Eleanor Roosevelt, Angela could say forever that she had known the First Lady. Other short-term jobs intervened before Angela, like many Americans during the Depression, got steady work with the New Deal's innovation to reduce unemployment, the WPA. She held that job, supervising recreation for children, until she got a better-paying government position with the FBI. So much for rugged individualism, and rugged individualists.[4]

Since *Red Masquerade* was trying so hard to be an anti-Communist tract, Angela had to soft pedal her dependence on anything that could be interpreted as "socialism." When Communists told her that Communism would bring "the abolition of greed, and higher standards of living for everyone," she thought "it all seemed a little too good to be true." Ever the hypocrite, Angela insisted, in her rough and ready style, that she should not "get benefits without earning them," and wondered "how they could be provided, for that matter." But finally it was her aspiration to a career as artist/photographer that made her suspicious, she tells us, of any sort of state control. Angela rejected the idea of being "a photographer under Communism" because her success would depend on "the whim of a Government agency," like "in Russia." Of course, while claiming that "wasn't the kind of success" she "was looking for," her success had, in fact, for years depended on the whim of an American government agency, the FBI, which took a greater interest in her photography than anyone had before.[5]

In the service of the FBI, Angela even joined a union and, to protect her cover, pretended to believe. At the time of the trial, she was a member, as she announced from the witness stand, of "Local 16 UOPWA, the Advertising Guild." Thousands of office and professional workers, in such diverse arenas as social work, publishing, insurance, banks, and department stores were members, too. While the United Office and Professional Workers of America (UOPWA) sounded harmless enough, the union's enormous recruiting potential—an estimated six million eligible workers in the US at that time, 400,000 in New York City alone—made it a potential threat to big business.[6]

In his *I Led Three Lives*, Herbert Philbrick, the other white-collar prosecution informant/witness at Foley Square, pinpointed the threat. As Philbrick was leaving Boston to take the stand in New York, he tells us that UOPWA had launched "an organizing campaign" against none other than the John Hancock Life Insurance Company, to "needle the Hancock employees into sentiments of discontent with their pay and working conditions." Then as now, interference with insurance companies would probably have been considered un-American. And there was a "Wall Street Section" of the UOPWA for workers in brokerage houses.[7]

Even more subversive was the militant African-American

presence in the union, which had a distinguished record of pushing for more hiring and promotion of minority workers. Indicative of their politics was an invitation from social workers in a union local to the octogenarian W. E. B. Du Bois to address an affirmative action conference in 1949. Always a provocative character in his role as historian, civil rights activist, and a founder of the National Association for the Advancement of Colored People (NAACP), Dr. Du Bois became intolerably threatening two years later, as chairman of the Peace Information Center, and was indicted (at age eighty-three), by the federal government for failing to register as a "foreign agent." At around the same time, in the midst of the Red scare, the UOPWA was charged with "Communist domination" and expelled, along with ten other left-leaning unions, from the CIO (Congress of Industrial Organizations). Other unions expelled in 1949-50 included the West Coast International Longshoremen's and Warehousemen's Union (ILWU), the Mine, Mill and Smelter Workers Union (Mine, Mill), the Farm Equipment Union (FE), the Food and Tobacco Workers, and the Fur and Leather Workers. The United Electrical, Radio and Machine Workers (UE) left under its own power.[8]

This swing to the right came on the heels of a period of intense labor unrest in America. Going back a few years, when the country had been at war, labor's relationship to management had improved, and in the interest of an Allied victory, unions had agreed to a no-strike pledge for the duration. But after 1945, all bets were off, as the transition from wartime to peacetime economy triggered industrial production cuts, which in turn prompted slowdowns and massive layoffs. The crisis hit American workers hard, as they watched plants shutting down, jobs disappearing. At war's end, for example, North American Aviation, manufacturers under government contract of combat aircraft, had orders for 8,000 planes. A few months later, they had orders for twenty-four, and employment in their various plants had dropped from a wartime high of 91,000 to 5,000 in 1946.[9]

Testimony at the Foley Square trial chronicled what the shutdown of the great American war machine had meant, and especially to the most vulnerable, minority workers who had found good union jobs for the first time. Thomas Aaron Younglove, the prosecution witness who followed Angela on the stand, had worked undercover for the FBI in St. Louis, and quoted from Missouri Communist Party notes on the drying up of industrial employment. It was reported at a "Small Arms" factory, "where 3,000 Negroes were employed, and where some Negroes rose to supervisory jobs, the entire plant is closing down." Later in the trial, another story came to light in the testimony of defense witness Yolanda Hall, a Party member and graduate of Chicago Teachers College, who had worked as a tool grinder for Bendix Aviation Corporation during the war. Immediately after the Japanese surrender, the plant closed down completely, and "Negro women," Ms. Hall testified, were told "to take work as domestic workers instead of at their regular occupations of drill press operators, instead of as assemblers and other jobs that they had."[10]

While some people had little or no recourse, others vented their ire in an unprecedented wave of strikes by auto, steel, and electrical workers. In the twelve-month period following the war's end, five million American workers participated in work stoppages, and government action against them was swift. When coal miners walked off the job in 1946, President Truman issued an Executive Order seizing the coal mines. And when railroad workers rejected a settlement of their strike, he seized control of the railroads and threatened to draft the workers into the armed forces, because they were jeopardizing national security and the postwar economic recovery.[11]

From the witness stand, Angela helped the prosecution by trying to tie one very recent and notorious strike action to Communist Party plotting. Pages and pages of reading from Marxist-Leninist texts, the last selection focusing on strikes by industrial workers in Russia under the Czar, also helped the jury make the connection. Then Angela took the spotlight with her own experience "on the waterfront," the West Side piers on the Manhattan banks of the Hudson. She had set the stage in the first few minutes of her testimony when she introduced herself as a member of a West Midtown club, whose territory included "the Hell's Kitchen area from 38th Street to about 50th or 52nd Street from Eighth Avenue to the river west."[12]

Back in the days when New York harbor was at the zenith of its power, with hundreds of piers and nearly as much traffic as all the other Atlantic and Gulf Coast ports combined, that demarcation meant a lot. In *Red Masquerade*, Angela sounded the alarm by categorizing that "lower West Side quadrant south of Seventy-second Street, and west of Eighth Avenue" as "of strategic importance to world Communism." It was an area that boasted "docks, railroads, freight yards, teamsters and warehouses," and, in Angela's estimation, more Party members ("disciplined comrades") than "any other comparable plot of ground in the United States." If they wielded influence in those industries, Angela said, the Communists could conceivably "make a revolution."[13]

At the time of the trial, her message would have resonated throughout the Foley Square courtroom. The latest labor unrest on the docks had the city, in fact the entire country, including the federal government, on edge. A wildcat dockworkers' strike that began November 10, 1948, had closed down the port of New York for eighteen days. The federal government had tried to head it off by invoking the Taft-Hartley Act, passed the year before, which had forced the East Coast International Longshoremen's Association (ILA), and the shippers, the New York Shipping Association, to continue negotiating a new contract into the fall. But once an agreement had been reached, the majority of the union rank and file, unhappy with the terms and convinced the vote to accept had been fixed, launched their strike action. It was not the first time that dockworkers had opposed the leadership of the ILA, notorious for mob connections, anti-communism and underhanded dealings with local politicians. But timing was particularly bad in 1948, because Marshall Plan cargo bound for Europe piled up on the docks, and perishable goods rotted in the holds of idled ships as the strike spread to other East Coast ports. Since Marshall Plan aid was intended to combat the postwar spread of Communism in Europe, the strike looked more suspicious. Truman denounced it as damaging to the national economy and a threat to national security.[14]

Angela, to be sure, pulled out all the stops in *Red Masquerade*'s version of the months leading up to the 1948 strike. "The Red battle for the docks" she calls it before outlining her branch's efforts "to convert individual longshoremen to Communism and eventually gain control of the union." According to her, the Party gave it their best shot, betting that controlling the longshoremen "meant control of every ship that came in or out of New York harbor." And in terms yet more menacing, she argued that "control of shipping throughout the world would be crucial in the event of another war"—the one that would be fought with our new enemy, the Soviet Union.[15]

At the Foley Square trial, Angela went on to link labor unrest on the New York docks to Communist "infiltration," and to offer details of a conspiratorial program that would paralyze transportation. From a New York County convention of the Party she had attended, in July 1948, she brought news of a recruitment drive. It was announced, she testified, that "the Party was gearing itself for concentration particularly in the basic industries" and mainly those in New York "the waterfront, and the railroads, and the Railway Express." Her West Side club's assignment, she explained, was "to concentrate on Pier 84, 86, and 88, concentrate on the recruiting of longshoremen in those—in that territory." They also "had the Railway Express Company at 42nd Street and Twelfth Avenue."[16]

The Court took note. In an unusual exchange, Judge Medina and Angela discovered a rising tide of conspiracy that supported the indictment. "You say the waterfront, the railroads, and the Railway Express?" he asked her.

"That is right," she told Medina. "The waterfront included longshore, seamen, Railway Express workers, and there was one other—trucking."

"Trucking?" the Judge exclaimed, doubtless sensing the potential threat.

"That is right," Angela replied, "teamsters, as we called them," then upped the ante a bit by adding that her section was "the Yugoslav community section," with "a lot of longshoremen in the Yugoslav group."[17]

At a time when there still was a Yugoslavia, a Socialist People's Republic under Marshal Tito, a Yugoslav presence on the waterfront might have been perceived as a potential fifth column. In *Red Masquerade*, since she was not under oath, Angela went on to suggest that a genuine plot was afoot, spearheaded by Yugoslav seamen she was sure were bringing "messages from the Motherland of Socialism" (the Soviet Union) to the Party leadership in New York. She regretted that she was "never able to prove it." A bit later, it was Tito's differences with the Russians that distressed Angela, who feared her Yugoslav comrades would abandon the Party role she had envisioned for them. "If we lost the Yugoslavs we might never win the waterfront," she exclaimed, as though she really meant it.[18]

As it turned out, instead of fomenting insurrection on the docks on orders from Moscow, Angela was only distributing the *Daily Worker*. But another witness, the last one for the prosecution, came forward to back her up on the dangers of Communist "infiltration" on Manhattan's West Side. Balmes Hidalgo, Jr., identified through his testimony as a person of Spanish descent, was representative of what Angela called that "Balkanized population of Italian, Negroes, Yugoslavs, Puerto Ricans, Spanish, Greeks and Irish" on the New York docks. According to her analysis in *Red Masquerade,* they all retained "the nationalistic passions of Europe," hard to explain in the case of the "Negroes" and Puerto Ricans, but implying once again that leftist politics led to chaos and was probably un-American.[19]

Because he was Hispanic, Hidalgo's testimony seemed a good time to re-introduce references to the Spanish Civil War (1936-1939), which was mentioned from time to time during the trial by both sides. The defense team cited the Party's opposition to US relations with Franco's Spain, while the prosecution portrayed the rise of the former Republic as a dangerous example—"the Spanish Revolution"—in terms intended to recall the even more dangerous Russian Revolution. One of the American Communists named by Hidalgo, Larry Cane, was a veteran of the "Republican Army in action in Spain." He also landed on Utah Beach on D-Day, lived through the Battle of the Bulge, and won a Silver Star for bravery. In keeping with the tone of the indictment, Balmes Hidalgo claimed to quote Cane's wife, Grace Cane, who had threatened that "soon they were going to have another revolution in Spain led by the Communist Party, much like the one that we will have here in the United States when the time is ripe." According to Hidalgo, she added that there were "10,000 veterans of the Second World War in the Communist Party now," and that "when the time comes" the Party will fight "the FBI, police, and Army and National Guard."[20]

Grace Cane's very threatening rhetoric would have been hard to match. Hidalgo did his best by highlighting the Communist plot to enroll minorities (like himself). The organizer, he testified, who went by the name of "Julie. J-u-l-i-e" spelled into the court record, had divided the Party faithful of the Thomas Jefferson Section, with headquarters on West 72nd Street, into groups with specific assignments. One was to "concentrate on the Spanish-speaking neighborhoods, recruit them and incite them." Another would "take the Italian-speaking group." Other assignments, that harkened back to Angela's testimony, included "to concentrate on power stations and communications, to infiltrate those industries [...] so that if at any time they wished to control power and communications, they would be ready and able to do so," and "to aid in transportation recruiting, specifically the New York Central Railroad."[21]

"Julie," Hidalgo insisted, sometimes went by his real name, "Katz," but sometimes, like so many other Communists named throughout the trial, used an alias. In Julie's case, the unlikely choice was "O'Donnell," claimed Hidalgo. This use of pseudonyms, referred to by various witnesses, contributed, of course, to the portrayal of Party members as basically dishonest, and up to no good. Only people with something to hide assumed false names and identities, it was believed. Angela testified that she "was told to take an assumed name," and was known as "Angela Cole," at least through the completion, in 1942, of her first course at the Marxist Summer Day School. Other witnesses pointed to the widespread use of false names. William Cummings, the African-American auto worker from Toledo, Ohio, testified about a list of nominees at an Ohio State Party Convention. "Some here," said Cummings, referring to that list, "didn't carry the correct names. [...] It's that the—they wasn't identifying these people by their real names."[22]

As the trial progressed, witnesses for the defense were brought in, at great expense and personal risk to themselves, to refute testimony by prosecution witnesses they had known in the Party. It was an almost inevitable strategy in a trial where paid informants took the stand and, besides their own impressions, were allowed to quote their version of what instructors in classes and speakers at meetings had said. The defense consistently objected "on the ground that it is all hearsay." But Judge Medina's response was to declare admissible "testimony relative to co-conspirators"—that is, most anybody in the CPUSA. Gladstein for the defense said it put the Party "as such on trial and its ideas and all of its members," not just the eleven defendants. Medina overruled all objections.[23]

In these exchanges, both the truth and the defense came off badly. For one thing, by the time the defense witnesses came to the stand, the jury had been sitting for so many months, they probably neither remembered nor cared much anymore who had said what. Nevertheless, Yolanda Hall, the war-time tool grinder at Bendix Aviation, came forward in late July to say that she had been invited to the same national Party training school, in Chicago, in December 1945, as William Cummings, and that she did not share his impressions. Students attending a Communist school, she said, always ran the risk of being "attacked and maligned," or losing their jobs, and "had a perfect right to use their first name or be called by a nickname or however they chose." And like many Red Scare witnesses in different settings, from committee hearings to Smith Act trials, Yolanda Hall, "as a trade unionist," denied the Foley Square prosecution more names of participants and instructors at the Chicago training school. Because, she declared, she did not "want to involve anyone in possible persecution or prosecution for being mentioned in this trial."[24]

Everyone knew it was all about the names, and many went to considerable lengths to avoid betraying comrades past and present. From the witness stand at Foley Square, Howard "Stretch" Johnson of Harlem, refused to "name names, [...] because people have been fired from their jobs precisely because their names have been mentioned in the courtroom." Angela, on the contrary, made it a point to offer up as many names as she could fit into her answers. At one moment in her cross-examination by Gladstein for the defense, she began to "string off this list of names." "There was Matti White. There was Vita Devyatkin and Paul Devyatkin," she began. "There was Bernice Levine. There was Sylvia Chuse, Sidney Howard [...] or Sidney Masters, as he was known, too. I believe there was Tony Schwartz, Florence Lipowsky or Tamisky. Both of them are her names," she continued, then added, "Reina Klein went along with us once." After several attempts to silence her, Gladstein asked, "And you knew all these people?" "Oh, I know still more," replied Angela. She was the ideal witness.[25]

Another defense witness came forward to refute Balmes Hidalgo's testimony, probably doing himself and his career no favors. Wilbur Broms, originally from Minneapolis, Minnesota, knew Hidalgo, he testified, from the Thomas Jefferson Section, and swore that the organizer Julie Katz had never used the name O'Donnell. Broms also denied Hidalgo's assertion that the "concentration activities" his group engaged in were related "to peculiarly the Spanish-speaking people in the area." And, yes, the section's interest in "assisting the workers at the New York Central yards, specifically" was often discussed, because "there was speed-up in this yard, there was discriminations [sic], as most of these workers were Negroes." But no one was ordered to "infiltrate" the local transportation industry.[26]

As though Wilbur Broms had not had enough exposure, Angela took pains to identify him in *Red Masquerade*, as "a slow-thinking Irishman with a Swedish name" who "came to New York City to study music on the G.I. bill of rights, a favorite Communist meal ticket." She was right about the music. Besides being active in the Party since his freshman year at the University of Minnesota, later a city organizer in St. Paul and state Party chairman of Minnesota, Broms had worked for WPA art and music projects in Minneapolis. He went on to have a career as a singer in the chorus at New York's Metropolitan Opera.[27]

Leaving behind Manhattan's West Side piers, and Angela's white-collar union, it is Wilbur Broms' life in the CPUSA that directs attention back to the American Midwest and the industrial heartland, whose militant labor movement most concerned the FBI and prosecution. Witnesses at Foley Square came forward, one after another, to testify to the threat posed by powerful unions "infiltrated" and controlled by Communists. John Victor Blanc, of Cleveland, Ohio, had been a member of the Party in the 1930s, and re-joined in 1944, when he began working for the FBI. Employed for the previous eight years by Park Drop Forge Company in Cleveland, one of many plants throughout the Midwest that produced parts for the assembly lines of the major automakers concentrated around Detroit, Blanc was also a member of the powerful United Auto Workers (UAW). Thanks to that connection, he could provide insider details on the union at a critical moment in its history. The court was all ears.[28]

Blanc backed up Angela's "concentration" story about expanding Party influence with news of a "Building Campaign" to increase membership. Launched early in 1946, he said, it targeted vital industries—steel, rubber, auto-aircraft, electrical radio, mining, and railroads. But Blanc had more information to offer about Communist strategy. As a delegate to the historic UAW International Convention of 1946, where Walter Reuther was elected to the presidency over the incumbent R. J. Thomas and his Secretary-Treasurer George Addes (who was branded by Reuther as a Communist before the convention), Blanc was in on discussions.[29]

Over the objections of Gladstein for the defense about the prosecution's inquiries into union business, Blanc offered up his version of a meeting of Communist UAW delegates held in Detroit before the convention. There, said Blanc, they were instructed by Nat Ganley, a Communist and future defendant at the Michigan Smith Act trial, that "we was to go to this convention with the intention of backing R. J. Thomas and George Addes against the Reuther forces." While this was not startling news, Judge Medina was always on the alert for additional conspiracies. In overruling Gladstein's objection, Medina reminded him of the importance of Blanc's testimony, which revealed that "they were in there planning the tactics they were going to pursue at the United Automobile Workers convention, these Communists."[30]

It was a reminder that national security was bound up with Detroit and the auto industry. Back then (not unlike today), what was good for General Motors (and Ford and Chrysler) was good for the country, and a radical labor movement was not necessarily an asset.

But what may have looked just as threatening in the 1940s as wage and benefit demands, was the long-standing UAW policy of eliminating racial segregation and inequality in the union. The CPUSA proposed eliminating them in American society in general. Several Foley Square prosecution witnesses had been part of those movements at one time or another, but had ended up on the FBI's payroll. Union members who took the stand for the prosecution in the order of their appearance at the trial were: William Nowell (Detroit, UAW), Charles Nicodemus (Maryland, United Textile Workers), Garfield Herron (Chicago, UAW), William Cummings (Toledo, UAW), and John Victor Blanc (Cleveland, UAW). Of these five, four had been UAW, and three of them were African-American. Signaling the importance of racial policy and auto making to the life of the nation, they were apparently part of an extensive web of surveillance. While FBI informers came from a variety of backgrounds—even from the lesbian subculture of Greenwich Village—many of them were African Americans. For money and the hope of a job, they watched closely the influence of the CPUSA among the country's largest disenfranchised minority and reported back to their handlers. The Bureau took that internal threat very seriously, saw it perhaps as even more fearful than the imminent Soviet attack—when the Red Army would "invade Alaska down through Canada and they could even destroy Detroit"—predicted, as noted previously, by a union man and prosecution witness, Charles Nicodemus, United Textile Workers, CIO.[31]

9. The Negro Question

In America, given a long history of slavery, the issue of race is always present. This was true at the Foley Square trial, where the American Communist Party's commitment to recruiting African Americans and raising them to leadership positions became a principal theme for both prosecution and defense. For the latter, it was about how the CPUSA—in response to a decades-old mandate to take up the cause, as defined by poet and writer of the Harlem Renaissance Claude McKay, of "the most oppressed, exploited, and suppressed section of the working class of the world"—had rallied to the African-American quest for first-class citizenship, and made it a priority. The prosecution, and mainstream politics, took a dim view of the African-American struggle, because it demanded real change. With Communist backing, it could even trigger destabilization, or "the overthrow of the US government by force and violence," which would leave the way open for the Party and its recruits to deliver the country over to the Russians. At least, that was the argument.[1]

From his lofty perspective, Judge Medina saw discussion of the issue as just another delaying tactic, and, by about the middle of Angela's testimony, he despaired that he had heard enough about "price control, rent control, discussing the Negro question, and abolishing all these unfair things that have to do with Negroes" which he felt "are not the issues here." The only question for the court, Medina said, was whether the Communists had "conspired as charged in the indictment [...] to teach and advocate the overthrow of the Government of the United States by force and violence." Later, George Crockett, the only African-American attorney on the defense team (the prosecution had none), politely reminded presiding Judge Harold R. Medina that he had ruled he did not "desire to hear any more testimony about Negroes," or "the Negro question."[2]

If Judge Medina did not want to hear, the FBI did. Hoover himself had a reputation of long-standing for opposing civil rights and maintaining the racial status quo. Few things would have seemed more subversive to him than enlisting African Americans under the banner of international socialism, a threat he later identified with Martin Luther King, Jr.—"the most dangerous Negro of the future in this Nation from the standpoint of communism." Hoover also opposed integration of the Bureau, and responded to pressure from the NAACP by appointing his long-time chauffeur as the first African-American FBI agent.[3]

Angela, who had been reporting for several years to her handlers, undoubtedly knew the FBI's official attitude on racial issues, and perhaps shared it. In 1946, she disclosed the latest about ongoing postwar Party discussions on racism at home, which seemed harder to defeat than fascism abroad had been. While her reports are not preserved, a Bureau memo—that also praised Angela's usefulness as a spy and asked that her salary be continued at the same rate ($180 per month)—passed on her story that "the negro question" was "considered the main theoretical problem before the National Board [of the CPUSA]." The Board, Angela reported, was asking that all Clubs "form conclusions" regarding "the negro and what has been accomplished for him by the Communist Party" and "make recommendations" for a "future program and policy."[4]

By 1949, members of that Board were on trial at Foley Square. While Angela was not asked to comment on the Party's "program and policy" from the witness stand (the prosecution had others for that purpose), the "Negro question" did arise repeatedly in *Red Masquerade*. In fact, the book is filled with stories about the Party's recruitment of African Americans in New York City—how "crocodile tears of sympathy for the discrimination they suffered" were used to "court" them, including "a special code of conduct toward Negroes" that treated them like "social cripples." This view was not original with Angela, but, on the contrary, fairly typical Red Scare rhetoric.[5]

Race in America was an issue of grave importance during the postwar period, with foreshadowings of the national civil rights movement of the 1960s. Angela would have done well to reserve comment, but, of course, she could not if she wanted to tell her story. To her chagrin, everything she said, whether sincere or contrived, placed her, along with the incorrigible bigots, on the wrong side of history. In one of her delusional moments in *Red Masquerade*, Angela falls back on an old familiar argument for preserving the status quo, vaguely defined as "what's all the fuss about?" The answer for her is that there is no "Negro problem," a variation on the "Negro question," because Angela "had grown up with" African Americans, with "Irish, Italian, Negro and Spanish children" on the streets, and "had the advantage of colored children" when she went to school on the Lower East Side. Claiming to be no stranger to diversity, Angela judges herself free of the guilt and hypocrisy that, she says, plagues well-to-do supporters of the Communist cause who have domestic servants. By contrast, Angela insists that she "always ate" with her "Ellie" (the help) as a matter of course, and never thought she "was proving anything by it."[6]

Of course, the idea that Angela might have retained a "cleaning woman" (Ellie) for her Village apartment seems a bit of a stretch, if not pure nonsense. But such ramblings doubtless resonated with an audience of Americans who agreed that there would be no "Negro" question, and no problem, except for the meddling Communists—precursors to the "outside agitators" of the 1960s. They allegedly stirred up anger and resentment, especially in the South, where before there was none. Another hole opens up in Angela's argument around the good fellowship and ethnic makeup of the old neighborhood she remembers in *Red Masquerade*, "Avenue B on the lower East Side of New York City." While cataloging the population ("Irish, Italian, Negro and Spanish"), she omits the largest component by far—immigrant Eastern European Jews. If her playmates really were

"Negro and Spanish children" instead, perhaps the explanation lay in repressed memories of those years spent in the Bronx orphanage, the Sevilla Home for Children, specifically for orphan girls, which she had banished from accounts of her childhood.[7]

On the other hand, while denouncing recruitment campaigns up in Harlem as just another of those "tricks all Communists use" to make people think they are concerned for "Negro and labor rights," Angela, quite by chance, gives us a glimpse in *Red Masquerade* into that lost world of leftist activism. The issues addressed by "specially prepared speakers" who give potential recruits "the works" include "the poll tax, discrimination in employment and in right wing labor unions, the Ku Klux Klan, high rents and gouging food prices in Negro sections." These abuses, largely ignored by mainstream politics, would have been all too familiar to an African-American audience. Likewise, Angela's spy mission to Washington, DC, to the convention of the Civil Rights Congress (CRC), a major force in the legal defense of victims of racism, provides a look at our nation's "Jim Crow" capital in 1949. "Non-segregated restaurants" were few, she reports, as were hotels that "accepted both Negro and white guests."[8]

In racist America, many would have shared Angela's attitude toward Communist activism in the African-American community. It was an activism, unique in a country where "segregation forever" was the motto, that brought everyone together to study, protest, and socialize. For the edification of her right-wing readers, *Red Masquerade* trots out the usual arguments against all that, and any other movement toward integration. Chief among them are sexual threats to American womanhood and the specter of miscegenation, ideas that served the Ku Klux Klan and its lynch mobs well. Part of the Communist recruiting pitch, Angela explains, gave the audience "to understand, in a tactful way, that several prominent Negroes in the Party had white wives," and that laws in states where "Negroes are not allowed to marry whites" are unfair. Proof that the Party "deliberately assign white girls to canvass Harlem" surfaces at a fundraiser Angela throws for her comrades at her Village studio, where the crowd includes "three girls escorting a somewhat bewildered Negro youth." Finally, because such a story affirms the straight identity she had adopted for her FBI career, Angela features herself as the unlikely object of desire when "a Negro comrade tried to make a date" with her. Because the invitation is for an expensive restaurant, she interprets it as "bluntly speaking, a proposition." She hesitates to refuse for fear of being accused of "white chauvinism," that failure to show interracial solidarity the Party frowns upon.[9]

Making light of racism in America, Angela, from time to time, ran into trouble. When she tells us about someone at the fundraiser in her studio who shared "a purported eyewitness account of a lynching allegedly suppressed by the New York papers," she is implying that such stories were, at best, exaggerated; at worst, more Communist deceit. In fact, a rash of very real lynchings had swept 1940s America, complicated by returning African-American GIs who had fought a foreign war hoping to win support at home for the reform of racist legislation and sentiment. At a time of national crisis, following the brutal lynching of four young African Americans, two men and two women, near a small town in Georgia, Truman was pressured to appoint a National Committee on Civil Rights in 1946. Later he went so far—and under considerable pressure from African-American protest leaders—as to order the desegregation of the American armed forces (1948). There were too many terrible incidents to make valid Angela's claim that the Communist Party was just inventing "lynch terror and police brutality" [...] "in order to attract Negroes" to their recruitment drives. While "these crusades," as Angela defines them, may have seemed to her, and to the FBI, just another way, and an easy "very economical way of stirring up unrest that might lead to revolution," eye-witnesses told a different story.[10]

At the Foley Square trial, Henry Winston, Party Organizational Secretary, one of the defendants and one of two African-American members of the National Board, testified about his experience. Taking the stand in his own defense, Winston told of witnessing, in 1931, a lynching "where Raymond Gunn was tied by rope and burned on top of a school building, together with the school building in Marysville, Missouri." He began to explain to Judge Medina how, "knowing that racial tensions were being fanned by various elements in the community," he had tried "to take some form of positive action" by joining the Young Communist League and later the Party. In the Party he had sought allies, he began to explain to the judge, among "humanitarians, people who were interested in decency and justice" to prove "that Negro and white in the City of Kansas City, Missouri, could unite on the basis on an intelligent program of democratic action."[11]

But Winston was talking too much, Judge Medina decided, and cut him off—as he did many defense witnesses whose testimony veered off into Party policy, or what he often called other "peripheral matters." Medina's argument, which he repeated with increasing frequency as the proceedings dragged on, was to save time in what had become for him "an endurance contest" where he could not permit things "on the fringe of relevancy [...] without unduly prolonging the trial." Likewise, the judge stuck by the declaration he had made in the middle of Angela's cross-examination, that he was "not going to have the whole case get off on to rent control and anti-Semitism and the Negro question, and Jim Crow and rent control and price control." All Medina wanted to hear from Henry Winston, he admonished the witness, was an answer to the original question about "the incident which you say also contributed to your joining the Communist Party."[12]

Meanwhile, Ben Davis, New York City Councilman from Harlem, and the other African-American member of the National Board on trial, seated at the defense table, had a different story about his conversion to Communism. Angela repeats, in *Red Masquerade,* a story from one of her first Party meetings, told by "a comrade from the South" who talked about "the conviction of a Negro in Alabama by an all-white jury." But while she made it sound like just another example of Communist alarmism, to be dismissed out of hand, as an attorney in Atlanta, Georgia, Ben Davis had lived such a story.[13]

His client was a young African American named Angelo Herndon, brought to trial in 1932 for "attempting to incite to insurrection" by leading an integrated protest of unemployed Georgians. In another example of law enforcement's interest in Party literature, Communist pamphlets found in Herndon's possession resulted in his detention under a 19th-century statute originally drafted to discourage slave rebellions. It had later been revised and revamped by the state to prosecute labor organizers. Herndon stood accused of intending to overthrow the Georgia state government and, according to the indictment, to set up a new one "known as United Soviets Soviet Russia, sometimes known as 'The Dictatorship of the Propertyless People.'" He was spared the death penalty but sentenced to twenty years on the chain gang. Herndon's appeal went all the way to the US Supreme Court, where his conviction was overturned. Toward the end of the Atlanta trial, Ben Davis turned in an application to become a member of the Communist Party.[14]

It was also no coincidence, and certainly symptomatic of the times they lived in, that both Angelo Herndon (in Atlanta) and National Board Member on trial Henry Winston (in Kansas City) had also joined another organization that, early on, sought to lessen the impact of the Great Depression on the working class. Beginning in 1930, when unemployment benefits did not exist, Unemployed Councils (UCs) set up by the American Communist Party went into the streets and marched on local government offices demanding help. Some relief, in the form of city funds, was forthcoming for the unemployed. But in Detroit, for example, marches and protests by the UCs and the Young Communist League targeted car factories, where layoffs had precipitated a crisis. The young Communist recruit William Odell Nowell, who had come from rural Georgia to Detroit in the 1920s, and later appeared as a prosecution witness at the Foley Square trial, was almost certainly a participant in those demonstrations.[15]

William Nowell, more than any other working-class prosecution witness, had been a dedicated Communist, active in the early struggles of a union committed to racial equality in the labor movement. Nowell had once sat at the right hand of UAW leadership. But, as one version of the story goes, he was later expelled from the union for collaboration with Harry Bennett, "a combination of Dracula and J. Edgar Hoover," who ran a union-busting army and extensive labor spy network inside Ford Motors. Like other ex-Communists, Nowell went over to the other side with a vengeance, beginning in 1939, with testimony before HUAC claiming UAW pioneers from Detroit were Communists. His own story was complicated by schisms within the UAW leadership, and serious infighting that had ultimately weakened the union and perhaps made him vulnerable to FBI overtures.[16]

By contrast, those other African-American witnesses for the prosecution at Foley Square—Garfield Herron and William Cummings—claimed they had no such history of being "genuine Communists." Like Angela, who, according to *Red Masquerade*, had "never, at any time [...] believed in Communism," it was a difference they insisted on. While Herron seemed a little fuzzy on details, he remembered being recruited by the FBI as an informant before he was approached by a Party member at Douglas Aircraft, United Automobile Workers CIO in Chicago. In a scenario that parallels the FBI's 1942 visit to Angela's Greenwich Village apartment, described by her in *Red Masquerade* and on the witness stand, Herron told about agents coming to his home, in the spring of 1944, out of the blue to ask him if there were Communists in the union. The Bureau was not anti-union, Herron assured Gladstein for the defense on cross-examination, because "they wanted strong unions." They just wanted to find out what the Communists were doing there. The prosecution, and the judge, accepted that distinction, but defense attorneys maintained that sitting in on meetings where union business—better working conditions and wages, elections for officers—was discussed went beyond "just watching Communists."[17]

Cummings also swore that he had not reported to the FBI on "trade union matters" or the activities of Communists at "trade union meetings," just on their "activities in the Communist Party." It seemed a fine line, difficult to draw, especially since his first assignment for the Bureau had been "to get some information" on the whereabouts of a former organizer, a Communist, for the Food and Tobacco Workers Union. And like Herron (and Angela), Cummings had talked to FBI agents before joining the Party in 1943. During six years of service as an informant, he had conscientiously recruited other African Americans into the Party, including relatives of his, and just as conscientiously turned their names in to the Bureau. On cross-examination, in a rare moment that might have elicited a wry smile from the defense, attorney George Crockett asked Cummings, "At the time you recruited these Negroes into the Communist Party, did you tell them that you intended to report their names to the FBI?" "No, I did not," was Cummings' solemn answer. "All the names that I recruited into the Party was [sic] reported."[18]

The defense promptly accused Cummings of being both a stool pigeon and a labor spy. The stool pigeon part was fairly routine for prosecution witnesses who had worked as FBI informants in the Party. Early on, Angela had been labeled "lowly spy and stool pigeon," and in *Red Masquerade*, she complains that the defense had tried to make it look as if she "had been spying on labor unions and political parties"—the American Labor Party and Henry Wallace's Progressive Party. But the FBI, according to Angela on the witness stand, had taken no particular interest in her joining, or not joining, the United Office and Professional Workers (UOPWA). Instead, she testified, it was her old friend Leona Saron who had "instructed" her to join the union, and work for the Party. Judge Medina knew where the defense was going, and asked a question of his own to shut them down. "Did all your reports to the FBI have to do with Communist activities?" he wanted to know. This implied that regular union members, non-Communists, were off limits, and Angela replied, "Yes, your Honor." Gladstein for the defense objected to "the leading question" from the judge, and asked that the answer be stricken and the question be withdrawn. Medina overruled the objection and denied the motion, which closed the book on the "labor spy" issue as far as Angela was concerned.[19]

The term "labor spy," in fact, had a special meaning back then, when unions and union organizing were at their height. Although the 1935 National Labor Relations Act (Wagner Act) and the National Labor Relations Board (NLRB) had been designed to curb corporate labor abuses, it soon became apparent that industrialists were continuing to interfere with legal union activities. One of their chief strategies was to send in hired informants, to identify organizers and report on what was said in meetings. To break this cycle, a Congressional committee, the La Follette Civil Liberties Committee (1936-1941), for Senator Robert La Follette (Republican-Wisconsin), took up the problem and unearthed a wide range of anti-labor tactics, including espionage and provocation. The findings of the committee were widely publicized, Gladstein for the defense reminded Judge Medina, and showed that "employers throughout the country used their own stool pigeons on their own payroll to filter into trade organizations, union organizations, and break them up."[20]

This impassioned speech, from the seasoned labor lawyer Gladstein, came in the middle of testimony by prosecution witness William Nowell, whose long career in the labor movement, the Communist Party, and the UAW (from "janitor at the Dodge Brothers Motor Company" to "punch-stamping press operator" at Ford), had ended badly. According to his own testimony, Nowell's fellow workers had pegged him as a company spy, "attempting to drop things out of cranes on me," he told the court, "and push things off stockpiles onto me." Maybe that was because he had been bumped upstairs to the "employment office," where he had access to personnel files, and could identify Ford employees who were Communists (or just union organizers). Gladstein identified that operation as part of the Ford Service Department, the agency Ford used to prevent the organization of its workers into a trade union, defined by Philip Dray in his *There Is Power in a Union,* as a "private army and extensive spy network."[21]

But Nowell was just getting warmed up, and would become a star witness with sensational revelations designed to make the Party look even more dangerous. Both Herron and Cummings had attended courses and leadership trainings where Marxism-Leninism and "The Importance of the Negro Question"—one section from a study outline cited by Herron—held center stage. Nowell, who had joined the Party in 1929, had a more extensive background. There could have been no more damning evidence of the CPUSA's collusion with our Soviet foe than Nowell's trips to the USSR, not once but twice—in 1929, and for a year's study in 1931 in Moscow at the Lenin Institute. He identified for the court several defendants—Jack Stachel, Irving Potash, Gus Hall—he had met along the way, and in Moscow. Defense lawyers recognized that the Russian connection put them in a bad light and protested that Nowell's story and his Party membership pre-dated not only the period covered by the indictments (from 1945 forward) but also the passage of the Smith Act in 1940 under which the defendants were charged. Harry Sacher moved to strike Nowell's testimony as "altogether too remote," while Gladstein suggested it was "most highly prejudicial and has no probative value whatever." That is, it would prove nothing.[22]

More electrifying news that went a long way toward explaining

Nowell's presence on the witness stand was yet to come and outstripped by far the impact of his Soviet study trips. His job was to outline the Party's "theory of what is called self-determination for Negroes in the Black Belt in the South." This theory would, according to Nowell, establish "a separate Negro nation in what is called the Black Belt, extending from Virginia to the Mississippi Delta in which they said that Negroes constitute a majority of the population." Thus, in one fell swoop Nowell expanded the Communist Party's plot, as stated in the indictment, from just overthrowing the US government to breaking up the country itself. All of this, he said, "to be executed through utilizing the legimate [sic] grievances of people there [...] as a means of mobilizing them and using them as a part of and preparatory to a proletarian revolution in the United States." Apparently, the long-awaited rebellion was at hand. It probably would not have helped much for the defense to stress the theoretical nature of the Black Belt Nation proposal, and much less to mention that it had its roots in the Comintern's early support for the rights of national minorities in the Soviet Union. Nowell, at any rate, testified that he had rejected the theory because he thought the separation of "Negroes North and South" would sabotage the improvement of conditions generally.[23]

Maybe a few reporters waited till the end of the day to file their stories, but most of them probably raced for the nearest phone while Nowell was still talking. His testimony, devastating for the defense, hit the front pages of New York dailies the next morning. The *New York Sun* sounded the alarm—"Reds Planned a Negro Nation. Witness Asserts They Discussed in 1930 Establishing It in the South." The *Herald Tribune* and *Times* echoed the distress cry, citing the "U.S. Reds' Plan for Negro State in South" and a "Plan for Negro Nation in U.S. [...] Plot for Rebellion and New Regime in Southern States." Almost a month later, in May 1949, during his testimony at the Foley Square trial, William Cummings revived the "Negro Republic" theme as part of the 1945 curriculum at the training school in Chicago where he was sent by the Ohio State Party. Perhaps less shocking and more democratic, Cummings' version suggested that "the Negro people would have to determine themselves whether they wanted the establishment of a Negro Republic in the Black Belt in the South or not," on land "which they had toiled on for years and years for the landlords." All this, according to Cummings, "after the dictatorship of the proletariat was set up in America."[24]

Let it be emphasized that the Black Belt Nation theory meant many things to many people over the years. Foley Square defendant Ben Davis, during Angelo Herndon's trial, defended it as "simply majority rule under the traditions and principles of both the federal and state constitutions." At a time when most African Americans in the South could not vote because of the poll tax, literacy tests, and intimidation, Davis insisted that, based on population and "by every principle of democracy, the Negroes should be governors, mayors, congressmen, senators, local and county officials." He did not see "self-determination for the Black Belt" as "insurrectionary or revolutionary." Others, of course, did. During his New York City Council re-election campaign, in 1945, political enemies made use of the Black Belt Nation theory to claim that Davis was laboring "diligently to carry out the orders of his foreign master to undermine and destroy the American government and way of life." Calling it a "ploy for segregation," opposition propaganda asked, "Must we all go back to the Black Belt?" Davis won the election anyway, hands down. He was sitting on the City Council when he was arrested for conspiracy to advocate the overthrow of the government.[25]

William Nowell only lived a few more years after his Black Belt Nation testimony at Foley Square. According to the FBI, he was dead by 1955 (presumably of natural causes), after a short run of testifying at Smith Act trials, where he specialized, David Caute has remarked in *The Great Fear*, "in flourishes of brazenly invented but marvelously detailed information." Cummings had a much longer run as an anti-Communist witness, rising to the ranks of "the perennials." Apparently, Garfield Herron never testified again. It is not hard to imagine why they, and other African-American informant/witnesses, would have gone over to the FBI. Like Angela Calomiris, they were outsiders looking for a way into American society, and what better way than a prestigious organization like the FBI, with money to spare? It is also possible that they were intimidated by Bureau agents, and could not, under duress, refuse to spy, or refuse to go on the witness stand.[26]

Despite the space Angela dedicates to the "Negro Question" in *Red Masquerade,* she does not mention Garfield Herron, William Cummings, or William Nowell. Of the prosecution witnesses, in fact, she only names Budenz and Herbert Philbrick in passing. After all, *Red Masquerade* was Angela's own story, where sharing space and the spotlight with other informants made no sense. If she did not have a show-stopping tale like Nowell's Black Belt Nation, or even Budenz's "Aesopian language"—where everything Communists said was a lie—she did have something the prosecution wanted mentioned at trial. It was testimony that nobody else in the FBI's pay was able or willing to give.[27]

In fact, while her reports from the New York waterfront helped to build the case for Communist meddling in union affairs, Angela's appearance on the witness stand was really bound up with her early membership in the New York Photo League (1936-1951). The organization itself consisted of pioneering documentary photographers. Berenice Abbott, Margaret Bourke-White, and Paul Strand were on the Advisory Board. Members included W. Eugene Smith and Arthur Fellig (Weegee), while Dorothea Lange, Robert Capa, and Edward Weston, among others, visited and lectured. In the spirit of the Farm Security Administration (FSA) out in the rural American heartland, Photo Leaguers had chosen to document urban life in the shadow of the Great Depression. They had photographed poor people, including poor African Americans, and Harlem was one focus. The League was already suspect before Angela testified, for these and other transgressions, and had found a place on a December 1947 list, issued by the US Attorney General, of organizations labeled "totalitarian, fascist, Communist, or subversive." Angela provided additional ammunition with names of Photo Leaguers the prosecution wanted spoken from the witness stand.[28]

While going public in that way was risky, Angela had hoped, in exchange, for a good job. At least something as steady as the job with the Immigration and Naturalization Services provided by the Justice Department in 1948, just before the trial, for William Nowell. There he assisted in deportation and denaturalization cases, identifying Communists and former Communists. Angela wanted more, in the guise of a big boost to her photography career, but it was not to be. Her career, like the careers of the people she named on the witness stand, would not recover after the Foley Square trial. As with other would-be insiders who had served the Red Scare well, Angela would all too soon find herself back on the outside, and struggling to survive.[29]

10. The Photo League

Angela Calomiris lied about a lot of things. Some were fairly obvious lies—that she was not paid for her FBI work, that her father died when she was fifteen instead of seven. And, like other informant/witnesses of the period, she mastered the art of the half-truth on the witness stand and in *Red Masquerade*, exaggerating the influence of Communists on the New York waterfront, downplaying the role of racism in American society. But one thing she did not lie about was her desire to be a photographer.

"The important thing" about herself, she wrote in a long article for *True: The Man's Magazine* in April 1950, was her photography. As proof of that, she showed the FBI agents who first came to her Village apartment her make-shift darkroom—"my very first"—and some of her work. "They said it was good and I think they really meant it," she wrote. When applying for the job of Confidential Informant, she went further, and told the FBI that she had been studying photography for a year and had "a dark room and photographic enlarger at her residence."[1]

During the trial, a few minutes into her testimony, Angela replied to the question "What is your occupation?" put to her by Special Assistant US Attorney Edward C. Wallace, that she was a professional photographer. "My formal training," she continued, "I took at the Photo League and the New School of Social Research." Later, when she was looking for a job, she would claim that she had done "individual study" with Berenice Abbott, one of the principal photographers of her generation, who produced the groundbreaking volume of photos documenting *Changing New York* (1939) for the Federal Arts Project. Abbott had worked as an instructor at the New School since the early 1930s, and perhaps Angela had attended one of her classes.[2]

In that same résumé, she would also claim "individual study" with Hal Phyfe, great grandson of Duncan Phyfe the 19th-century American furniture designer, who was the "official photographer to High Society" and for a time to Florenz Ziegfield. When she told the story to Eleanor Roosevelt, during their radio conversation, the connection was more tenuous. In that version, Angela had worked in Phyfe's "studio anywhere from six months to a year." Like the job Angela had in the late 1930s with Mrs. Roosevelt's good friend Esther Lape, the job with the rather eccentric Phyfe might well have come through a gay connection, as Phyfe has been routinely called "a life-long bachelor" and "one of the best amateur cooks in Manhattan." To call her temporary work in his busy studio "individual study" was the kind of exaggeration to which Angela was prone.[3]

Her trial testimony contained more dangerous exaggerations, especially regarding her involvement with the Photo League and its co-founder, World War II veteran and freelance photographer Sid Grossman. He had been for years director of the League's school, a pioneering figure in the "New York School" of photography, and, in the opinion of many, "the heart of the Photo League." An interest in documenting reality inspired several group projects that were dubbed "documents," depicting diverse aspects of contemporary urban reality. Based on the premise that pictures could tell a story with minimal text, the League produced its "Harlem Document" (1939) with forty photographs of Harlem life that were exhibited at the Harlem YMCA, the New School, and a CIO Union Headquarters; and subsequently five panels of a "Chelsea Document" (1940), in cooperation with neighborhood residents of the Chelsea Tenants' League, when Chelsea was still a residential slum that bordered the New York waterfront.[4]

Just as it is impossible to determine exactly how Angela came to work for the FBI, so too it is difficult to say with certainty how she found her way to the League. The most likely connection was a woman named Peggy Vaughn, about whose photography career little is known. She was, however, for a brief period editor of *Photo Notes*, the League's more or less monthly publication, and someone identified in conversation with old friends of Angela as a "girlfriend" or lover. She lived, at least for a time, in the same Village apartment building as Angela, at 9 Jane Street, and probably, like Angela, had no political agenda and a limited income. Both women would have recognized the Photo League's reputation as "the best buy of the country's many photography schools." It would not "quickly turn you into a big shot commercial photographer," but costs were kept low. Membership was $5.00 per year with darkroom privileges, and the League offered classes at $15.00 ($5.00 for members) for a 16-week course. It was also a welcoming place where, according to a former League member, enrolling in a beginning class was simple, and despite the bare-bones décor, the simple fact was that you could emerge a "brand new photographer."[5]

Likewise, despite working most of her career in portrait or commercial photography, Angela seems to have sympathized with the Photo League's ideal of making "pictures that get across what you think and feel" while "documenting" contemporary reality. In *Red Masquerade*, she insists that "like most serious photographers," she "didn't want to take flattering pictures of people dressed up to sit for a portrait." Instead, in harmony with the Photo League aesthetic, she says she loved the streets of Manhattan, and wanted to show others "the many human dramas" she witnessed, "with no false props and no sentimental angles." Or, as she put it in her article for *True* magazine, she wanted "to be the best photo-journalist" she could be. As mute testimony to her ambition, among the papers she saved for almost fifty years, was a note written to her in April 1949 after her appearance on the witness stand. A former camper from the summers Angela spent working in camps that belonged to the Young Women's Hebrew Association and the Edwin Gould (son of financier Jay Gould) Foundation, recalled her determination "to be a journalist even if it meant starting as an office boy."[6]

Ideals aside, it is significant that Angela only began to take an active role in the Photo League after she had gone to work for the FBI in March 1942. Probably to impress her handlers and to gain access to insider information, she tried to make herself useful—tending bar at the League's "Spring Hop" in April where Zero Mostel provided entertainment, and getting herself elected in May 1942 Executive Secretary of the League, a position she held for little more than a year. After that initial flurry of activity, Angela only put in sporadic appearances at the Photo League if there was an event, or a party, especially one with guests of some celebrity status. People who came into the League after the war did not know who she was before she took the witness stand at the Foley Square trial.[7]

But there was one Photo League project where Angela— spelling her name "Angy" back then, doubtless for artistic effect— lowered her guard, forgot she was spying, and truly found a place. Coinciding with the brief period when she was most active, and with the League's effort to mobilize people to greater participation in the war effort, the "War Production Group" of 1943 put together four large photo murals of nursery schoolchildren. It served as a background for a booth staffed by the Committee for the Care of Young Children in Wartime (CCYCW) at Madison Square Garden during an International Women's Exposition. The Committee represented a cross-class alliance between left-wing women and philanthropists who advocated for government-funded child care.[8]

While many New York street scenes from the Photo League repertory featured children—because they liked being photographed, were open and spontaneous—it's likely that the innocence and vulnerability of childhood would have resonated especially with Angela. Her work as a counselor and recreation assistant in camps and settlement houses, and, of course, those years in the Bronx orphanage had taught her too much about the harshness of life. Even more poignant is *Red Masquerade*'s description of another project, one probably unrelated to the Photo League. Originally established in 1940 under the patronage of Eleanor Roosevelt, the U.S. Committee for the Care of European Children (USCOM) hoped to rescue British children from the dangers of constant bombings, and German Jewish children from the Nazi terror. Angela, on the other hand, claims that she worked with the Committee in the preparation of "a series of pictures of refugee youngsters orphaned in the Spanish war" and "brought to this country in 1943 for adoption." The series gave her great satisfaction, she reports, because—without acknowledging the personal trauma that underlay her claim—the pictures of Spanish orphans "were often the basis on which foster parents chose a child."[9]

Part of Angela's ongoing tragedy was that her years of working for the FBI distorted, beyond recognition, what may have been a nascent desire to produce photography of some worth in the pursuit of "social betterment." By the time of *Red Masquerade*, of course, in the midst of the Red Scare, it was politically correct to declare that she had been altogether out of step with League activist aesthetics. Not for her, she insists, that somber Communist doctrine which taught that "a good picture was a picture that illustrated social injustice" and trained students "to document the seamy side of American life." But because she was intelligent, she must have known that FBI assignments—photographing Leona Saron, and members of the IWO (International Workers Order)—meant nothing artistically. They did, however, get praise from her handlers, who recommended her for a raise, in 1942, on the basis of "good pictures of the speakers' stand at this [Communist Party] rally, in addition to shots of other individuals." She supplied their office "with enlargements of all pictures that she took." Besides her IWO photos, by 1944 she was furnishing the New York FBI office with "several good photographs of various persons in various places in New York who were canvassing for Congressman Vito Marcantonio during the primary campaign."[10]

Other assignments included pictures of big protest rallies during the war, "when comrades even made way" for her as she "came through the crowd" with her camera, according to *Red Masquerade*. At the annual May Day Parade, she photographed everything and shared eight-by-ten prints with the FBI, that were combined with those of other photographers and bound in a "thick 'May Day Parade' book." "Every identifiable face on every print was numbered," Angela reported in *True*, "and all undercover agents and other sources of information queried in order to connect each face with a name." At least one shoot would have demanded a bit more stealth. Three undated sheets of paper Angela preserved, with both handwritten and typed notations, gave names, some addresses, and construction details—"white clapboard, brown shingle, modern ranch"—for houses, most of them in a neighborhood of Croton-on-Hudson, New York, that had been for many years a home to artists, nonconformists, and progressive thinkers of all sorts. One paper labeled "Sequence of Photos" had each shot numbered alongside a list including prominent Communists like Joseph North, editor of the weekly *New Masses*, and Alexander Bittelman, who was convicted in 1951 (at age sixty-one) of "conspiracy to advocate the overthrow of the US government by force and violence" at the second New York Smith Act trial.[11]

Both of them lived in the Mt. Airy section, an address they shared with others on a list that included Adolph Elwyn with a note "Prof. N.Y.U. or Columbia," author and publisher Albert Kahn, and Richard Boyer "of New Yorker." The names of Paul Robeson, Rockwell Kent, and Dashiell Hammett also appear, with referrals to suburban locales beyond Croton. Besides keeping tabs on these suspicious characters, who had probably been identified as "subversives," the photographs might have been intended to aid in their arrest in the event of a national crisis. The Internal Security Act of 1950 (also labeled the McCarran Act), which included an Emergency Detention section, referred to as the "Concentration Camp" amendment and modeled on the internment of Japanese-Americans during World War II, had authorized such detentions.[12]

What is certain is that the FBI knew Angela was in the Photo League when they recruited her. "And you're studying photography at the Photo League?" Angela's original handler, Kenneth M. Bierly, later a friend to whom she dedicated *Red Masquerade*, asks during their first encounter. What is highly likely is that, for the Bureau, having someone inside the League was more urgent than having just another informant inside the CPUSA, and her photo skills were useful. *Red Masquerade* makes it sound as though it were a "sudden inspiration" on Angela's part, that she could provide the Bureau with "pictures of some of these people" she had been telling them about. But that was probably part of the plan from the beginning. An organization with the Photo League's history and pedigree as defined in a 1945 FBI report—"originally organized as the Film & Photo League" with officers who are "mainly Communists or Communist sympathizers," a group "used for recruiting Communist Party members and follows the Party line" [...] "believed to be Communist controlled and believed to be existing for the benefit of the Communist Party"—could not have escaped notice. An internal FBI memo had also described the League as "progressive, liberal, even radical in their policy, pro-labor, anti-fascist, very much interested in the protection of civil liberties and better conditions for the working people." Certainly a group to watch out for! League president Walter Rosenblum had never made any secret of his intentions, urging photographers to "go to the people, to the auto workers in Detroit, to the transport workers in New York, to the Farmer's Union in Oklahoma. Let us photograph the people who are making America a finer place for us all. These are the things which our pictures must show."[13]

Back at the trial, Angela's FBI career of seven years came full circle. After a long-term absence, when she had been busy establishing herself as an officer in local branches of the CPUSA, with greater access to more information, she recaptured the intrigue of her original assignment inside the Photo League. Responding from the stand to the first questions from the prosecution, that yes, she was a photographer, a professional photographer, and "a member of the Photo League" in 1942. Immediately after that, to establish the connection between the League and radical politics, US Attorney Wallace asked when and where she had been asked to join the Communist Party. It was a well-designed and effective strategy to bolster the Attorney General's 1947 designation of the Photo League as "subversive," and put another nail in its coffin. Obviously, that had nothing to do with the case against the defendants, but explained the prosecution's choice of Angela as witness. "Who asked you?" the prosecution wanted to know, and Angela, who was adept at naming names—which she did whenever possible in five days of testimony, and 400 pages of text in the trial transcript—answered promptly: "I was asked by Sid Grossman, Marion Hillie, and Leona Seron, all three of whom were responsible for my recruiting." Immediately after that, Grossman was identified as "the director of the Photo League" who told Angela "to take an assumed name" when she joined the CPUSA. A few minutes later, she identified the Photo League as a "mass organization [...] an organization that is often set up by the Party." "We also used the term 'front,' in reference to these organizations, she continued, "quite interchangeably, as a matter of fact."[14]

For Sid Grossman's wife, Marian Hille, who took care of administrative duties at the League (sometimes Executive Director of the League, sometimes editor of *Photo Notes*), Angela used an alternative version of her name, carefully spelled into the court records—"Marion H-i-l-l-i-e." Leona Saron's name was also misspelled into the record as "S-e-r-o-n," which, once again, makes one question how well Angela really knew her. But the prosecution obviously wanted her named at the trial. As for Marian, in its long-term surveillance of the Grossmans, the FBI consistently referred to her as "Marion," and "Hillie" was one suggested spelling for the last name. By the time of the trial, however, Marian Hille was no longer with Grossman or the Photo League, and had probably returned to the Midwest.[15]

Grossman, however, took the full brunt of the attack. After he was named by Angela from the witness stand, he never worked in New York again, left the Photo League to keep from endangering it further, and watched former acquaintances cross the street to avoid speaking to him in public. Three days after he was named at the Foley Square trial, while Angela was still testifying about other matters, the FBI prepared a Security Index card for Sidney Grossman— "Aliases: Sid Grossman [...] 7 West 24th Street, New York City." The Security Index was J. Edgar Hoover's own substitute for the custodial detention classification that FDR's Attorney General Francis Biddle had officially canceled in 1943 because it was "unreliable." The Index kept track of citizens, many of immigrant background, whose loyalty to the US the Bureau considered suspect, "who might be a source of grave danger to the security of this country." People on the list might be immediately arrested and interned should war break out.[16]

Grossman and his second wife, Miriam, survived on the GI Bill until his premature death in 1955, in the Manhattan VA Hospital of a heart attack, at age forty-two. Soon after, an FBI agent visited Miriam at the 24th Street apartment, but she did not let him in. That same year Grossman's name was removed from the Security Index.[17]

The supreme irony of it all is that Angela's place in history, and particularly in the history of photography, was secured, not by the quality of her photography, but by a betrayal—similar in style and effect to the attack on Judy Holliday's girlfriend Yetta Cohn. With bitterness and anger, former Photo Leaguers denounced Angela for her pillorying of Sid Grossman. Fifty years after the fact, and a year before his own death, Sol Libsohn, co-founder with Grossman of the Photo League, remembered that what Angela "did to Sid was really horrible" using "whatever stories she made up." In praise of Grossman, Walter Rosenblum spoke of his generosity as a teacher who "was never paid for any of his services to the Photo League," and did not mince words when he accused Angela of the "terrible crime" of ruining Grossman's life.[18]

Nevertheless, in recent retrospectives of the Photo League, Angela has found a place, which would have pleased her mightily. She was not represented in the New York Public Library 2006 retrospective *Where Do We Go From Here? The Photo League and Its Legacy (1936-2006)*, possibly because those in charge of the Library's very important Picture Collection would have known the story of the League's betrayal, and never bothered with work by Angela. While not all-inclusive, that exhibit featured a cross-section of Photo League membership. They ranged from well-known figures who lent their support—like Berenice Abbott, Ansel Adams, Margaret Bourke-White, Dorothea Lange, and Edward Weston—to artists tied more directly to the League's New York operations—like Sol Libsohn, George Gilbert, Aaron Siskind, Arnold Eagle, Walter Rosenblum, Dan and Sandra Weiner, Rosalie Gwathmey, and Sid Grossman. *The Women of the Photo League* show at Higher Pictures Gallery, New York City in 2009 included Angela's work, as did the definitive exhibit *The Radical Camera: New York's Photo League, 1936-1951*, which opened in November 2011, at New York's Jewish Museum. There Angela was immortalized with her own exhibition case, containing memorabilia from her spying on the League. She also gained some notoriety for her less than illustrious legacy by inclusion in a catalog essay alongside female photographers like Lucy Ashjian and Sonia Handelman Meyer, who would not have tolerated an informant. Despite a history of government blacklisting and the fear that at least some of the members may have been Communists, the Photo League has survived, and Angela alongside them, her name forever linked to Sid Grossman's.[19]

It remains unclear how well Angela knew him, whether she really ever sat in his photography class or not, or where the story that he had recruited her into the CPUSA came from. In *Red Masquerade,* she acknowledges getting "a lot of pointers on the art of photography from teachers at the Photo League." She may have experienced what she calls Grossman's "sarcasm" first-hand, even the "iron hand" with which he ruled the students. But Angela could have known all that and more about him without attending his class, since his reputation seems to have circulated freely around the League and become something of a joke—as in "the tyrant, dictator, Gruesome Grossman." On the other hand, he was rather universally acknowledged, according to former Photo League president Walter Rosenblum, to be "everyone's photographic conscience, [...] an inspiring and talented instructor." Perhaps because he had the respect of so many, for publication in *Red Masquerade,* Angela disguises her attacks on Grossman by calling him "Joe," an "excellent photographer" who never seemed to have a job, whose "attitude was: to hell with the world if it 'don't realize how good I am.'" All this led Angela to the conclusion, she writes, that "Joe was a typical Communist," one of those she later branded as moochers "who were on relief, collecting unemployment insurance, or 'studying' on the G.I, bill of rights." The latter she describes as "a favorite Communist meal ticket." It was typical of her depiction of all things she labeled "Communist" as slightly dirty and bedraggled, from the "bare, rugless [meeting] room, drab and forlorn, whose floor had not been swept in earnest" to Photo League headquarters "in a dilapidated old town house" where "everyone complained of the dirt" and "the stairs were grimy." And because the Red Scare had declared open season on American Communists, in the magazine article for *True,* she added offensive details (later deleted in *Red Masquerade*), to describe "Joe"—"not the most careful young man about the cleanliness of his person [...] with a thick lower lip and bad teeth." Walter Rosenblum corroborated the bad teeth, but added that Grossman had "no money for a dentist." His widow, Miriam Grossman Cohen, always doubted that Angela had ever studied with her husband, and insisted that she was never around the League after the war.[20]

It is interesting that the blame for recruiting Angela into the CPUSA, the charge she had lodged against Grossman at the trial, seems to have shifted by the time she published *Red Masquerade*. There the culprit is Leona Saron, who had "courted" Angela with "a very dull movie on collective farming in Russia" and "dinner in a little restaurant on the second floor of a brownstone house near Irving Place […] a favorite eating place of the [Party's] 'top leadership.'" She writes that by the end of April 1942, having been approved by one and all, she was inducted into the Party. Even the FBI, in an internal memo, expressed admiration for the speed with which she had "gained admittance to the Party after a little over five weeks concerted effort on her part." In fact, a closer look indicates that maybe nobody recruited Angela, that her attempt "to become an affiliated member of the Communist Party" had required some "active work," that maybe they had not wanted her at all.[21]

The FBI's careful surveillance of Sid Grossman seems to bolster that suspicion, while explaining a lot about his early association with Angela. To judge from a curious half-page document in his FBI file, a month into Angela's appointment as Confidential Informant she had yet to get herself recruited into the local Communist Party— perhaps because she was a rather obvious lesbian, perhaps for some other reason. Instead of being courted by Leona Saron, who is not mentioned, Angela apparently faced stiff resistance. The brief report dated April 16, 1942 recounted a conversation with Grossman and "Marian Hill" at their home after Angela had attended "a class at the Photo League on April 15, conducted by Sidney Grossman." She told the Grossman's that she "was annoyed at the treatment" given her, and went on to quote "Sidney," who assured her "that everything the Communist Party did was done for a reason." Angela reported that he had then stated, "That there was no question as to whether or not I would be desirable as a [P]arty member—he would see to that." Years later, she repeated the same story for the FBI, recalling that Grossman had assured her "he would see to it that she would be acceptable as a CP member." Maybe he did, using whatever influence he may have had as a Party member, according to the FBI, since

1936, and thereby helping Angela launch her spy career. He could never have imagined what disaster would befall him as a result of that friendly gesture.[22]

While the informant's name on both reports was thoroughly blacked out, in FBI style, there can be no doubt it was Angela, and little doubt that Sid Grossman initially trusted her. Further proof comes in a document from the war years, a report by an Army officer of an "Interview with Subject [Grossman] under subterfuge" where he denied being radical and claimed to be a "liberal" registered member of the American Labor Party. Among the people Grossman named from the Photo League, who would presumably speak well of him, the League's mission, and its loyalty, he included "Angela Calomiris, Secretary, Jane Street." If she had been drafted by the FBI for her Photo League connections and assigned specifically to shadow Grossman, she was good at the job. She certainly seemed to fit *Red Masquerade*'s description of "the ideal plant [...] able to inspire confidence without ever giving any in return." And Sid Grossman was probably a nice, even trusting person.[23]

In the last analysis, Angela became a tool of the prosecution and the FBI in a campaign against Grossman that had been going on for almost a decade before the Foley Square trial. Arriving somewhere in the middle, Angela evidently put in an appearance on the fringes of that "culture of the left" that flourished in America before McCarthyism, a cultural milieu where Grossman had many friends and felt at ease. A reliable witness, Walter Rosenblum, placed Angela in Grossman's apartment before both men went off to war, for a social evening unrelated to Photo League business. As Rosenblum confided, back in those days he did not know what a lesbian was, but a good friend of his and Grossman's, a Villager named Suzy Harris, had brought Angela along to hear music. Those evenings featured African-American folk singers, born in the Deep South, who had begun to make a name for themselves in the nascent folk music movement that had arisen out of the Great Depression. Among others, Folkways recording artists Big Bill Broomzy and Lead Belly performed at Grossman's home and received a big welcome there, as they generally did among white leftist urban audiences. This musical interaction between races, and the political overtones it generated, would have been of special interest to the FBI, of course.[24]

Sid Grossman's connection to folk music was not casual, but direct and personal through his wife Marian Hille. Unfortunately, all that, plus bad timing and bad luck, led directly to his early targeting by the FBI. While the Bureau's interest in Hille extended back several years, documenting her work for the WPA, and how she had taught photography in an Adult Education Program in the Bronx, her family in the Midwest also attracted attention. Her father was a minister with a church outside Chicago, and Marian's brother, the FBI said, was studying for the ministry. At some point the brother, Waldemar Hille, had shifted gears slightly and become deeply involved in leftist politics. After the war, he became an activist in the People's Songs movement, which included Pete Seeger and Lee Hays (late of the Almanac Singers) and other notable members of the folk community (such as Woody Guthrie). A pianist and composer, Hille moved in leftist cultural circles, edited *The People's Songs Newsletter* and subsequently the folk and protest musical reference work known as *The People's Songbook*.[25]

But before that, in the late 1930s, Waldemar Hille, billed as "dean of music at Elmhurst College in Chicago," had spent time at Commonwealth College, an alternative community that lasted from 1925 to 1940, near Mena, Arkansas. In the style of other communities set up by Americans of a socialist orientation during the last century, Commonwealth ran a school and farm where students and faculty shared the work load. Lee Hays, an Arkansas native, spent time at Commonwealth, as did the New Theatre League, originally based in New York, which produced left-wing plays about unions and against war. But Commonwealth attracted hostile attention, and the school was charged with Bolshevism, "Sovietism," communism, and free love. Later, after Commonwealth merged its interests with those of the Southern Tenant Farmers' Union (STFU), charges of anarchy and failure to fly the American flag were added. The school was fined for these and other so-called un-American activities, including bringing white tenant farmers together with their African-American counterparts, and closed down.[26]

During the last months of Commonwealth College's existence, sometime in the summer of 1940, Sid and Marian Grossman passed that way, inspired by connections through Marian's brother to the folk music movement, Lee Hays, and perhaps the New Theatre League. While contact with Commonwealth would have been enough to arouse suspicion, the Grossman's next stop, Oklahoma City, Oklahoma, sealed their fate. Home to a burgeoning oil industry and the Depression-era "Dust Bowl," Oklahoma also boasted the Progressive Book Store, run by American Communists, in the state capital. In August 1940, the bookstore was raided by local police on a preprinted official warrant that authorized a search for liquor on the premises (Oklahoma was a dry state at the time). A typewritten addendum authorized a search for "books, records, papers and articles which are used in and are evidence of the commission of criminal syndicalism or any other crime against the laws of the State of Oklahoma and of the United States." Thousands of books and pamphlets were seized, including fifteen copies of the US Constitution, and the Progressive Book Store was closed down. Several people connected with it were jailed, and four of them tried and convicted in the fall, under the state criminal syndicalism laws against conspiring to advocate crime, sabotage, and violence to effect political, industrial, and social change.[27]

Grossman had been photographing in both Arkansas and Oklahoma, and had produced at least two iconic photographs that survive—*Henry Modgilin, Community Camp, Oklahoma, 1940* and *Emma Dusenberry, Arkansas, 1940*. The Oklahoma City neighbor, who had "called at the Oklahoma City [FBI] Office to make a complaint," told agents that Grossman had "made photographs for different magazines," and had a "large amount of photographic equipment and flash bulbs." There were also "several photographs of poor people in tents and shacks as well as negatives of oil well pumps and equipment." Because of his affiliations with leftist culture and the Party, he would have known people in the local Oklahoma City Communist organization, all of whom were under heavy FBI surveillance. In fact, they were probably the only people he knew there. Among other suspicious rumors, the FBI determined that "Mrs. Grossman, on several occasions contacted a woman at the Humpty Dumpty Store, near West 16th Street," and that a mysterious trunk "weighing forty-five pounds" had been shipped from Oklahoma City to Mena, Arkansas, to be picked up by Sid Grossman himself.

Not recognizing Grossman right away, the FBI agonized over his identity, checking and cross-checking their files, while the friendly neighbor brought them mail addressed to Grossman bearing the return address of the Photo League, in New York City. All of that landed the Grossmans (and the Photo League) in the dragnet the prosecution laid out in what was becoming a major case, with national ramifications.[28]

The convictions of the Oklahoma City Communists were eventually thrown out on appeal. But years of their lives were lost, financial resources exhausted, while the FBI typically continued to spy on them for years. Likewise, the Oklahoma episode cast a spotlight on Sid Grossman that was never extinguished. He was under surveillance during his wartime military service and quizzed about his political beliefs by Army Intelligence. Grossman was finally obliged to sign a brief statement swearing that he was "not a member of the Communist Party" and had "never been a member of that organization." He swore the same regarding his wife. Having volunteered to fight Fascism, Grossman found himself in Panama for the duration of the war, far from any battlefield.[29]

Except for her FBI assignments, Angela's photographic career did not blossom during the war years. Instead of breaking into photojournalism, she photographed children, sometimes pets, for Upper East Side matrons. A less than flattering assessment of her career appeared in the *New York Times*, on the first day she took the witness stand at Foley Square, where she was described as a "girl photographer" who "specializes in animal pictures." She had hoped for more, and perhaps the heady world of FBI intrigue had inflated her ambition. If she had harbored some illusion that betraying Sid Grossman and the Photo League would open doors for her, time would show that she had dramatically miscalculated the odds.[303]

11. Angela in the Anti-Communist Network

When Angela came down off the witness stand at Foley Square, a world of uncertainty was waiting. Could it be true what the *Daily Worker* said, about an informant/witness being only "a tool to be used for a while and then discarded unceremoniously when his [or her] value as a sneak and a snooper wears out"? Angela had no intention of being discarded. She wanted some of the rewards she saw others getting, rewards she had perhaps been led to expect. But things had a way of working out badly for her.[1]

What she had really wanted was government employment, and asked for it upfront. She must have known that fellow Foley Square prosecution witnesses William Nowell, of the Black Belt Nation testimony, and Louis Budenz, of the "Aesopian language," had both worked for Immigration and Naturalization, providing information in proceedings designed to deport known Communists. Budenz went on to academic appointments at Notre Dame, then Fordham University. None of that interested Angela, but, still unemployed a year after testifying at Foley Square, she did want the Bureau to help her arrange interviews with "government agencies," those that had "some jobs in her field," like "the Economic Cooperation Administration, State Department, etc." New York agents initially informed her that "the FBI could not assist her" in obtaining government employment.[2]

She would have settled for a job in her field, something that corresponded to "her position as a commercial photographer" and not the "clerical position" the FBI hinted might be easier to come by. Angela was also feeling unsafe in her old neighborhood, Greenwich Village, and thought she would like to travel, leave New York. If the Village had been a refuge and safe haven for a butch lesbian, it was not for an FBI informer. Once word was out about her spying for the FBI, reporting on members of the Photo League, some locals, who took a dim view of anyone who participated in Senator Joseph McCarthy's witch hunt, wanted nothing more to do with her. Former comrades, of course, were outraged. Angela told Bureau agents that her apartment was vulnerable to attack, with "windows on the first floor, as well as a fire escape entrance." When she asked for protection, prosecution attorneys "felt sure some arrangements could be made to insure her safety during the trial and for a short period thereafter," but that did not sound very reassuring.[3]

Maybe that was why she thought a job "in any private industry, particularly Standard Oil Corporation," because it "had assignments for photographers in various parts of the country," would be a smart move. But Angela must have suspected that she would be at a disadvantage. In the first place, old Photo Leaguers, like Berenice Abbott, Arnold S. Eagle, and Sid Grossman's friend Sol Libsohn, worked on projects for Standard Oil under the direction of Roy Stryker, former director of the influential Farm Security Administration (FSA) photography program. They had not forgotten Angela's testimony, and would, in fact, remember it for decades after. But, typically, she had an answer for that, confiding to FBI agents "that the Standard Oil Company was attempting to clean out the Communist sympathizers from the Photographic Department," opening the way for "a person such as herself whose political thoughts were known."[4]

At the same time, she let the Bureau know that she had connections. The big news about Standard Oil cleaning out "the Communist sympathizers from the Photographic Department" had come to her from a source close to Victor Riesel, the notorious labor columnist for Hearst's *New York Daily Mirror,* and a militant anti-Communist. It was his secretary, Angela claimed, "a former roommate" of hers who had passed on the information. Riesel himself, she added, had asked her "to work with him in preparing a book on labor management" by taking "photographs of the various plants throughout the country."[5]

Whether there was truth to that story or not, the FBI was not impressed. Whereas she had been "an excellent confidential informant" before, her behavior after her testimony indicated that she was just the type of person they had feared—one "who might be inclined to capitalize on her position as a former Bureau informant" and "the publicity resulting from the Communist Party trial." Hoover himself, who did not tolerate any behavior that might jeopardize the FBI's reputation, went from anger to outrage over Angela's statements to the press—starting, as noted here, with articles by Frederick Woltman, Pulitzer Prize journalist and chief Red-baiter for the *New York World-Telegram*—about how she had not been paid for her spying and having no work after the trial. Time passed, but the story would not die. Other anti-Communist journalists, like Victor Lasky, also a top reporter for the *New York World-Telegram,* plugged the sad tale of Angela working for the FBI without compensation, and having no "permanent job" more than a year and a half after her trial testimony.[6]

When the New York Office reported back to Hoover that "the impression had been created," by comments in the press and on radio, that Angela was "being treated badly by the FBI," bringing down criticism on the Bureau, the Director was furious. In handwritten notes he appended to memos from the New York Office, Hoover wrote, "I don't like the way she has acted," and added that, "it has put us in a bad light." Later, he was "pretty well disgusted with this woman," who was "doing us great harm." Because federal prosecutors and the Bureau wanted to keep Angela quiet, and under control, they were still paying her through the Foley Square defendants' appeal to the Supreme Court. Any hint of proof that she had perjured herself on the witness stand about money paid to her would have aided the defense on appeal. Hoover, who understood all that too well, concluded most of his hand-written comments about Angela with a threat "to discontinue further payments to her," and especially when she was being "extremely argumentative and contentious."[7]

Because she reminded the FBI that she was "still in need of a job" every chance she got, agents finally, but somewhat halfheartedly, contacted "a top official" at Standard Oil (name blacked out) for Angela. They noted that despite "outstanding patriotism," she had not been a regular FBI employee, not subject to the customary thorough investigation "as to background and qualification." In other words, she could prove unworthy of trust, or worse (a lesbian?). In turn, the official they contacted offered several excuses—recent cutbacks in Standard Oil's Photographic Department, business trips out of the country—and nothing more came of that.[8]

Since nobody at the FBI seemed to be doing anything about her photography job, Angela adopted a different tack. With a little help from a friend, she set about regaining the spotlight, something the Bureau was dead set against. It was a fellow Villager and supporter, Fred Woltman of the *New York World-Telegram*, who once again gave her a boost by providing the press pass that got her back into the Foley Square courtroom as the trial drew to a close. To the Bureau agents, Angela pleaded "curiosity and a desire to hear the summations of the trial." But the agents considered her presence prejudicial and hustled her out, adding a tidbit of far-reaching significance to their report. Angela had not been alone, and on further investigation, her companion was identified as "Myrtice [sic] Johnson, sister-in-law of former SA (blacked out but known to be Kenneth M. Bierly)."[9]

The FBI was on the alert at the mention of former agent Ken Bierly, originally from Peoria, Illinois, recruited during the Bureau's wartime expansion and assigned to the New York Communist Squad. There he had specialized in recruiting informants to work inside the CPUSA, keeping in close touch, collecting and evaluating the information they brought to him. An early, loyal, and diligent recruit had been Angela Calomiris, who names him in *Red Masquerade* as one of the FBI agents who came to her Village apartment in 1942, then dedicated the book to him. It was an acknowledgement of a great debt and deep affection, because Ken Bierly had been a steadfast friend. Whereas other anti-Communist connections had proved useful and willing to help, quite simply, without Bierly and his family, Angela would never have risen to the rank of Cold War celebrity.[10]

What had begun as a relationship between handler and informant developed over the years into a real friendship, where Angela—as Melva Wade, executrix of her estate confided—"always talked about Ken," and he nicknamed her "Angelus" in a letter from the mid-1950s. According to *Red Masquerade*, "Ken Bierly and his wife, Billy" were among Angela's "very best friends," and it was to the Bierlys' home on Long Island (Flushing, Queens) that Angela, "tired and tense," retreated when she was done testifying at Foley Square. After they moved to Greenwich, Connecticut—a big step up from Flushing—Ken and Billy invited Angela over. Visiting relatives from Peoria, Mr. and Mrs. Richard D. Bierly, Ken's brother and sister-in-law, remembered meeting her at a barbecue, where "it was all big estates, you couldn't even see the other houses, they were so far apart." Besides what was on the grill, Angela and Ken—as Ken's brother remarked—"were cooking up something about that newspaper they published. What was the name of it?" That would have been *Counterattack: A Newsletter to Combat Communism* (1947-1968), published by Bierly's firm American Business Consultants, Inc. After leaving the FBI in 1946, he had set up offices in New York in partnership with two other former FBI agents, Ted Kirkpatrick and John Keenan.[11]

Much to Hoover's chagrin, the three of them became important players in an anti-Communist network of newspaper columnists, radio commentators, the American Legion, religious leaders, and professional blacklisters. Hoover did not like the idea of former agents like American Business Consultants branching out, taking over work that should have been left to the FBI, possibly using information acquired from people on the FBI payroll. A file on *Counterattack*—supposedly self-supporting through subscriptions from businesses and corporations, and mailed out regularly to Hollywood studio heads—was immediately opened at Headquarters. Hoover repeatedly denied any connection between the Bureau and *Counterattack's* newsletter. He would have especially deplored and resented its reference in a *Counterattack* newsletter from May 1950, to the jobless state of a young woman after she had spent "7 years as an underground agent for the FBI [...] and testified against the 11 CP leaders in their NY conspiracy trial last year." The Bureau's New York Office hastened to point out that "this obviously refers to Angela Calomiris."[12]

In fact, backing Angela was probably not in the best interest of the *Counterattack* team. Hoover was not one to forget a slight. When Ken Bierly applied for admission to the Pennsylvania bar, after the family moved there around 1954, the FBI tried to block his application. Bierly had pirated, they said, Bureau information from "active undercover agents," which meant Angela, possibly others. Bierly's "Angelus" letter to her followed, a plea for help. In reply, she immediately fired off a letter to the State Board of Law Examiners in Philadelphia, saying she had never shared with Ken Bierly any "information gathered for the F.B.I." Maybe they believed her in Pennsylvania. Hoover most likely did not.[13]

The mission of American Business Consultants and its weekly newsletter was a familiar one for the times—to alert the public to "the specific techniques that Communists used to gain influence in America." In practice, *Counterattack* was another blacklisting tool. Armed with references to petitions signed, memberships in organizations gleaned from reading back issues of leftist publications, especially the *Daily Worker,* it printed exposés of prominent individuals, claiming links to Communism. Many of these people had demonstrated sympathy before and during the war for the Soviet Union, the American Communist Party, or just for causes no longer tolerated in the postwar political climate.[14]

Media personalities got top billing in *Counterattack.* Actors Fredric March and his wife, Florence Eldridge, were branded "Communists" eight times, from 1947 to 1948. They finally sued *Counterattack* for libel, and got a printed retraction. Closer to home, the doyenne of talk-show hosts Mary Margaret McBride had been accused in *Counterattack* in December 1949 of flirting with treason by advertising Polish hams.[15]

Meanwhile, the partners at American Business Consultants/ *Counterattack* ratcheted up the policing of the airwaves in June 1950 with *Red Channels: The Report of Communist Influence in Radio and Television.* It included page after page of artists and writers—

from John Garfield to Lillian Hellman, Langston Hughes to Artie Shaw, Dorothy Parker to Aaron Copland—plus organizations (the National Negro Congress, the Sleepy Lagoon Defense Committee, the Book Find Club, for example) classified as subversive or Communist fronts. There was a positive spin to all this name calling and blacklisting for Ken Bierly and his partners. Early on, almost at the beginning of their enterprise—which paid better than the FBI—a memo attached to one folder in their "research files" helped explain how they had hoped to profit. The note concerned famous dancer/actor Gene Kelly, who was named in *Counterattack* (January 30, 1948) for being an "honorary chairman" of Young Progressive Citizens of America. The note suggested that "everything in our files on Kelly" be put together for the "Industrial Relations Director of MGM," which "might be just the chance we need," it said, "to get our foot in the door in the movie industry."[16]

As their plans matured, it became apparent to the *Counterattack* partners that, besides providing evidence of subversive inclinations, they could also help to rehabilitate their victims—for a price— through further investigation, preparing exculpatory statements, encouraging them to name a few names, plead ignorance, ask forgiveness. During Mary Margaret McBride's "Polish ham" scandal, *Counterattack* made her a nice offer to screen guests with possible subversive links "for a small sum" before they were invited on the radio show. But it was Hollywood that actively encouraged penance and shelled out big money to save careers and get stars off the Red Scare hook.[17]

One successful practitioner of the art of exoneration was none other than Ken Bierly, with his own breakaway firm Kenby Associates formed in 1951, "working to clear actors and actresses who have been previously charged by *Counterattack* with being mixed up in subversive organizations." With the promise of a hefty fee, Bierly launched his new career with Columbia Pictures boss Harry Cohn in May 1951, and Bierly's most famous client (possibly his only client) was that same Judy Holliday with whom Angela's story begins. Judy was Columbia's hottest property when she was hauled before the McCarran Committee (the Senate Internal Security Subcommittee [SISS], the Senate equivalent of HUAC) in March of 1952. To those in the know, it must have seemed too much of a coincidence that Ken Bierly should have been chosen for the job of clearing Judy. His friend Angela, who usually relished and bragged about any connection she had with a prominent person, had been able to make life unpleasant for Yetta Cohn, and through Yetta, for Holliday. It is not hard to imagine a conversation, or several conversations between Bierly and Angela, passing on insider information she was privy to as part of the Village lesbian community. Likewise, how Bierly got the job exonerating Judy has never been explained. Perhaps he approached Columbia Pictures (rather than vice versa) because he knew what was at stake, thanks, at least in part, to Angela's gossip. It is impossible to imagine that she stood by idly.[18]

Judy Holliday came to the 1952 committee hearing armed with a sworn statement, put together under Bierly's direction, that claimed she had nothing to do with Communism or Communists, and had lent her name to groups whose affiliations she had not understood. As further evidence of the disdain, threats and genuine nastiness to which the blacklisted were subjected, there is a draft version of Judy's statement in the file that American Business Consultants/*Counterattack* kept on her. Handwritten comments from Bierly's colleagues (Ted Kirkpatrick and John Keenan) respond to Judy's explanations with—"Wow, How weak can you get? J"/"Baloney."/"The 'official sources' were late in catching you. That's all that bothers you, just that you got caught." Also, in the attached analysis, organization by organization, event by event (Josephine Baker Day Rally, The Progressive Party, Scientific and Cultural Conference for World Peace, for example), where Judy says she does not remember, someone remarked, "Feeble-minded—but she can memorize 3 acts of a left wing show."/"She shouldn't be in a new play—with her failing memory." These remarks offer some idea of what a grim business blacklisting was.[19]

More bizarre, if possible, is Bierly's 1951 "Report" to Columbia Pictures on "the results of our research and investigation concerning the affiliations of Miss Holliday to Communist front organizations." It will never be known for sure what were the "two allegations [...] of a serious nature" Bierly claimed, because entire paragraphs have been blacked out by FBI censors. But one allegation had to do with

Judy's "friendship with [Person's name censored by the FBI. Known to be Yetta Cohn]," that same "female who was a cop" who was going with Judy, the one Buddy Kent accused Angela of turning in to the FBI. The censored paragraphs must have contained a mix of personal and political details, possibly even hints of lesbianism. In Judy's defense, Bierly saw fit to defend the friendship between Yetta and Judy as in no way "subversive or unpatriotic." It had been "completely misinterpreted," he said, and added that Yetta was not a member of the Communist Party.[20]

But Yetta did not escape so easily. In the course of the hearing, her name was put into the record by Richard Arens, a former Kansas City, Missouri, lawyer and staff director of the Committee, who asked Judy most of the questions. "Do you know a lady by the name of Yetta Cohn, C-o-h-n?" Arens asked Judy, who answered that "Mr. Bierly, who was investigating me and my friends," had said Yetta "was a Communist." In a show of veiled, or not so veiled, hostility toward Bierly, Judy insisted it was not true, because Yetta had "no interest in that sort of thing." To have one's name mentioned at all in a hearing could spell unemployment and disgrace, as it apparently did in Yetta's case.[21]

Gay screenwriter Arthur Laurents has said that "homosexuality had never entered into the Hollywood part of the Witch Hunt." But, in Judy's case, at least some lesbian drama played a role. A fellow policewoman who did not like Yetta much, and was a friend of Angela's, said in an interview that she would not have been surprised if Yetta was a Communist. As for Angela, Judy the movie star became something of an obsession. One of those curious documents that turn up in FBI files reveals that Angela continued her attacks. After the McCarran Committee hearing, someone, a "Miss Krasilovsky" wrote to Judy—the original letter is lost—warning her about a "Miss Kalomiris." We have Judy's response that she had already been tipped off about Angela, described "as a troublemaker and a liar." Judy reported that Angela was known "as vicious and irresponsible [...] in her own circles" and "those in authority" paid little attention to what she said. On the other hand, Judy added, "she has done much damage (to others) in the public relations area."[22]

Besides a passion for blacklisting, Angela and Ken Bierly

shared another vital connection. The "Myrtice [sic] Johnson," who accompanied Angela when she sneaked back into the Foley Square trial, still in progress, had been identified by the FBI as "sister-in-law of former SA (blacked out known to be Kenneth M. Bierly)." What they did not know was that Myrtis Johnson was Angela's lover. Divorced and a writer of newspaper and magazine pieces under the name "Marta Robinet," and a sometime editor of children's books, Myrtis made a living at her craft for some thirty years. For a woman of her background in those bygone days this was no small feat. Angela idolized her, thought her the smartest, most accomplished of women.[23]

Myrtis had undoubtedly been a happy addition to Angela's life, at a hopeful time when everything had begun going her way, and her spy career was about to pay off. No longer the abandoned waif from the Bronx orphanage, no longer the marginal Village character, earning just enough to get by, she was finding doors open. Depending on the timeline for their love affair, it might be possible that Angela had originally agreed to appear as a witness at the Foley Square trial, at least in part, to make herself more interesting to Myrtis. With Myrtis, she traveled to London in 1950, her first trip abroad, whose progress the FBI followed with their usual diligence. By March 1951, Angela and Myrtis were looking at houses to buy in Connecticut, and by June, had purchased one in Wilton, an easy drive from Ken and Billy. Always on the lookout for a new family—preferably all-American, non-immigrant, middle-class, professional—to temper the memories of poverty and rejection, Angela embraced the Bierlys and Thawleys from Peoria, who more than fit the bill.[24]

What Ken Bierly and his wife Billy thought of Angela and Myrtis is anybody's guess. It was a time when such things were not talked about, and lesbians, especially someone like Angela, with impeccable anti-Communist credentials, could remain invisible. Apparently the arrangement raised no eyebrows, and trust prevailed. A good-natured letter signed by Myrtis, that Angela kept for almost forty-five years, recalled that the couple had used their time abroad to recruit an au pair for the Bierlys in Greenwich, Connecticut. But the love affair did not last. It's not known if it was a lesbian lifestyle, Angela, or both that Myrtis decided were not for her. According to an old friend, the relationship ended after three years, and details are few. The last letter Angela saved with the address of the Connecticut house they had purchased together is from 1954. Nevertheless, she kept a Philadelphia address and phone number for Myrtis in her address book until the end, which would indicate that something vital had survived the breakup.[25]

Meanwhile, there is no mention of Myrtis/Marta in any correspondence about *Red Masquerade*. But it would have been remarkable, because she was a writer, had she not taken an interest in Angela's literary ambitions. Perhaps she was even the inspiration for the book, and a prime mover in the contracting for it. Fred Woltman, of the *New York World-Telegram*, would have lent his support, too, as well as Ken Bierly. Obviously someone had to step in, since Angela had neither experience nor connections in the publishing field, and, according to her closest friends, no talent for writing. The idea of writing about her spy career had taken shape by mid-summer 1949, a few months after her appearance on the witness stand, while the trial was still in full swing. It was then that she somehow secured the representation of one of New York's most prestigious literary agencies, Russell & Volkening, and the personal assistance of Diarmuid Russell, son of the distinguished Irish author George William Russell (A.E.). They entered into a contract for the proposed book on July 28, 1949, a contract Angela later sought to cancel when she, once again, saw a chance to move on. A contract with Lippincott for a manuscript "tentatively entitled UNDERCOVER GIRL" followed swiftly on August 5, 1949. The first public announcement that such a project was in the works came in mid-October, as the Foley Square trial came to an end, catching the FBI by surprise. Publication was promised for early 1950, which meant that the manuscript had already taken shape, and was well underway.[26]

That announcement and other subsequent publicity failed to mention that the real author of the book—who had labored over "mountains of tape" of Angela telling her story into a recording device (some eighty hours' worth), organizing, structuring, putting into grammatical and correctly punctuated English—was a young woman named Caroline Bird Menuez, later Caroline Bird Mahoney, later just Caroline Bird when she published several books, and played an important role in the women's movement of the 1960s and 70s. Angela was indeed fortunate to be paired with Bird, who confirmed that Angela "couldn't have written anything," and whose agent was also Diarmuid Russell. She was not a novice. As a working writer she had cut her teeth on magazine articles for *Fortune* as part of a male-female, writer-researcher team, where all too often it fell to the female half of the combo to finish the work she had started because her male writing partner was indisposed, sometimes drunk and disorderly.[27]

Bird, who was named in the *Undercover Girl* contract as "Editor," continued to play a secondary role, this time to Angela, referred to as "the Author." Though the publisher opted not to mention Bird anywhere, she was consulted about matters contractual to do with *Red Masquerade,* and got a share of money earned. Angela, however, garnered all the praise for "a literary gift of high order" and the "best-written, the most literate" work of its kind, according to George Sokolsky of the *New York Journal-American*, with no word about a ghostwriter. It should come as no surprise that Angela did not like to share.[28]

The FBI's opposition and the publisher's fear of being sued for libel—by any of those Angela named outright as Communists, or failed to disguise convincingly with pseudonyms—delayed publication. All things considered, it was remarkable that *Red Masquerade* made it into print at all. Promised in early 1950, the weeks stretched into long months, with letters flying back and forth from Angela's agent and Ken Bierly, acting as her lawyer, to Lippincott. Satisfactory modifications of the clause saddling her with court costs should a suit be brought were secured, and "some six full pages of corrections" to the manuscript were mandated by the publishers to head off problems. Through the US Attorney's Office in New York, the FBI gained some ground, asking to see an advance copy of the book and recommending changes. At all times, the Bureau intentionally and carefully avoided being "placed in a position of endorsing this book." A target date for publication was finally set for September 13, but was postponed until October 25.[29]

Readers favored with advance copies responded enthusiastically. Unlike the usual dry anti-Communist prose, most of it from former Communists, *Red Masquerade* was "fast and fascinating reading," proclaimed Eugene Lyons of the *Reader's Digest* editorial staff. A former fellow-traveler himself, who had swung sharply to the right by 1950, Lyons praised Angela's book as "living adventure hot off the griddle of history in the making." Angela was sure her book, in condensed form, would be ideal for the magazine, and depended upon Lyons ("a close friend") to make it happen. After all, as another sympathetic reader—Irene Corbally Kuhn, author and NBC radio personality—declared in a letter to the promotion team at Lippincott, *Red Masquerade* was "as exciting as a mystery thriller," and the narrator was someone you could trust, a "courageous young woman" who had never believed in Communism, who had done it all out of "patriotic self-sacrifice." It looked like Lippincott, Russell and Volkening, Angela—and Caroline Bird—had a hit on their hands.[30]

12. Almost a Brilliant Career

Red Masquerade came along at just the right moment, that same moment informant/witness Harvey Matusow remembered when informers were "national celebrities." "I just joined the hit parade," he told his biographers. So had Angela. Her interview on Mary Margaret McBride's ABC show, the first of many radio appearances, gave the book an early and generous boost on October 25, 1950, the day of its release. Walter Winchell followed up the next day in the *New York Daily Mirror* with a brief but tasteful "orchid" (from his "orchid garden") for "*Red Masquerade* (Lippincott) by Angela Calomiris. She was an F.B.I. undercover-agent within the Communist Party for seven years and helped convict the leaders." He sent out more good wishes to Angela and her book on his Sunday radio broadcast, with a reminder to "John Edgar" that she "hasn't had a job since." Hoover would not have been amused. One of Angela's oldest friends, who had known her since 1940, described the book many years later as "a pack of lies."[1]

But truth was not the issue. On the contrary, it was the fervent embrace of powerful players in the anti-Communist network, genuine luminaries, that put Angela and *Red Masquerade* over the top. Most of them had been flaming radicals in their youth, supporters of the Russian Revolution and socialism, who had become flaming reactionaries long before her book appeared. But they recognized it for what it was, a smashing piece of Red Scare propaganda that told a story they wanted told, and they gave it their stamp of approval. J. B. Matthews—former chief investigator for HUAC and future research director for McCarthy's Senate Committee (Permanent Subcommittee on Investigations)—gave the book party for *Red Masquerade*, with old friend Fred Woltman and labor journalist Victor Riesel, who championed Angela's search for work as a photographer, attending. It was also a chance for Angela to meet and charm new friends among the most influential of New York's press corps.[2]

George E. Sokolsky—a friend of J. Edgar Hoover and Roy Cohn, a supporter of McCarthy and an enemy of Roosevelt and Social Security (among other things)—is someone whose name means nothing today. But as "the high priest of militant anti-Communism," he preached for years from such lofty podiums as the *New York Herald Tribune*, the *Sun*, and at the time of Angela's emergence as a "literary personage," the *Journal-American*. Sokolsky came to the book party, a gathering he described as "a party of Red-baiters […] men and women who over the years and at great sacrifice fought Stalin's stooges," met Angela—who impressed him as "sharp-eyed, with a gay humor"—went home and read the book. As a result, a few days later he dedicated his regular column to her, calling it "Urges All to Read 'Red Masquerade.'" Repeating the story about Angela working for the FBI and the country for nothing ("with no protection, with no compensation, with only her expenses paid"), Sokolsky called her book "a heroic tale" of one who "served this country as valiantly and as dangerously as any soldier at the front in the worst of battle." Yet more striking was his insinuation that the *Herald Tribune* and the *Times* had organized a "cartel" to ignore and reject *Red Masquerade*, because they had not reviewed it. For those times, and coming from the all-powerful Sokolsky, it was almost as bad as accusing the editors of the book review magazines of Communist sympathies. Did they "desire that this important book should not be read"?[3]

Angela was home free. Anxious to avoid any suspicion of conspiracy or ill will, all major New York newspapers, including the *Daily News*, rallied around immediately to evoke memories of Angela's "unimpeachable testimony about the Communist conspiracy." Both the *Times* and the *Herald Tribune* swung into action, with reviews and interviews. Among common themes were Angela's working for nothing, and her unique revelations about "day-to-day life in the grimy lower depths" of "Communism at the curbstone level." Since previous insider publications about goings-on in the Party had come mostly from near the top—from the same Louis Budenz, leadoff witness at the Foley Square trial and former managing editor of the *Daily Worker*—reviewers found Angela's stories from the branch level, from the average Party member's perspective, new and different. She could also explain "why people became Communists" when what they really needed was psychiatric treatment. For *The Nation*, and from the postwar "liberal" point of view, future author and Special Assistant to President Kennedy, Arthur Schlesinger, Jr. found "why people become Communists" an "ever perplexing and fascinating question." Because "free society" failed "to fill people's lives" with hope, Schlesinger implied, Communism had an appeal to those, like Angela, of an immigrant, impoverished background, frustrated by the Depression. Another topic, that made the book "an absorbing spy story," was the danger involved, with numerous "anxious moments" and "close escapes" when she could have been discovered. "Phone calls in the middle of the night" still threatened, but she claimed did not bother her. She accounted for her lack of remorse at betraying people she had worked closely with to John Hutchens of the *New York Herald Tribune*. "The Party doesn't believe in friendship," she told him. "There aren't any friends there."[4]

A lot of this was an echo of her radio appearance with Mary Margaret McBride, where Angela had replied in stronger terms that "none of those people were really my friends. And not people I would've ever known or mixed with. They're misfits, and they lie, make promises to poor people that they can never keep." And on the issue of danger, she had told Mary Margaret quite simply that if a spy was discovered in the Communist Party, "they would kill them." The safety question was broached again by Angela's friend Fred Woltman, who—despite having gotten into trouble with Hoover before for writing about her—dedicated a feature article (with photo) to the publication of *Red Masquerade*. Talk of Angela's "hiding out on public thoroughfares," a meeting on "an obscure street corner," and the Bureau's meticulous "security precautions" infused a fairly mundane tale with a dose of mystery. If that did not make for a best seller, another useful angle was sex, a stronger selling point for a female spy story. Angela's photo was captioned "Sex was Topic B in social conversation," with assurances that "Marx was Topic A," and that "no one in the party really regarded sex as important." Of course, *Red Masquerade* had its own slant on sex, which consisted mostly of Angela "not planning to marry in the immediate future," attracting "some attention from off-duty seamen" on the Hudson River piers, avoiding "romantic entanglements" with Party comrades—"a drab and serious lot," not "people who would naturally have attracted me."[5]

Probably because it unmasked the evils of atheistic Communism, *Red Masquerade* also became an instant favorite of some church people. Angela's anti-Communism won her, before the book was out, a paid commitment from the *Catholic Digest* to publish a 7000-word condensation. The *Christian Herald* joined the chorus of Angela's supporters with a timely review, which celebrated her "quiet courage and loyalty" and compared her to Molly Pitcher, who had loaded and fired a cannon at the Battle of Monmouth during the American Revolutionary War. All this talk about heroism in battle and military prowess was not coincidental, coming as it did in the shadow of World War II.[6]

Other reviewers gave considerable praise to the style and pace of Angela's spy thriller. It was like "a well-constructed murder or spy novel," not "stiff," not "melodramatic or sloppy," the *New York Daily News* insisted, and not the work of "some ghost writer." "This lady can write," the *News* added. Such irony cannot have escaped Caroline Bird, the unsung star of this drama, especially when, midway through her interview with John Hutchens of the *Herald Tribune*, Angela made a claim for "the writing—three revisions."[7]

But what Fred Woltman, in the *World-Telegram*, called "the newsworthy feature" of Angela's continuing saga was still the lack of a job. Complaining that "she is unable to get a foothold in her profession," Woltman left the field open for others to treat her as photographer and frustrated artist. Picking up the theme, poet, editor, and future playwright Harvey Breit of the *New York Times*, in his "Talk With Miss Calomiris," focused on Angela the artist. He understood her desire "to be behind a camera" and recorded the list of big names whose example she hoped to follow. These included the old master Alfred Stieglitz, Edward Steichen, and Walker Evans. Evans, formerly with the Farm Security Administration, did "fine and clean and honest work," Angela said, that was documentary but "not the ash-can school which the Photo League taught." It was another unkind cut at the nearly-defunct Photo League, and a way to distance herself from their activist aesthetic of the 1930s and '40s.[8]

Meanwhile, the media blitz around *Red Masquerade* sold books. By December 1950, only a month into the advertising campaign, a fifth printing was going to press, which meant, Angela told the FBI proudly, that almost 20,000 copies had been sold. A devoted fan, one of Myrtis Johnson's relatives in Pennsylvania, wrote to say she "was thrilled to see *Red Masquerade* among the best books of the year in N.Y. Times Book section." The *New York Daily News* responded in February 1951 by running eight installments of *Red Masquerade*, with photographs intended to refresh the public memory—of Party protests at Foley Square, NYPD detachments outside the courthouse, the Communist leaders and other personalities from the trial. Even if Angela's spy story was a bit more fantasy than fact, "author" and publisher were happy, and the reader was none the wiser. The book had rapidly become part of Red Scare mythology.[9]

Since Angela did not seem to be going away (as hoped)—on the contrary she was becoming a media personality—and the press kept talking about her having no job, the FBI was forced to respond in some way. A couple of weeks after the book's release, the Bureau office in New York put together a six-page report on her "desire to work as a photographer" and how the job search was progressing. As usual, Angela was aiming high. The names bandied about ranged from the aforementioned Standard Oil of New Jersey, to *Newsweek*, to 20th-Century Fox in Los Angeles, to Ford Motors in Detroit. Since all the names of FBI (and Angela's) contacts are discreetly blacked out, it is hard to tell how high up the requests went. A lot of good will was evident in the responses to FBI overtures. Even if, early on, Angela had been baptized "a difficult person, […] strong-willed, independent" who would better be employed as an "efficiency manager," everyone wanted to help out in the struggle against Communism. But in Angela's case, no one came through. 20th-Century Fox did not hire still photographers, women did not operate movie cameras, and one prominent individual (name blacked out) said "he would not hire a woman photographer." Someone (name blacked out) did, however, offer her a contact with *U.S. Camera* magazine, which, in fact, published a feature article in March 1950, called "Versatile Is the Word for Angela Calomiris," accompanied by a series of Angela's photos.[10]

It was great publicity, identifying Angela as a "gifted young woman" and "very talented photographer," her work as "technically excellent [...] first-rate." A second photo spread for *Modern Photography*, which Angela said would appear about the same time, never materialized. The J. Walter Thompson advertising agency, where Angela's friend Ruth Parish had worked on the office staff for many years, had contrived to arrange the latter, but apparently to no avail. Nevertheless, J. Walter Thompson continued to go to bat for Angela, offering her connections at Ford Motor Company, one of their big accounts, and probably promoting a contact for her with Edward Steichen, Director of MOMA's Department of Photography. To the FBI she proclaimed, rather optimistically, that "she was making an appointment with (name blacked out) of the Museum of Modern Art, for the purpose of arranging an exhibition of some of her work." If none of that worked out, it was not for lack of trying. This was, after all, the big leagues.[11]

But the promises, plus the kind of flattery *U.S. Camera* dispensed, were probably pure hype—rather like the assignments listed on a professional resume Angela put together when no job came of her new contacts. A more accurate assessment of her accomplishments would be that Angela's career in commercial photography had not earned her a lot of money during the previous decade, when her real income had come from the FBI. The Bureau's investigation into her IRS returns, noted previously, had been triggered by Angela's insistence that she had earned a lot of money ("from $8,000 to $10,000" annually) as a big-time photographer prior to her Foley Square testimony. Those statistics she offered in support of the theory that a promising career had been placed in jeopardy by her patriotic service. It was an idea that dated back to Fred Woltman's original front-page article about Angela, "Girl Photog Cut Career to Expose Reds' Plot." As months passed, and this idea grew in Angela's imagination, she concluded that the FBI should spare no effort to find her a steady, lucrative position. Unfortunately for her, meticulous records kept by the IRS and the Bureau did not support her story, and Hoover himself calculated "that her annual income from her self-employment as a photographer was quite meager."[12]

It is possible that Angela actually came to believe that fame had been within reach when she sacrificed it all for national security. Or, more likely, she just decided to pad her resume, which listed assignments for *Time, Newsweek, Coronet,* and the New York trade journal *Tide: The News Magazine of Advertising Marketing,* where she claimed to have been a staff photographer. *Tide,* for one, did not credit its photos. Humbler associates, like the Manhattan-based Advertising Council, where she listed herself as a contractor for "publicity work," did know her, and responded warmly to her appearance at the trial "for doing a wonderful job for our government." At least an assignment with the Janssen Piano Company, listed on her resume, is verifiable from photos still in a professional portfolio she used for job interviews, which came to rest, years later, in the Lesbian Herstory Archives. On the other hand, assignments listed for the Office of War Information—three of seven photos included in the *U.S. Camera* spread make that claim—raise other questions. If there is truth to that, it undoubtedly stems from a 1943 general appeal to the Photo League from the OWI for "Win the War photos and general Four Freedoms photos." Maybe Angela responded with submissions, and maybe some of her photos were selected.[13]

An assignment that can absolutely be verified is probably more typical of Angela's accomplishments in the photography field. A *Parade Magazine* spread in 1944 recommended the conversion of rubber lifeboats, US Navy issue, to peacetime civilian pleasure craft, and while there is no individual photo credit, Angela did claim to work for the Black Star Agency at one time. Authentication of the *Parade* feature came quite accidentally from Angela's old friend Ruth Parish, who shared her own faded copy of the article. A 1940s bathing beauty, she was one of the young women who appeared sunning herself on the gunwales of the lifeboat with a male companion. This was Angela's work, she said.[14]

More telling was the tag Sid Grossman's widow Miriam used to define Angela's place in the Village photography world. Angela worked as "a nightclub photographer," Miriam said, which was a good business back then, taking pictures of cabaret customers at their tables, processing and returning them quickly. So did Suzy Harris, an old friend of Sid and Miriam, who had brought Angela to Sid's apartment to listen to folk music. The nightclub business, an honest, reputable enterprise, explained how Angela and Suzy knew each other, but it was not world-class photojournalism.[15]

Modest professional success—the odd magazine assignment, portraits of children, industrial photography, studio portraits of Party comrades, and numerous photo shoots for the FBI—was not enough for Angela anymore. The wave of publicity that had come her way after the trial, together with her rapid rise in anti-Communist circles, fed a restless ambition. Never particularly stable, success seems to have gone to her head.

The most notable entry in the FBI's analysis of Angela's job search was *Life* magazine, where she was aiming not for "mere assignment work" but a position as "Staff Photographer." And while it is possible to dismiss this as idle fantasy, there is evidence that Angela had imagined herself quite seriously in the role of top-notch woman photojournalist. At least one scene in *Red Masquerade* says that her anti-Communist celebrity had blurred the boundaries between truth and fantasy. It reads like something out of a Hollywood movie with Angela in the starring role. She is photographing a war-time rally in Madison Square Garden, staged to pressure the Allies to come to the aid of the Soviet Union during the Battle of Stalingrad by opening up a Second Front. To identify participants—probably for the FBI— she "was trying to catch all the speakers on the stand when "a woman with a full skirt and a peasant shawl over her head tapped me timidly. 'Please to tell me,' she said. 'Are you Margaret Bourke-White?' Margaret Bourke-White had just published her *Shooting the Russian War*. My questioner was obviously from the old country. [...] She was so anxious to go home and tell her family that she had stood beside the famous woman photographer that I couldn't help obliging her. I smiled and nodded my head."[16]

Because of mounting evidence, it seems unlikely that this was just an amusing story of mistaken identity. It was, instead, an apocryphal anecdote engineered to make Angela look interesting. Always on the lookout for another new identity, she had made a good choice in Margaret Bourke-White. As the first female photojournalist hired by *Life* magazine, Bourke-White had an extraordinary record. She had been the first Western photographer allowed to work in the Soviet Union in 1930, and had collaborated on a picture-book of the Great Depression *You Have Seen Their Faces* (1937) with her husband, author Erskine Caldwell. As the first female war correspondent and the first female permitted to work in combat zones, she had crossed Germany with General George Patton, and photographed Buchenwald concentration camp. While Angela was light years away from Bourke-White in politics and achievement, she believed, and told the FBI, "that her work was equal to that of the Staff Photographers" at *Life*. The Bureau's contact at *Life* (name blacked out), unfortunately for Angela, disagreed and judged "her talents not up to our standards for a full-time Staff Photographer."[17]

Once again, the anti-Communist network came to Angela's rescue in the person of Westbrook Pegler, another career journalist of the period, highly respected in conservative circles, an implacable enemy of President and Eleanor Roosevelt, labor unions, and the New Deal. In Hearst's *New York Journal-American,* he rose to defend "an active patriot, with a record as enviable as Bourke-White's," (in Mr. Pegler's opinion) who "has been having a difficult time." That would be Angela, of course, "practically banished from the profitable practice of her profession," while Margaret Bourke-White, "with a long record of flagrant association with Communist fronts," enjoyed success with assignments that could well endanger national security.[18]

The very next day, in "Girl Spy for FBI Recounts Insult by a Picture Editor," Pegler went out on another limb for the "competent and patriotic" Angela. Promoting her to "professional news photographer," he chose to by-pass the question "whether she is better or worse than Margaret Bourke-White." More urgent and to the point, he said, was the fact that Angela had "suffered a great deal for her patriotism in spying on the Communists and testifying against them" and "gotten a pushing-around from magazine editors." It was great publicity and confirmation for the story Angela had been telling the FBI for months— "that the real reason that she had not been able to obtain suitable employment in the photographic field during the past year and one-half has been that the Communists and 'fellow-travelers' in this field have effectively obstructed her efforts." There was no escape, she told the FBI, because of "Communist cells" in all the major publications, and cited *Time, Newsweek, Life,* the *New York Herald Tribune,* and the *Times.* Casting herself in the role of outsider/victim, a role she knew well and, in this case, savored, she explained her failure to get the plum job in photography she had expected. It was not because she lacked skills and talent, but because, in an age of conspiracies, she was the victim of a conspiracy. Another of Angela's anti-Communist connections, labor columnist Victor Riesel, also publicized the tale of "a skilled photographer" who "can't find work because the Party's friends have influence in the field," arguing that American Communism still had the power to punish, and that even the FBI could not protect its own.[19]

By that time Hoover almost certainly was not very interested in protecting or assisting Angela. But he was ever alert to Communist sympathizers in the print media, because they could be concocting enemy "propaganda." And one picture, then as now, was worth a thousand words. As the war raged against the Photo League, he called upon Walter Winchell to ferret out so-called dangerous photographers working for major publications, and Winchell replied that there was W. Eugene Smith, who had taken over the presidency of the League after it was declared a "totalitarian, fascist, communist or subversive" organization on the Attorney General's list, and was on "the photographic staff of *Life* magazine." Winchell also named Elizabeth Timberman, among others, who had worked for *Life* and *Fortune* magazine, and "given a course this year at the Photo League school." He went on to name several "lecturers" at the Photo League, including one who would go on to a long and distinguished career in photography, John Godfrey Morris, a longtime friend of Robert Capa, later with him at Magnum Photos, then at the *Washington Post, New York Times,* and *National Geographic.* Back then, reported Winchell, Morris was "Picture Editor of *Ladies' Home Journal.*"[20]

The name of John Morris rang true for Westbrook Pegler, who was happy to target him as one of the principal offenders among, as Angela argued, "photographers connected with the Photo League" who had "formed a boycott against her." Once again, it was a story that she had been telling for a while, since late November 1949, before *Red Masquerade*, before the FBI got involved in her job search. At that time the J. Walter Thompson advertising agency had secured an interview for Angela with John Morris, at the offices of the *Ladies' Home Journal*. Not the best choice for her, Pegler indicated, because its editors had supported the New Deal, particularly "during the long reign of Eleanor Roosevelt as queen of the magazine."[21]

As a matter of fact, the interview was a disaster. In the course of her brief encounter with Morris, well-documented by Angela for the FBI, he more or less dismissed her with the admonition that he could not be objective in judging her work because she had done a disservice to the country and harmed innocent photographers. He could not work with her because he did not trust her, and thought that there should be room in the country for "a Communist Party, a Shredded Wheat Party, or any other kind of minority group that wished to express their own political views." *Counterattack* said he denounced Angela "as a 'stool pigeon.'" For these and other opinions expressed, Morris got his own FBI file, which he obtained years later in 1991 under the Freedom of Information Act. It let him know that he was spared a Security Index card because there was no information "to date" that "he is or ever had been connected with the Communist Party." Angela, on the other hand, got some satisfaction out of pointing to the John Morris affair as the prime example of "a boycott against her." More than forty years later, and two years before her death, she would still be insisting that she had been "black listed by most magazines and media."[22]

As 1950 faded into history so did Angela's hope of reaping the rewards she felt she was due. Too many dead ends marked her search for a career in photojournalism, and she was running out of leads. As each and every one petered out, only the patriotic *American Legion Magazine* stepped up, on the recommendation of someone (name blacked out) at the *World Telegram and Sun*, probably Woltman, and began to offer her serious assignments. For Angela, who had expressed a passionate desire to travel and see the world, it was a promising arrangement. First, she went around the country, doing a series on Army, Navy, and Marine Corps life. Then they sent her back to Europe in 1953 to photograph major battlefields of both world wars. With cordial optimism, Angela let the FBI know about her trip, just in case the Department of Justice, State Department, or Voice of America might have some work for her to do over there. Since she was no longer on the Bureau's payroll, had not been for some time, this would have been a special assignment. In fact, Angela had asked the FBI to stop paying her before the Supreme Court appeal of the Foley Square defendants was settled. Between sales of *Red Masquerade* and her American Legion work she was feeling more secure, she said. The Bureau, in turn, felt they could depend on her "friendliness and cooperation" even if they did not pay.[23]

Despite her failure to secure a government post, or the photojournalism position she wanted, the Red Scare was beginning to show a profit for Angela. The article in *True* magazine had paid $2,250, and the *Daily News* had offered $2,000 to serialize *Red Masquerade*. But Angela's total income from book sales, magazines, and the press was only a little more than $1,700, because some money had gone to Lippincott, some to her agent, and half the rest to "Editor" Caroline Bird Menuez. It was an arrangement probably not to Angela's liking, one she would try to remedy in future negotiations. Foreign sales lagged. While Angela's literary agent could find no likely publisher in England, he confided, where "the Communist problem is a different thing from here and is being handled differently," a Swedish publisher picked up the translation rights to *Red Masquerade*—its only foreign-language edition. For extra cash, Angela signed up with a booking agency run by someone described by his peers as a man "who loves the Commies about as much as the devil loves holy water." It was an ideal match. Angela went on the national lecture circuit to spread first-hand news of the Red Menace.[24]

As her FBI career was ending, she had a few more cards to play. For example, Angela could hardly ignore the "good fortune" that had befallen her fellow informant/witness Matt Cvetic, a veteran of HUAC hearings and Communist trials who had worked undercover in Pittsburgh. His story had found a publisher in the *Saturday Evening Post* in July 1950, and even more tantalizing was the news that Warner Brothers had purchased the rights to the *Post* story for the production of a feature film that would be released in 1951 as *I Was a Communist for the FBI*. Despite some fanciful moments and a general demonizing of all things Communistic, the film was nominated for an Academy Award for "Best Documentary."[25]

Not to be outdone, Angela, as it turns out, had been way ahead of Cvetic, trying to sell *Red Masquerade* to the movies before its publication. But she hit a snag. Her friends at *Counterattack* discouraged her cooperation with the Russell & Volkening agency's representatives in Hollywood. Some of them had what *Counterattack* considered suspicious backgrounds, donating money to Progressive Citizens of America (forerunners of Henry Wallace's Progressive Party) and to the Committee for the First Amendment, which had protested HUAC and the treatment of the Hollywood Ten. *Counterattack*'s Ted Kirkpatrick and John Keenan counseled that she proceed very slowly with the agency, Famous Artists Corporation, and offered more help as needed. But all was not lost. A year later, Angela got very positive feedback from Columbia Pictures Corporation, where her story—"one of the most potent indictments of Communism at this critical stage"—seemed a good bet for screen adaptation. Even the Los Angeles Office of the FBI, through their contacts in the movie business, thought she might "be able to sell her story to a major motion picture company." Unfortunately for Angela, FBI Headquarters was not supportive. In a hand-written note on the memo from the Los Angeles Office, someone in Washington had cautioned, "I don't think we should become involved in this."[26]

Hollywood was put on hold, perhaps because there were so many pressing engagements back East. She took time out to receive a "Medal of Honor" from the Freedoms Foundation of Valley Forge, Pennsylvania, "for outstanding achievement in bringing about a better understanding of the American way of life." And if she was not lecturing to a variety of audiences, from Catholic labor organizations to local synagogues, she was making the rounds of New York radio shows. Audience response was generally on her side, like a stationery store owner in Brooklyn who wrote in to thank "Big Joe" Rosenfeld's late-night *Happiness Exchange* program for placing Angela—"a real fine American girl"—in a class with "our gallant G.I.'s." There were strident dissenting voices, too, but not many. A housewife from Newark, New Jersey, wrote to the sponsors of the *Nancy Craig Show* complaining about the abuse of good radio time to dignify what "workers call 'a rat' and 'stool pigeon.'" Angela, she said, was "a cheap liar" who will "make a million by peddling her lies." On the other hand, Angela proved the ideal radio guest on NBC's *We, the People*, a show that featured real people telling their unusual and extraordinary true stories. Months later, they brought her back for the TV version, and fans wrote in to say that her performance "was finished far too soon."[27]

The number and variety of Angela's engagements explain a lot about how anti-Communism had taken hold in the American conscience. Programs dedicated to the theme, like the CBS network show *You and Communism*, hosted by news analyst Dwight Cooke, gave her a warm welcome. NBC's nighttime espionage thriller *David Harding, Counterspy* usually depended on stories about fictional heroic Americans fighting subversives. Angela, on the other hand, was (supposedly) the real thing. But the appearance that gave her the biggest boost turned out to be Bill Slater's *Inside Communism*, confirming for its audience the "priceless American privilege to speak up for freedom." There Angela appeared with Victor Lasky, reporter for the *New York World-Telegram*, who had covered the Alger Hiss trials. The script for the show, which Angela kept for forty-four years, indicated that a warm relationship already existed between her and Lasky. For one, as part of the campaign to provide "conclusive evidence of the Red conspiracy," he had generously reviewed *Red Masquerade* a few months before, reminding readers that Angela had received no compensation for her work, and had no permanent job a year and a half after testifying. It was an old story, but it still angered the FBI. Angela repeated for *Inside Communism*'s radio audience that she had "received no income from the FBI—not a cent."[28]

Then in 1954, time and a business venture would bring Lasky and Angela together again, with Martin Berkeley as an ally. Berkeley was a Hollywood screenwriter who—according to drama critic Eric Bentley's classic *Thirty Years of Treason*—"specialized in movies whose main characters were horses," and had named, in HUAC hearings, 162 people in the entertainment field as Communists. As for *Red Masquerade*, it seems that negotiations for a film deal had continued behind the scenes, moving through channels at Columbia, up to legendary producer and screenwriter Jerry Wald, whose screen credits include *They Drive by Night* (1940) and *Mildred Pierce* (1945), among many others. All he needed to see was a synopsis of the book to decide it was a story that had, by 1954, "been told and re-told so many times in films, on TV and on the radio" that it "would be lacking in the requisite drama or suspense." Angela would have been left to consider how much difference a few years might have made, and to reflect on the success of fellow informant/witnesses Matt Cvetic and Herbert Philbrick, whose timing had been better. Besides the movie, Cvetic had gotten a radio series (1952-1953) out of *I Was a Communist for the FBI*, while Herb Philbrick's *I Led Three Lives* (1952) had blossomed into a long-running TV series (1953-1956) based on the book.[29]

They would not get all the glory (and the money) if she could help it. Angela swung into action, and had, in fact, already put out feelers to Ziv Television Programs, producers for Cvetic and Philbrick. But it was vital that she find allies, which she did in Victor Lasky and Martin Berkeley. The three of them were, by February, deep into a partnership to sell *Red Masquerade* to television (or to radio, or the movies) with Angela providing the raw material and Berkeley presumably bringing the Hollywood know-how and connections. Lasky, who wrote early on that "we might get some action on TV for *Red Masquerade*," had almost certainly brought Berkeley on board. From Hollywood, the new partner advised that "some people will like the idea because of the success of the Philbrick series, others will say they are not interested because of it!" Lawyers were engaged, contracts exchanged. Berkeley proposed to write "2 crackerjack episodes to sell the deal," and Angela tried to get a letter from Hoover, saying "how important such a series is to acquaint the American people with the true facts." While it was hard, Berkeley said, to get first-rate actors for TV, Angela thought Ida Lupino would be "the perfect girl" to play her role, with Ann Baxter (of *All About Eve* fame) as second choice. Whoever it was, Angela insisted, they had to be "an unquestionable American," untainted by past connection with any front organization.[30]

But those hopeful plans quickly went awry. It did not take FBI agents long to answer her query that "as a matter of policy" there would be no letter from Hoover. Reminding each other of Angela's service to the Bureau, they remarked that "after testifying," she had become "extremely difficult to control." While she was being pushed out, Philbrick, on the other hand, moved to the inside track. The FBI had long since acknowledged that, over the years, he had furnished information for "patriotic motives" (while Angela had done it "for financial reasons"). But "since the trial" Philbrick had risen higher in everyone's estimation because he had "maintained such a decent attitude," and not rushed his book into print before the Supreme Court appeal of the Foley Square defendants was disposed of. His new boss, the *New York Herald Tribune*, gave Philbrick full credit for turning down offers not "in the best interest of the country" and conforming "to the high standards set by the Bureau." Hoover's note at the end of the FBI memo discussing Angela's request for a letter of support for her project sums up her fate—"I frankly am pretty much fed up with this individual. (Calomiris). H."[31]

There would be no rewards for her. As soon as Berkeley was advised that no trophy letter from Hoover to show around Hollywood was coming, his interest waned. He must have known instantly that the project was doomed. While he kept up a show of anti-Communist network solidarity by mentioning dinner with Angela's old supporter J. B. Matthews, and "a short visit" with Lasky's co-author, Ralph de Toledano, he also took a studio job ("must eat, you know") and went out on location.[32]

But there was, if possible, worse news. While drawing up contractual agreements between Angela and Lasky, Angela's lawyers had hit a "serious snag" whose name was Caroline Bird Menuez, who figured in the original Russell & Volkening contract at compensation of 15% of any money "paid by a motion picture company." Angela reacted swiftly. She dumped Russell & Volkening, Inc., saying she wanted to be free to act as her own agent. They apparently acquiesced, and the following day she registered her book with the "Motion Picture Assn of America Inc.," enclosing the nominal fee for full motion picture rights. Caroline Bird Menuez was apparently not so cooperative. Months later, Angela's lawyer wrote to say that Angela could not enter into a contract with Berkeley (or, presumably, anybody else) until she got a release from that "other party." There is no further mention of Caroline Bird Menuez in Angela's papers. With no legal agreement possible for the six-month option on *Red Masquerade* as a TV property that Berkeley had proposed, he and Lasky gave up. They took with them Angela's last chance at the big time and the big money.[33]

Five years of sporadic celebrity had passed since her appearance at Foley Square. At times she had felt important, with a place among powerful, influential people, and a bright future. No one seemed to mind that she was a closeted lesbian, obvious enough for most anybody who cared to look. But perhaps, as her former Party comrades had warned Angela and the other informant/ witnesses from Foley Square, instead of valuable, they had only been expendable, exposed on the witness stand because the FBI had no more need of them. Reality would take some getting used to.[34]

Epilogue: Land's End and Other Endings

Angela's life unraveled quickly. By 1956, she was calling the FBI again to say that her job as a staff photographer for the *American Legion Magazine* "had 'fizzled' and was no longer a paying proposition." She was "deeply in debt and in dire need of immediately finding employment," she said. Applying for work through an agency, she had listed herself as an "undercover agent for the F.B.I., 1942-1949," hoping to qualify for a job in personnel, screening applicants for potentially sensitive positions in whatever company (Western Electric, U.S. Rubber) might employ her. The Bureau sent an agent out to tell the employment agency that Angela had never been "a duly constituted Special Agent of the FBI." The New York Office further advised headquarters in Washington that they were not going to help her secure a job in those fields where she had asked them to use their contacts—"research, personnel, teaching or photography." As usual, there would be no hint of "official endorsement or recommendation."[1]

A year went by, and Angela approached her former employers one more time. Would they come to her residence, she asked, to discuss matters of undisclosed importance? The New York Office reminded itself who she was—"one of the government witnesses in the first Smith Act trial against the National Board members of the

CP, USA." The remainder of this single-page entry in Angela's FBI file, more than two-thirds of the page, is completely blacked out, the story of whether they got together or not lost forever.[2]

If 1957 was not a banner year for Angela, the Red Scare had nothing to celebrate either. Senator Joe McCarthy died, more or less in disgrace, having been censured by the Senate in December 1954 for conduct contrary to Senate traditions. His demise had begun during the televised Army-McCarthy hearings from April to June 1954 when his pursuit of suspected Communists and security risks in the US Army, and especially the Signal Corps, was exposed to public scrutiny. The Red Scare suffered another setback in 1957 when the US Supreme Court, with Earl Warren as Chief Justice, voted 6 to 1 to overturn the Smith Act convictions of fourteen California Communists in the appeal of *Yates, et al. v. US*. The Court decreed that even radical speech was protected under the First Amendment, and did not pose a "clear and present danger." The Smith Act remained on the books, but indictments were dropped, and there would be no more prosecutions. By that time, most of the original Foley Square defendants had already served their prison terms, as had several others from later trials. The highest count of American Communists prosecuted under the Smith Act gives 160 indictments (which includes those accused of harboring a fugitive, or just being a member of the Party) and 114 convictions.[3]

The CPUSA had mostly ceased to exist by the end of the decade, its demise hastened by Nikita Khrushchev's 1956 revelations before the 20th Party Congress "On the Cult of Personality and Its Consequences" about Stalin's purges of the 1930s and the cult of personality Stalin fostered during his years as Party leader. Many of those remaining CPUSA members, who had survived McCarthy-era Congressional committee hearings and the Smith Act trials, finally quit in disillusionment. By the late 1950s, not much remained of the militant American Left that had led union organizing during the 1930s and '40s, and helped formulate New Deal policy. From a record high membership of 50-80,000 during the Depression and World War II, the CPUSA had dwindled to around 5,000 members—many of them FBI agents, in 1961, according to Attorney General Robert F. Kennedy—and hardly worth prosecuting. J. Edgar Hoover, on the other hand, still saw the American Communist Party as a threat in the 1960s, "a greater menace to the internal security of our Nation today than it ever was since it was first founded in this country in 1919." It was part of his long-standing feud with Attorney General Kennedy.[4]

Angela, too, like her former boss Hoover, was continuing the fight. She reminded the FBI of her existence one more time, rather pathetically, by sending along the proofs of a forthcoming article, "Communist Party, U.S.A.," which was scheduled to appear in January 1962, in the *American Legion Magazine*. While no author is named, and the photos are not credited, Angela may, in fact, have done the photo layout for the article. It suggested that she still had skills to offer the FBI should they choose to contact her. They did not, and showed little enthusiasm for the article, "very short, consisting primarily of pictures." They did note that "the over-all impression" was "most favorable to the Bureau," but apparently did not acknowledge receipt of it from a "Former Confidential Informant." Had her old FBI handlers replied to her directly, Angela would certainly have saved that correspondence. The last entry in her FBI file, in 1965, concerns some confusion at Bureau headquarters about whether or not "Beatrice Siskind was the sister-in-law of Gus Hall, Communist (CP) leader." Angela was cited as one reliable source of information. Then there was silence. For Angela, it was over, and even for those who had turned "professional witness," there was less demand for their services. The Red Scare had a limited life span simply because the CPUSA had not been hard to crush and dismantle. There were not so many Party members, after all, and most were disheartened or terrified.[5]

Angela, too, had no choice but to acknowledge the end of an era, and move on. The support she had enjoyed from old friends, her lover Myrtis Johnson, and the anti-Communist network was fading to nothingness. Myrtis was gone. One last letter from her tells Angela that Myrtis "would like to see you again sometime […] but we cannot pick up the tarnished pieces of a shattered experience and be friends." There is a reference to Myrtis' "move from Wilton [CT]," while another reference to "Ken's spirit" suggests the letter dates from the late 1950s or after. Because Kenneth Bierly was dead by 1958, age forty-two. The rigors of the Red Scare seemed to take a toll on hunters as well as hunted. Likewise, at the height of his career, in 1953, Angela's long-time friend and supporter Fred Woltman had suffered a serious heart attack, followed over the next few years by paralytic strokes that forced him into early retirement in Florida, where he died in 1970, age sixty-four.[6]

Left with few skills and fewer friends, but possessed of an agile mind and a ruthless will to survive, Angela looked around for a way to re-invent herself. Why real estate proved the answer to her problems is a matter for speculation, but it began years before she settled in Provincetown. Her first purchase was a brownstone on 12th Street, just west of Greenwich Avenue in the Village. But a changing Provincetown, in the early stages of its transformation from fishing village to world-class resort, where she had vacationed in the years prior to her informant/witness celebrity, beckoned. Perhaps Angela felt safer there, and prices before the boom were attractively low. She discovered that she had a real knack for business. A major coup was the purchase of 353 Commercial Street, which would become rental units (now luxury condominiums) called "Angel's Landing," which she later sold at a hefty profit. Other purchases over the years included additional properties on Commercial Street, a house on Nickerson Street, lots in Wellfleet, and seaside cottages (later the Wind and Wave Cooperative) in North Truro. In her heyday, Angela Calomiris was one of the area's most successful "wash-ashores"—a local term for those who come to Provincetown for a brief vacation and stay on as residents.[7]

Her career in real estate, like her spy career, did not earn her a lot of friends. The late Willa Levitt, a lesbian from New York, told the story of shopping for property in Provincetown, and settling on "a row of cottages next to the beach." She thought it would be a good business deal to make them into condos for sale, keeping one for herself. Willa went to a friend for advice about what seemed to her a reasonable asking price. That friend was Angela, who advised caution and then went immediately to the real estate office and made an offer of $5,000 above the price Willa had cited. It was a quick sale, and the sort of maneuver that spelled success in business. It did not, however, make for lasting friendships. Willa described Angela as "a person with no conscience, no scruples." There were other real estate stories regarding Angela, of deals gone wrong, where a handshake could not be trusted.[8]

But the big news about Angela predated Provincetown. If she felt secure on Land's End, a past as colorful and deadly as hers was hard to hide for long. The truth began to leak out, even if no revelations were forthcoming. Long-time Wellfleet resident Gloria Nardin, for example, spoke out in an article about the Schoolhouse Center exhibit in 2004 of Sid Grossman's Provincetown photography. Going back several years, Gloria recalled looking for a place to stay for herself and her children. She followed up on a recommendation for "Angel's Landing," and thought the apartment would do nicely. But a glance at the business card the owner handed her shocked her speechless, and brought up terrible memories of the demise of the Photo League, where she had studied, and of her good friend Sid Grossman. There was no confrontation, and "Nardin," the article reads, "fled in horror."[9]

Grossman had, in fact, preceded Angela to Provincetown. Her denunciation of him from the witness stand at Foley Square had made life in New York intolerable, and he chose to escape, using the benefits of the GI Bill, to study under the direction of German-born abstract expressionist painter Hans Hoffman, a pivotal figure in post-war American art, at his Provincetown Summer School. If Angela was visiting or vacationing, Grossman never saw her. He spent the summers until his death teaching the few students who enrolled (Gloria Nardin among them) in his Provincetown School of Photography. To make ends meet, Grossman's widow confirmed, they fished and afterward sold their catch (flounder) on the street.[10]

Other Provincetown residents knew bizarre details of Angela's past, and avoided her. Roslyn Garfield remembered that Angela had identified other lesbians in the Village as Communists or fellow-travelers, friends of Garfield who had attended Village Party meetings many years before. Back then, when she was put on the spot, Angela had an original excuse. Her family in Greece had been threatened by the FBI, she told her accusers, and, as a result, she had had no choice but to cooperate and turn informer. It was the kind of story her fertile imagination might have dreamed up, and maybe she even believed it. Roslyn Garfield did not.[11]

Time was running out for Angela. During the 1970s to '80s, as real estate values increased exponentially in Provincetown, her health grew precarious. "Too many cigarettes," recalled a friend, and the diagnosis was emphysema. Following medical advice, Angela began to investigate warmer, sunnier climates where breathing might be easier. After a few exploratory trips, she settled on San Miguel de Allende/Guanajuato, in the hill country of central Mexico. In the process of liquidating her small Provincetown real estate empire, she must have realized remarkable profits. During the 1980s alone, according to those in the know, the value of real estate in and around Provincetown had increased by a minimum of 400 percent over the 1960s. At her death in 1995, in Mexico of COPD, her estate was valued at $900,000. Unfortunately for the executrix and her partner, to whom Angela left most of her money, a trip to Mexico to recover her remains proved harrowing because Angela had given out three different birthdates on official documents, and her passport was missing. The Mexicans did not believe she was American. A couple of well-placed bribes could have probably resolved the situation quickly, but Angela—at least her ashes—were liberated at last. They found a final resting place in Ulster County, New York, beneath a headstone that reads "Writer, Friend, Entrepreneur and Patriot." Obviously, when speaking of the dead, everyone is entitled to an opinion.[12]

But those who would celebrate Angela's accomplishments are a minority. Memories of that terrible time known as the McCarthy era tend to evoke in most Americans a profound shame and disbelief. Debate still rages over the extent of individual American complicity in Soviet war-time espionage, while the executions of Julius and Ethel Rosenberg continue to trouble people of conscience. As evidenced over the years, wars—back then World War II and Korea—breed deep irrational fears that can be exploited to generate more fear, wars, and destruction. And as far as FBI informants who placed the lives of fellow gay men and lesbians in jeopardy are concerned, the years have not erased their indiscretions. Ten years ago, a lesbian from bygone Village days, someone who had perhaps known Judy Holliday and Yetta Cohn, ran into an old friend of Angela's in a Florida restaurant. Without any preamble, by-passing niceties, one white-haired octogenarian screamed at the other, "How could you be friends with that squealer?" As historian Victor Navasky has said of all informers, "They named the names because they thought nobody would remember, but it turned out to be the one thing that nobody can forget."[13]

In this publicity photo, Buddy Kent appears as "Bubbles" Kent, *exotic dancer, who in the late 1940s played Jimmy Kelly's nightclub. Bubbles knew the Village cabaret scene, as well as a million stories about her lesbian community over several decades. In 1983, she shared stories about Angela Calomiris, Judy Holliday, and Judy's life-long friend Yetta Cohn. These stories led to a further investigation of Calomiris and her role in the Red Scare, and to the writing of this book.*
(Photo from author's Personal Collection)

Members and guests at a New York Photo League function *in the 1940s. In the foreground, Paul Strand, one of the pioneer figures in American documentary photography and film, and across the table, Beaumont and Nancy Newhall, curators of photography at New York's Museum of Modern Art, and later at the George Eastman House (now George Eastman Museum) in Rochester, New York.*

Angela Calomiris *singing along with* Jacob (Jack) Deschin, New York Times *photo page editor, in 1946 at a Photo League party. Angela was happy to be seen with a distinguished journalist at what was probably a Christmas holiday affair, to judge from the mistletoe suspended above their heads.*

A photograph entitled "Dusk" by Angela Calomiris from the 1940s, during the time she was taking courses at the New York Photo League. The low-light allure of the scene testifies to her artistic potential and professional competence as a photographer. This photo and others by Calomiris were recovered after her death, and are preserved in the Lesbian Herstory Archives, Brooklyn, New York.

(PHOTO BY ANGELA CALOMIRIS, © LESBIAN HERSTORY EDUCATIONAL FOUNDATION, INC.)

Acclaimed photographer Berenice Abbott walking with students around Washington Square Park in the Village, encouraging them to photograph street life and contemporary reality. Calomiris claimed to have studied with Abbott, who taught at the New School and was on the Board of the Photo League.

(PHOTOGRAPH BY GLORIA NARDIN)

J. Edgar Hoover, *first Director of the Federal Bureau of Investigation (FBI), testifying before HUAC in 1947. On his watch, undercover informants were positioned strategically to report on activities considered subversive. The American Communist Party was one target, but artists in many fields were also subject to scrutiny.*
(Courtesy Photofest)

Judy Holliday *was one of Hollywood's brightest stars in the 1940s and '50s. She began her career in the late 1930s at The Village Vanguard as one of The Revuers, alongside Betty Comden, Adolph Green and others, then moved on to Broadway.*
(Courtesy Photofest)

In the role of Billie Dawn *in the movie version of* Born Yesterday, *Judy as "dumb blonde" tries to better herself intellectually to please co-star William Holden. Fellow co-star Broderick Crawford disapproves. Judy won the Academy Award for Best Actress in 1950 for her performance, and in 1952 went before the Senate Internal Security Subcommittee (McCarran Committee), suspected of Communist sympathies.*
(Courtesy Photofest)

Founded in 1946 by African-American lawyer William L. Patterson to expose racial injustice in the US, the Civil Rights Congress staged this demonstration protesting the 1949 prosecution of the Communist Party leaders in front of the Foley Square Courthouse, New York City.
(DAILY WORKER / DAILY WORLD PHOTOGRAPHS COLLECTION, TAMIMENT LIBRARY, NEW YORK UNIVERSITY, COURTESY OF PEOPLE'S WORLD)

Harold R. Medina was born in Brooklyn and was appointed a Federal judge in the Southern District of New York in 1947 by President Harry Truman. He achieved lasting fame for his handling of the 1949 trial of the Communist leaders, and served on the Federal bench until his retirement in 1980 at age 92.
(LIBRARY OF CONGRESS, PRINTS & PHOTOGRAPHS DIVISION, LC-DIG-DS-09970)

The defendants looking optimistic before the Foley Square trial. From left to right: Henry Winston, Eugene Dennis, Benjamin Davis, Gus Hall, John Williamson, Carl Winter, Irving Potash, John Gates, Robert Thompson, and Jacob Stachel. Gilbert Green, the eleventh defendant, is not pictured. All of them were convicted and served time in federal prison.
(DAILY WORKER / DAILY WORLD PHOTOGRAPHS COLLECTION, TAMIMENT LIBRARY, NEW YORK UNIVERSITY, COURTESY OF PEOPLE'S WORLD)

Another demonstration at Foley Square in support of the Communist defendants. The placards, complete with a portrait of former President Franklin Delano Roosevelt, express the belief that the issue is freedom of speech, with recollections of the recent war against fascism in Europe.

(DAILY WORKER/DAILY WORLD PHOTOGRAPHS COLLECTION, TAMIMENT LIBRARY, NEW YORK UNIVERSITY, COURTESY OF PEOPLE'S WORLD)

Angela Calomiris at her typewriter, where she would have presumably written a draft of her book, Red Masquerade: Undercover for the F.B.I. *Contract details and other documentation from her papers in the Lesbian Herstory Archives, however, put her authorship in doubt.*

(COURTESY OF RAE SKINNER)

Attorneys for the defense in the Foley Square trial in January 1949. Left to right: Abraham Isserman, Harry Sacher, George Cockett, Louis McCabe, Maurice Sugar, and Abraham Unger. The team would later be joined in the courtroom by San Francisco labor lawyer Richard Gladstein. At trial's end, Judge Medina found defense lawyers in contempt of court and sentenced each one to from four- to six-month jail terms. One, Louis McCabe, got off with thirty days.

(PHOTO BY JOHN DE BIASE)

Headlines *on the front page of the* New York World-Telegram, *October 1949, billed Calomiris as a "Girl Photog" who cut her career short to expose the Red Menace.*

(LIBRARY OF CONGRESS, PRINTS & PHOTOGRAPHS DIVISION, LC-DIG-DS-09971)

Mary Margaret McBride *was a pioneering radio personality and author from the 1930s until her retirement in 1954. McBride interviewed Calomiris immediately after the publication of* Red Masquerade *in late 1950.*

(COURTESY PHOTOFEST)

Walter Winchell, *for decades a renowned newspaper and radio commentator, raised gossip to an art form. In 1950, he offered Calomiris an "orchid" from his "orchid garden" for publication of her book, and sent wishes for its success on his Sunday radio broadcast.*

(COURTESY PHOTOFEST)

Eleanor Roosevelt, *First Lady of President Franklin Delano Roosevelt, also had a public life of her own. In late 1950, she hosted Calomiris on her radio program to talk about* Red Masquerade.

(COURTESY PHOTOFEST)

Sid Grossman, *a distinguished photographer and co-founder of the New York Photo League, taught at League workshops and later in Provincetown, Massachusetts. Here he relaxes with friends on the beach in nearby Wellfleet in the early 1950s. Grossman's career ended when Calomiris named him as a Communist from the witness stand at Foley Square.*
(Photograph by Gloria Nardin)

Calomiris in Provincetown in 1970, *at the large complex of rental apartments (now condos) on 353 Commercial Street she called "Angel's Landing." Purchased in 1961, at a modest price, the complex was sold decades later at considerable profit.*
(Courtesy of the Lesbian Herstory Educational Foundation, Inc.)

Calomiris in 1979, *in her own Provincetown apartment. Lucky and successful in real estate, perhaps in love, she takes a moment to sit for this portrait and reflect on fleeting fame, people hurt, and what might have been.*
(Photo by Ray Block, 1979, Courtesy of the Lesbian Herstory Educational Foundation, Inc.)

Endnotes

INTRODUCTION

1. Interview, Melva Wade, executrix of Angela's estate, Accord, New York, August 8, 2003.

2. For a glimpse of the origins of American documentary filmmaking, see http://www.youtube.com/watch?v=569mT2bCwRY for Reel 5 of "Passaic Textile Strike" (1926). Also see Russell Campbell, *Cinema Strikes Back: Radical Filmmaking in the United States, 1930-1942* (Ann Arbor: University of Michigan Research Press, 1982); and David Pratt, ed., *Celluloid Power: Social Film Criticism from "The Birth of a Nation" to "Judgment at Nuremberg"* (Metuchen, New Jersey: Scarecrow Press, 1992). The American Jay Leyda (1910-1988) who trained at the State Film Institute, Moscow, with Sergei Eisenstein, was influential, as assistant curator, in the creation of the MOMA film library.

3. For the Photo League, see Lili Corbus Bezner, *Photography and Politics in America. From the New Deal into the Cold War* (Baltimore: Johns Hopkins University Press, 1999). From Angela's book *Red Masquerade: Undercover for the F.B.I.* (Philadelphia: Lippincott, 1950), pp. 77, 23-24.

4. The Photo League's fairly extensive FBI file is Headquarters File #100-114718. There is also a New York File #100-79069, and an early New York Investigative File #100-392. The author is grateful to Prof. Fiona Dejardin, Department of Art and Art History, Hartwick College, Oneonta,

NY, for her PhD Dissertation, "The Photo League: Aesthetics, Politics and the Cold War" (University of Delaware, 1993), and for sharing these and other FBI files.

5. There had been a US Communist Party since 1921, when the Communist Party of America (CPA) merged with the Communist Labor Party (CLP), co-founded by John Reed, author of *Ten Days That Shook the World* (1919), to form the American Communist Party (ACP). In 1929, the ACP became the Communist Party of America (CPUSA), whose platform had always included support for Russia.

6. The trial was officially *Dennis et al. v. US*, for Eugene Dennis, General Secretary, CPUSA, referred to here throughout as *Dennis v. US*, five million words, 21,157 pp., in 28 volumes. This citation of prosecution witness Charles Nicodemus is from vol. 6, April 19, 1949, pp. 4804-4805. The likelihood of another heart attack or stroke excused defendant William Z. Foster, long-time labor activist, from standing trial with his 11 Party comrades.

7. Russell Porter, "Girl Aide of FBI Testified of 7 Years as 'Communist'," *New York Times*, April 27, 1949, p. 1. George E. Sokolsky, "Urges All to Read 'Red Masquerade'," *New York Journal-American*, November 2, 1950. See Michael J. Ybarra, *Washington Gone Crazy: Senator Pat McCarran and the Great American Communist Hunt* (Hanover, New Hampshire: Steerforth Press, 2004). The title says it all.

8. *Dennis v. US*, vol. 7, April 26, 1949, pp. 5023-5025. See Lewis Wood, "90 Groups, Schools Named on U.S. List as Being Disloyal," *New York Times*, December 5, 1947, pp. 1, 18.

9. Other biographies include: Daniel J. Leab, *I Was a Communist for the FBI: The Unhappy Life and Times of Matt Cvetic* (University Park, PA: Penn State University Press, 2000); Lauren Kessler, *Clever Girl: Elizabeth Bentley, the Spy Who Ushered in the McCarthy Era* (New York: HarperCollins, 2003); and Robert M. Lichtman and Ronald D. Cohen, *Deadly Farce: Harvey Matusow and the Informer System in the McCarthy Era* (Urbana and Chicago: University of Illinois Press, 2004).

10. For the complete history of this dramatic moment see Allan Bérubé's *Coming Out Under Fire: The History of Gay Men and Women in World War Two* (New York: The Free Press, 1990), on which this capsule statement is based. The clinical definitions are on p. 141. Zsa Zsa/Josh Gershick has given us an update in *Secret Service: Untold Stories of Lesbians in the Military* (Los Angeles: Alyson, 2005), with a "Foreword" by Col. Margarethe Cammermeyer.

11. For Miller, see *Congressional Record*, March 31, 1950, 4527-28, http://www.writing.upenn.edu/~afilreis my 1950s site, Gays in government, 1951. See David K. Johnson, *The Lavender Scare: The Cold War Persecution*

of Gays and Lesbians in the Federal Government (Chicago: The University of Chicago Press, 2004) for "lavender lads" (p. 18) and a detailed analysis of all related issues. Senator Kenneth Wherry (Republican-Nebraska) is quoted by Griffin Fariello, *Red Scare: Memories of the American Inquisition, An Oral History* (New York: W.W. Norton, 1995), p. 124, note. David K. Johnson, in *The Lavender Scare*, cites Washington, DC vice squad estimates of 5,000 homosexuals in the city, and 3,750 of them working for the federal government (p. 79).

12. David Ehrenstein, *Open Secret: Gay Hollywood 1928-1998* (New York: William Morrow and Company, 1998), pp. 114-115. Matusow recanted all his prosecution testimony at trials and committee hearings, and wrote a book after the fact—*False Witness* (New York: Cameron & Kahn, Publishers, 1955). He is quoted in Griffin Fariello, *Red Scare*, p. 101.

13. McCarthy's Senate committee is not to be confused with HUAC, the House Un-American Activities Committee, which lasted from 1938 to 1975. For Lillian Hellman, see Cheryl A. Bates, "The Gay McCarthyites," in *The Gay & Lesbian Review Worldwide*, vol. 17, no. 2 (March-April 2010), pp. 21-22.

14. For more Cohn, see von Hoffman's *Citizen Cohn* (New York: Doubleday, 1988) and *The Lavender Scare*. See www.ptowndiaries.com for the film (2009) directed by Joseph Mantegna.

15. See Sam Tanenhaus, *Whittaker Chambers, A Biography*, pp. 343-345, for the confession. Also, see Allen Weinstein, *Perjury: The Hiss-Chambers Case* (New York: Random House, 1997; orig. ed. Knopf, 1978), pp. 103-104; and *The Lavender Scare*, especially pp. 31-33.

16. For Timothy Hobson see http://algerhiss.com/media/audio-and-video/timothy-hobson/ including "Tim Hobson at 89. An essay by the last remaining eyewitness in the Hiss Case" (January 2016). Hobson did not take the stand for the defense at Hiss' trial, lest his homosexuality prejudice the case. Also see Ed Gold, "At Alger Hiss Conference, Gay Debate Gets Red Hot," *The Villager*, vol. 76, no. 46, April 11-17, 2007. In later life, Hiss concluded that his rebuff of Chambers had wounded him more deeply than he had realized at the time. The memoir *Recollections of a Life* (New York: Henry Holt and Company, 1988) contains these (p. 208) and other thoughts on Chambers.

17. The debate about Hiss' innocence or guilt continues, alongside greater questions around the postwar betrayal of the New Deal by conservative opponents. See Susan Jacoby, *Alger Hiss and the Battle for History* (New Haven: Yale University Press, 2009).

18. David Carter in *Stonewall: The Riots that Sparked the Gay Revolution* (New York: St. Martin's Press, 2004) quotes from a Ginsberg interview, pp.

94-95. Anthony Summers, in *Official and Confidential: The Secret Life of J. Edgar Hoover* (New York: G. P. Putnam's Sons, 1993), tells the entertaining story of Hoover in the black gown at an orgy staged by none-other-than Roy Cohn in a swell-elegant suite at the Plaza Hotel. Historian Athan Theoharis, *J. Edgar Hoover, Sex, and Crime: A Historical Antidote* (Chicago: Ivan R. Dee, 1995) provides a wealth of information about Hoover maneuvering through official Washington.

19. "Communist Trial Ends With 11 Guilty," *Life* magazine, October 24, 1949, pp. 31-35. "Record of Smith Act Cases," typescript with charts prepared by Simon W. Gerson, October 1, 1956, 11 pp., in Gil Green Papers, Box 7, 1st folder, Tamiment Library & Robert F. Wagner Labor Archives, New York University. "The Party's Over," as sung by Judy Holliday in the 1956 musical comedy *Bells Are Ringing*. Music by Julie Styne, lyrics by Betty Comden and Adolph Green. See George Kennan, architect of our policy to contain the Soviet Union, on CNN in 1996. www.johndclare.net/cold_war7_Kennan_interview.htm Also see his *At a Century's Ending: Reflections 1982- 1995* (New York: W. W. Norton, 1996).

CHAPTER 1

1. The audio tape of the interview with Buddy Kent is part of the Lesbian Herstory Archives collection, Brooklyn, NY, and is dated January 27 and February 8, 1983. All references are to that tape. For blackmail, see David Carter, *Stonewall*, especially pp. 91-100, and for 1940s Mafia-owned Village nightclubs with gay floorshows, see my novel *Under the Mink* (Los Angeles: Alyson, 2001; IntoPrint Publishing, 2015), and C. Alexander Hortis, *The Mob and the City* (Amherst, New York: Prometheus Books, 2014), pp. 166-172.

2. Boze Hadleigh, *Hollywood Lesbians* (New York: Barricade Books, 1994), p. 246, where she is cast as "lesbian or bi." For the complete Judy Holliday, see "The Judy Holliday Resource Center" www.judyhollidayrc.com, and also standard biographies, Gary Carey, *Judy Holliday: An Intimate Life Story* (New York: Seaview Books [PEI], 1982) and Will Holtzman, *Judy Holliday* (New York: G. P. Putnam's Sons, 1982).

3. New York: Hill and Wang, 2003. Orig. ed. The Viking Press, 1980. Navasky is a standard reference for understanding blacklisting and the Red Scare.

4. For the NYPD, Interview, Morry Baer, October 1, 2002, Whiting, New Jersey, who was in the first class to attend the Police Academy and train to be policewomen, not just "glorified matrons." Morry was on the women's

pistol team, and knew all the players in our drama. She regretted that another policewoman, Helen Ilona Bloch, was fired because her sister and brother-in-law were active Communist Party members.

5. *Naming Names,* pp. xxiii, 18-19, 12.

6. Interview, Miriam Wolfson, May 19, 2002, New York City. Interview, Morry Baer, October 1, 2002, Whiting, New Jersey.

7. *Naming Names,* p. xxiii. Angela Calomiris Papers, Lesbian Herstory Archives, Special Collections #99-02, Brooklyn, NY. Subsequently referred to as Calomiris Papers, LHA. See Albert E. Kahn, *The Matusow Affair: Memoir of a National Scandal,* with Introduction by Angus Cameron (Mt. Kisco, NY: Moyer Bell Ltd, 1987) p. 48, for these thoughts on Matusow.

8. Calomiris Papers, LHA. The back flap of the death-threat envelope reads: Martin Boyed 62 West 85 St. New York.

9. *Naming Names,* pp. xxii-xxiii.

10. Angela appeared with Dwight Cooke on *You and Communism,* and on *David Harding, Counterspy* in December, 1950; with Bill Slater on *Inside Communism* in April, 1951. Radio scripts in Calomiris Papers, LHA.

11. Script in Calomiris Papers, LHA. Victor Lasky's *Seeds of Treason* was published for *Newsweek* by Funk & Wagnalls Company, New York, 1950. Lasky's co-author was Rafael de Toledano, an assistant editor of *Newsweek* and "expert on Communist and Falangist espionage" who became a life-long advocate for conservative causes.

12. The author is indebted to Prof. Veronica Wilson, University of Pittsburgh, Johnstown, for a copy of the Calomiris file—Smith Act Prosecutions Gov't/Angela Calomiris File No. 100-HQ-3722384, hereafter cited as Calomiris file.

13. Memos SAC Edward Scheidt, New York, to Director, August 20, 1950; A. H. Belmont [one of Hoover's top assistants] to D. M. Ladd [one-time Head of the FBI's Domestic Intelligence Division], August 31, 1950; SAC Edward Scheidt, New York, to Director, August 31, 1950, p. 3; D. M. Ladd to Director, September 1, 1950; SAC Edward Scheidt, New York, to Director, September 8, 1950. Calomiris file. SAC = Special Agent in Charge. The Feinberg Law (1950), passed by the NY State Legislature, denied "subversives"—those who "advocate violent overthrow of the government"—the right to teach in New York's public schools. See Oliver Stone's 10-part Showtime series *Untold History of the United States* for the importance of Henry Wallace.

14. Memo SAC Edward Scheidt, New York, to Director, August 31, 1950, p. 4. Calomiris file. See Gary Carey, *Judy Holliday: An Intimate Life Story,* and Will Holtzman, *Judy Holliday.* Writer Arthur Laurents, in his memoir *Original Story By* (New York: Knopf, 2000), remembers a poker

game at Judy's with "her ex-girlfriend, Yetta Cohen [sic], and Yetta's new girlfriend, Ruth [Brooke]," pp. 158-159. According to Holtzman, p. 181, Yetta resigned.

15. For "Transcript of Judy Holliday's Testimony" before the McCarran Committee, see The Judy Holliday Resource Center www.judyhollidayrc. com, retrieved January 8, 2004. See, *Red Channels*, pp. 78-79, for Judy and Lena Horne. Vincent Harnett, later a founder of AWARE, Inc., "An Organization to Combat the Communist Conspiracy in Entertainment Communications," wrote the lengthy introduction to *Red Channels*.

16. Interview, Morry Baer, October 1, 2002, Whiting, New Jersey, a fellow policewoman, who did not like Yetta, but claimed to have met Judy at a social gathering at Yetta's apartment. Interview, Emma ("Jerre") Kalbas, April 10 and October 22, 2004, New York City, who worked for Yetta selling mail order vitamins, adored Judy, and visited at the Dakota, 72nd Street and Central Park West, after Judy moved uptown. Will Holtzman, *Judy Holliday*, p. 127. Writer and playwright Jane Bowles was the wife of Paul Bowles. La Touche wrote the lyrics for "Ballad For Americans" (1939), an American patriotic cantata, music by Earl Robinson, often performed by both Paul Robeson and Bing Crosby. Arthur Laurents wrote scripts for *The Way We Were*, *West Side Story* and many other dramatic sensations

17. Memo SAC P[ercy]. E. Foxworth, New York, to Director, March 10, 1942, for Angela's address. Calomiris file.

18. The memo, dated November 15, 1950, is from Barbara Frost, publicity manager of the New York office of Lippincott (based in Philadelphia).

CHAPTER 2

1. *Red Masquerade*, p. 23. In a phone Interview, August 21, 2010, Rhinebeck, New York, Melva Wade, executrix of Angela's estate, recalled that Angela always talked proudly about any connection she had to a prominent person.

2. McNulty wrote the Obituary for "Angela Calomiris, 79," in the *Provincetown Advocate-News*, February 17, 1995. For what the Ptown crowd did and didn't know about Angela, also see Veronica A. Wilson, "Red Masquerades: Gender and Political Subversion During the Cold War, 1945-1963," PhD Dissertation (Rutgers University, 2002), p. 206, note. *Red Masquerade*, pp. 25-26.

3. Phone interview, Melva Wade, August 21, 2010, Rhinebeck, New

York. For Esther Lape and Elizabeth Read, especially in Mrs. Roosevelt's life, see Blanche Wiesen Cook, *Eleanor Roosevelt, Volume I 1884-1933* (New York: Penguin, 1992).

4. See Judith Schwarz, *Radical Feminists of "Heterodoxy": Greenwich Village 1912-1940* (Norwich, VT: New Victoria Publishers, 1986), and especially "Heterodoxy and Politics," pp. 25-51. Also see Ross Wetzsteon, *Republic of Dreams. Greenwich Village: The American Bohemia, 1910-1960* (New York: Simon & Schuster, 2002) and especially "The Feminists of the Village," pp. 162-239.

5. For Esther Lape and Elizabeth Read, see Blanche Wiesen Cook, *Eleanor Roosevelt, Volume I.* The former Holly-Chambers apartment complex, now part of New York University, also bears a plaque honoring Eleanor Roosevelt's stay there. See Susan Ware, *Partner and I: Molly Dewson, Feminism, and New Deal Politics* (New Haven: Yale University Press, 1987) for Dewson's activism on behalf of minimum wage laws and Social Security.

6. Appropriately, the expression "through the grapevine" had Village roots, in a bar called The Old Grapevine at the corner of 11th Street and Sixth Avenue, where gossip was served up with the drinks. See Ross Wetzsteon, *Republic of Dreams*, p. xiii. Helen Tamiris (1905-1966), née Becker on the Lower East Side, helped establish the Federal Dance Project of the WPA, and is probably best known for her suite of dances called *Negro Spirituals*, which she created between 1928 and 1941. A dancer herself, Buddy Kent knew the New York dance world, and had studied with Pearl Primus, another pioneering student of African dance styles.

The WPA (originally the Works Progress Administration, later the Works Projects Administration) was a New Deal agency that gave millions of unemployed people jobs on public works projects. It extended from 1935 to 1943, when it was terminated because the war had eliminated the country's unemployment problem.

7. For Angela's work history, Memo SAC P. E. Foxworth, New York, to Director, March 10, 1942. Calomiris file. Jobs were not easy to come by. As Buddy Kent, who had graduated from high school in 1939, recalled "if you were a Jew, they didn't hire you, and if you looked like a lesbian, they didn't hire you."

8. Curt Gentry, *J. Edgar Hoover: The Man and the Secrets* (New York: W.W. Norton, 1991), pp. 299, 300-301.

9. "My Day," October 19, 1949, and August 19, 1948. As part of the Eleanor Roosevelt Papers Project, based at George Washington University, Mrs. Roosevelt's "My Day" columns (1935-62) are available online at http://www.gwu.edu/~erpapers/myday. All "My Day" references are to this site.

10. William C. Sullivan (the FBI's third in command, after Hoover and his very close associate Clyde Tolson), *The Bureau: My Thirty Years in Hoover's FBI* (New York: W.W. Norton, 1979), p. 37. Anthony Summers, *Official and Confidential: The Secret Life of J. Edgar Hoover*, p. 143. Liddy's memoir *Will* (New York: St. Martin's Press, 1980), p. 83. Quoted in Ovid Demaris, *The Director: An Oral Biography of J. Edgar Hoover* (New York: Harper's Magazine Press, 1975), p. 124.

11. "My Day," June 9, 1945, and June 26, 1951.

12. "My Day," January 25, 1947, and October 24, 1949.

13. Angela's interview is Recording RWC 5544 A1-3, December 1, 1950, Motion Picture, Broadcasting and Recorded Sound Division, Library of Congress. References throughout are to this recording. Since his committee hearings were broadcast live on TV in 1950 to 20-30 million viewers a day, Kefauver was a star in his own right, and would later run unsuccessfully for Vice-President on the Democratic ticket with Adlai Stevenson.

14. $200,000 in 1950 = $1,967,726.14 in 2016. http://www.bls.gov/data/inflation_calculator.htm

15. See Susan Ware, *It's One O'Clock and Here Is Mary Margaret McBride: A Radio Biography* (New York: New York University Press, 2005), p. 231, and throughout for more information about McBride and her career.

16. Angela's interview is LWO 15577 107B, October 25, 1950, Motion Picture, Broadcasting and Recorded Sound Division, Library of Congress. References throughout are to this recording. Broadcast on November 8, 1950, LWO 15577 14B is the same program, expanded a bit, for Chicago. See Susan Ware, *It's One O'Clock,* p. 34, and pp. 87-101, "Doing the Products." Also see Philip Hamburger, "Mary Margaret McBride. A Supersaleswoman Shares Adventures of Mind and Stomach with a Host of Radio Listeners," *Life,* December 4, 1944, pp. 47-52. http://books.google.com/books?id=1EEEAAAAMBAJ&source=gbs_all_issues_r&cad=1

17. See Mary Margaret McBride's autobiographical *Out of the Air* (Garden City: Doubleday, 1960), pp. 145-147, for the episode she described as the saddest memory of her radio life, and for Walter White, p. 144.

18. See Fred Jerome, *The Einstein File: J. Edgar Hoover's Secret War Against the World's Most Famous Scientist* (New York: St. Martin's Press, 2002), pp. 155-156, for Einstein on Eleanor Roosevelt's show, February 12, 1950. For Robeson, see Martin Duberman, *Paul Robeson: A Biography* (New York: New Press, 1989), p. 385. Robeson was to appear with Representative Adam Clayton Powell, Jr. and black Mississippi Republican committeeman Perry Howard. Many things had changed since 1942, when Mrs. Roosevelt had co-sponsored, with Mrs. Francis Biddle, wife of the US Attorney General, and Mrs. Hugo L. Black, wife of the Associate Justice of the Supreme Court, a concert of Robeson's in Washington.

19. See Susan Ware, *It's One O'Clock*, pp. 24-27, for Connolly, and pp. 130-131 for the intimate closeted nature of the relationship between Stella Karn and Mary Margaret McBride. Judith Schwarz states candidly that Stella was Mary Margaret's "long-time lover and friend," and identifies McBride among the ten (at least) lesbian members of Heterodoxy. *Radical Feminists of "Heterodoxy,"* pp. 62 and 85. Also see Barbara G. Merrick in "Estella Karn, The Tough-Talking Program Manager behind the Radio Talkshow of Mary Margaret McBride," paper presented to the Association for Education in Journalism and Mass Communication (AEJMC) conference, Washington, DC, August 1995. http://list.msu.edu/cgi-bin/wa?A1=ind9602b&L=aejmc

20. Mary Margaret McBride's *A Long Way from Missouri* (New York: Putnam, 1959), pp. 36-37, 50-51.

21. See Judith Schwarz, *Radical Feminists of "Heterodoxy."*

22. Postcards, Mary Margaret McBride to Angela Calomiris, October 28 and November 15, 1950. Calomiris Papers, LHA.

23. Enclosure, SAC Edward Scheidt, New York, to Director, November 10, 1950. 11 pp. Calomiris file.

24. For the Roosevelts and their scandals, see Blanche Wiesen Cook, *Eleanor Roosevelt, Volume I 1884-1933.* Also, for Mrs. Roosevelt's clandestine romance, see *Empty Without You: The Intimate Letters of Eleanor Roosevelt and Lorena Hickok*, ed. Rodger Streitmatter (New York: Free Press, 1998), and especially the passionate letter (1933) from Lorena Hickok to Eleanor: "Most clearly I remember your eyes, with a kind of teasing smile in them, and the feeling of that soft spot just northeast of the corner of your mouth against my lips" (p. 52).

25. See Susan Ware, *It's One O'Clock and Here Is Mary Margaret McBride*, p. 231. From the Harry Ransom Center collection, University of Texas, Austin, you can see Mike Wallace's 1957 *Interview* with McBride and assess the devastating effect that Stella Karn's death, some two months before, had on her. http://www.hrc.utexas.edu/collections/film/holdlings/Wallace

CHAPTER 3

1. *Red Masquerade*, p. 16.

2. "Girl Tells of 7-Year Role as FBI's Red 'Mata Hari,'" *NY Journal-American*, April 26, 1949, p. 1.

3. Quoted in Albert E. Kahn, *The Matusow Affair*, p. 34; and Matusow's *False Witness*, p. 29. His publishers, Alfred Kahn and Angus Cameron, had been targets of the blacklist, and the latter had been forced out of the editorship of the publishing house of Little Brown in 1951 for Communist

sympathies. Also see Robert M. Lichtman and Ronald D. Cohen, *Deadly Farce: Harvey Matusow and the Informer System in the McCarthy Era* (University of Illinois Press, 2004). Matusow, a former Communist, went to work for the FBI in 1950, and campaigned for Senator Joseph McCarthy and McCarthy-sponsored candidates in 1952.

4. Steinbeck, "The Death of a Racket," in *The Saturday Review*, April 2, 1955, quoted in *The Matusow Affair*, p. 287. Sylvia Thompson quoted in Griffin Fariello, *Red Scare*, p. 9.

5. *False Witness*, p. 29. By the mid-1950s, reporter Howard Rushmore showed signs of unraveling. Even Hoover wanted nothing more to do with him, and thought he "must be a nut." In January, 1958, Rushmore shot his wife in the head, then turned the gun on himself in a New York City taxicab. See Sam Kashner and Jennifer MacNair, *The Bad and The Beautiful: Hollywood in the Fifties* (New York: W.W. Norton, 2002), pp. 17-46. Walter Arm, "F.B.I. Agent Tells How She Posed as Red" and "Pay Is Doubled For 16 Jurors at Reds' Trial," *New York Herald Tribune*, April 27 and April 28, 1949.

6. Russell Porter, "Girl Aide of FBI Testifies of 7 Years as 'Communist,'" *Times*, April 27, 1949, p. 1; Walter Arm, "F.B.I. Agent Tells How She Posed as Red," *Herald Tribune. Red Masquerade*, p. 253.

7. *Red Masquerade*, pp. 253-254. The premises housing Straubenmuller have a long and convoluted history. It was renamed Charles Evans Hughes High School for the former Governor of New York and US Supreme Court Justice. Later it took the name of Bayard Rustin High School for the Humanities, after the Civil Rights leader, and is at present divided amongst several schools. As a Cold War note, the head of its Mathematics Department and an Executive member of the long-defunct Teachers Union, Irving Adler, was suspected of Communist sympathies and fired in 1952. Interview, Melva Wade, August 8, 2003, Accord, New York.

8. Calomiris Papers, LHA. "Surprise Witness in Red Trial," *New York Herald Tribune*, April 26, 1949, and Philip Santora, "Girl Counterspy Accuses 11 Reds," *New York Mirror*, April 27, 1949. *Red Masquerade*, p. 254. Contract with the Lee Keedick agency, June 2, 1950. Keedick was reported to love "the Commies about as much as the devil loves holy water" when he added "a speaker who should make the Communists squirm," in *Program. The Magazine of the American Platform*, November-December, 1950, p. 13. Calomiris Papers, LHA. $200 in 1950 = $1, 967.73 in 2016 http://bls. gov/data/inflation_calculator.htm Interview, Melva Wade, August 8, 2003, Accord, New York.

9. William C. Sullivan, *The Bureau: My Thirty Years in Hoover's FBI*, p. 133. Sullivan was involved in the investigation of the assassinations of John F. Kennedy, Martin Luther King, Jr., and Robert F. Kennedy. In 1971,

Hoover fired him for insubordination for suggesting that Hoover retire. Sullivan met with an untimely and suspicious death when he was shot by a hunter in the woods near his home in New Hampshire in 1977. Among many other revelations, Sullivan's book stated that the FBI spent a million dollars maintaining informants in the antiwar movement of the late 1960s and early 1970s (p. 129). *Red Masquerade,* p. 37.

10. *Red Masquerade,* pp. 13-15, 29-30, 82. One of the most successful and far-reaching efforts of the New Deal to lessen the impact of the Great Depression on the average American was the WPA, 1935-1943. Angela was only one of millions to whom it provided employment.

11. Interviews, Emma ("Jerre") Kalbas, April 10 and October 22, 2004, New York City. Jerre repeated the story several times, always with the same details.

12. *Red Masquerade,* pp. 35, 55. The importance of photographer/ informants to the FBI was recently confirmed by revelations about Ernest C. Withers, one of the most celebrated photographers of the civil rights era, close to Martin Luther King Jr. and his intimate circle. Reports obtained under the FOIA show Mr. Withers passing information to agents of the Memphis, Tennessee, office. Photos, of course, are valuable tools for the identification of those under surveillance. See Robbie Brown, "Civil Rights Photographer Unmasked as Informant," *New York Times,* September 13, 2010.

13. One of the most damning exposés is M. Wesley Swearingen's *FBI Secrets: An Agent's Expose* (Boston: South End Press, 1995). He was in Chicago, 1952-62, and Los Angeles, 1970-77, with postings in Kentucky and New York. Swearingen talks about informant quotas and the development of fictitious informants to fill them (pp. 54, 99, 164). In addition, he notes that the main purpose behind developing informers was to prepare them as witnesses in a court case (p. 104). Memo D. M. Ladd to Director, October 19, 1949, p. 3. Calomiris file. See Ellen Schrecker, *Many Are the Crimes: McCarthyism in America* (New York: Little, Brown, 1998), p. 196, for the selection of informant/witnesses for the trial.

14. *Red Masquerade,* p. 59.

15. Memo D. M. Ladd to Director, October 19, 1949, p. 7. Calomiris File. Budenz went on to publish more books but became, like other informers, difficult for the FBI to handle. See Robert P. Newman, "Agony at the FBI: Louis Budenz," in *Owen Lattimore and the "Loss" of China* (Berkeley: University of California Press, 1992). $70,000 in 1955 = $619,319.78 in 2016 $100,000 = $884,742.54 http://www.bls.gov/data/inflation_calculator.htm

16. *New York World-Telegram,* "Editorial," October 21, 1949, p. 22.

17. Memo SAC Edward Scheidt to Director, October 26, 1949, in Woltman's FBI File, #62-85195, October 23, 1947-March 6, 1970. Cited here as Woltman file. Other sources on Woltman include comments by fellow *World-Telegram* reporter Fred Cook from "The Nightmare Decade" (pp. 19-25) in *Maverick: Fifty Years of Investigative Reporting* (New York: G. P. Putnam's Son, 1984), "Introduction" by Studs Terkel; and Brad Hamm, Dean of the Northwestern University Medill School of Journalism, "From College Expulsion to Pulitzer Prize: How the *New York World-Telegram's* Fred Woltman Became the 'No. 1 Newspaper Specialist' on Communists," Unpublished paper presented at the American Journalism Historians Association Conference, September, 1995.

18. See *The Matusow Affair*, pp. 176-177, for recollections of Matusow's conversation with Bentley. Her book was *Out of Bondage* (1951), and she has been the subject of two recent biographies: Kathryn S. Olmsted, *Red Spy Queen: A Biography of Elizabeth Bentley* (2002) and Lauren Kessler, *Clever Girl: Elizabeth Bentley, the Spy Who Ushered in the McCarthy Era* (2003). Bentley also lived in the Village (58 Barrow Street), and was accused of making homosexual advances to a female comrade (*Red Spy Queen*, p. 68).

19. *Red Spy Queen*, p. 125. The articles on Bentley appeared July 21-28, 1948.

20. Woltman, Frederick. "Girl Photog Cut Career to Expose Reds' Plot." *New York World-Telegram* (October 17, 1949), pp. 1, 10; and "Leading Double Life No Picnic." *New York World-Telegram* (October 18, 1949), p. 8. Rosemary Dew, *No Backup: My Life as a Female Special Agent* (New York: Carrol & Graf, 2004), p. 1.

21. "Girl Photog Cut Career to Expose Reds' Plot." *New York World-Telegram* (October 17, 1949), pp. 1, 10; and "Leading Double Life No Picnic." *New York World-Telegram* (October 18, 1949), p. 8. Some of Angela's acquaintances remember the policewoman but not her name, and that she and Angela ended up having an affair. Interview, Morry Baer, October 1, 2002, Whiting, New Jersey, late of the NYPD. Interview, Ruth Parish, October 2, 2003, Hallandale, Florida.

22. Interview, Ruth Parish, October 2, 2003, Hallandale, Florida. Ruth knew about Angela working for the FBI and considered it a "patriotic thing." Like some others who had known Angela, Ruth was willing to talk once. But the political implications of the story did not escape her, and she refused further comment and contact.

23. Quoted by Brad Hamm, "From College Expulsion to Pulitzer Prize," p. 22, from a prepared obituary (dated February 20, 1958) found among Woltman's papers that never ran in the *World-Telegram*, which ceased publication in 1966. Frederick Woltman, "Cruising Car Best for FBI

Contacts, Woman Spying on Commies Found: 7-Yr. Assignment Related in Book," *New York World-Telegram*, November 13, 1950, p. 4. Teletype (Urgent) from SAC Edward Scheidt, New York, to Director, October 26, 1950, reported that "Woltman was present in Calomiris' home on the two occasions when an agent of this office today telephonically contacted Calomiris." Calomiris file.

24. "Leading Double Life No Picnic," *New York World-Telegram*, October 18, 1949, p. 8.

25. Fred Cook, *Maverick*, pp. 22-25. Cook was also the author of *The FBI Nobody Knows* (New York: MacMillan, 1964). Other journalists who opposed the Red Scare, and whose work is largely forgotten today, included James Aronson, *The Press and the Cold War* (New York: Monthly Review Press, 1970), and George Seldes, author of many books and editor of the newsletter *In Fact* (1940-1950), which served I(sidor) F(einstein) Stone as a model for his *I. F. Stone's Weekly* (1953-1967). In 1940, in *Witch Hunt: The Technique and Profits of Redbaiting* (NY: Modern Age Books) George Seldes explained that when "he threatens to tamper with the status quo, not even the President of the United States is immune to the charge of being a red" (p. xi). He was talking about FDR. Fred Woltman's FBI File contains Hoover's message to him (April 6, 1953) when he was hospitalized. Woltman wrote to "Dear Lou" (Nichols), on September 19, 1950, recalling the visit to the ranch house.

26 . Memo L. B. Nichols to Clyde Tolson, November 1, 1949, and prior undated memo to all executive staff in Hoover's handwriting. Woltman file. Also see Schrecker, *Many Are the Crimes*, p. 216, for the citation from an internal FBI memo, and the names of favored journalists—Drew Pearson, Walter Winchell, Fulton Lewis, Jr., and Hollywood gossip columnist Hedda Hopper, among others—to whom the Bureau routinely leaked information. The name of George Sokolsky of the *Journal-American*, who figures prominently in Angela's story, heads the list.

CHAPTER 4

1. "My Day," June 22, 1945, and "Liberals in This Year of Decision," where she talks about her experience with the American Youth Congress (1934-1940), collected in *Courage in a Dangerous World: The Political Writings of Eleanor Roosevelt*, ed. Allida M. Black (New York: Columbia University Press, 1999) p. 249.

2. Radio broadcast *Today With Mrs. Roosevelt*, December 1, 1950.

3. *World-Telegram*, "Leading Double Life No Picnic, FBI Girl Found,"

October 18, 1949, p. 8; "Editorial," October 21, 1949, p. 22; "Girl Photog Cut Career to Expose Reds' Plot," October 17, 1949, pp. 1, 10;; Letters from Stuart L. Vandervort, Summit, NJ (October 21, 1949) and Isidor E. Prussack, Brooklyn, NY (October 24, 1949). Calomiris Papers, LHA.

4. In February, 1942, Angela was "making twenty-seven dollars a week" (*Red Masquerade*, p. 12). $25 in 1942 = $365.23 in 2016; $225 in 1949 = $2,251.25 http://www.bls.gov/data/inflation_calculator.htm Memo SAC, New York, to Director, June 24, 1944. Memo D. M. Ladd to Director, October 19, 1949, p. 1, provides a detailed summary of Angela's salary history. Calomiris file. Without the Freedom of Information Act (FOIA) of 1967, all of this would have remained secret. "Girl Photog," *World-Telegram*, October 17, 1949, p. 10.

5. Long selections from Lenin's *The State and* Revolution, Stalin's *Foundations of Leninism, The History of the Communist Party of the Soviet Union (Bolsheviks), The Communist Manifesto,* and Georgi Dimitroff's address (*United Front Against Fascism*) to the 7th World Congress of the Communist International (1935) were read into the record of *Dennis vs. US.* Memo D. M. Ladd to the Director, October 19, 1949, pp. 3-4. Calomiris file.

6. Memo SAC Edward Scheidt, New York, to Director, October 19, 1949, pp. 3-4. Calomiris file.

7. "Temperamental" was often contemporary code for gay, at least for men. It probably does not have that connotation in Angela's case, though one can never be sure. SAC New York to Director, December 30, 1949, p. 2. Memos D. M. Ladd to Director, October 19, 1949, pp. 3-4; L. B. Nichols to Clyde Tolson, October 21, 1949. Calomiris file.

8. "Story of Girl FBI Undercover Agent Is Odd." *Washington Daily News* (October 19, 1949), p. 32.

9. Anthony Summers, *Official and Confidential: The Secret Life of J. Edgar Hoover,* p. 142. Memos D. M. Ladd to Director, October 19, 1949, p. 7; L. B. Nichols to Clyde Tolson, October 20, 1949, pp. 1- 2. Calomiris file.

10. Memos SAC Edward Scheidt, New York, to Director, October 19, 1949, p. 5; L. B. Nichols to Clyde Tolson, October 20, 1949, p. 2; L. B. Nichols to Clyde Tolson, October 21, 1949; SAC New York to Director, November 1, 1949; SAC New York to Director, November 7, 1949; SAC Edward Scheidt, New York, to Director, October 19, 1949, p. 5. Calomiris file.

11. *New York Daily Mirror,* October 23, 1949, p. 10. Memo SAC Edward Scheidt, New York, to Director, October 19, 1949, p. 6. Calomiris file.

12. Letter from Herbert E. Krugman, Research Associate, Yale University, Institute of International Studies, January 25, 1951. Calomiris Papers, LHA. *Red Masquerade,* pp. 48, 160, 179, 207, 179.

13. *Daily Worker,* April 10, 1949, p. 5. *Spartacus* became a major motion picture (1960) starring Kirk Douglas in the title role, directed by Stanley Kubrick, with screenplay by the blacklisted Dalton Trumbo working under a pseudonym. Fast, who had written for the Voice of America during World War II, joined the CPUSA in 1943, was imprisoned for three months, in 1950, for contempt of Congress for refusing to name names before HUAC, and left the Party in 1956. Jimmy Randall Grant, "Louis Francis Budenz: The Origins of a Professional Ex-Communist," PhD Dissertation (University of South Carolina, 2006), p. 239. Daniel J. Leab, *I Was a Communist for the FBI: The Unhappy Life and Times of Matt Cvetic.* Cvetic survives in the Warner Brothers movie version (1951) of his story, *I Was a Communist for the FBI.*

14. Memos SAC Edward Scheidt, New York, to Director, October 19, 1949, pp. 3, 5; L. B. Nichols to Clyde Tolson, October 20, 1949. Calomiris file.

15. *Dennis vs. US,* vol. 7, April 29, 1949, p. 5212; May 2, pp. 5308, 5311. Louis F. McCabe of Philadelphia, part of the legal defense team, represented Henry Winston, one of two African-American Communists serving on the National Board. Richard Gladstein had defended Harry Bridges of the ILWU against accusations that he was a member of the Communist Party, and (Bridges was Australian) had kept him from deportation. Here he was counsel for Robert Thompson, serving as New York State Party Chairman, recipient of the Distinguished Service Cross, the country's second highest military decoration, for his service in New Guinea during World War II, and Gus Hall, Ohio State Party Chairman.

16. Interview, Melva Wade, August 8, 2003, Accord, New York. Interview, Emma ("Jerre") Kalbas, April 10, 2004, New York City.

17. *Dennis vs. US,* vol. 6, April 11, 1949, pp. 4354, 4320. "FBI Aide Says Reds Taught Treason," *Times,* April 13, 1949. *I Led Three Lives,* pp. 294-295. See Veronica A. Wilson, "Red Masquerades: Gender and Political Subversion During the Cold War, 1945-1963," who has seen Philbrick's complete FBI file (the one sold by the FBI under the FOIA dates only from 1952) and says that Philbrick received $50/month, 1944-48, and $100/ month from 1948 through the appeals (pp. 157-158, note 30, 169-170, note 62). In 1951, the FBI gave him the cash sum of $1000 ($9158.92 in 2016) in appreciation of his loyal service (Wilson, p. 169, note 62).

18. *Dennis v. US,* vol. 8, May 12, 1949, pp. 5947, 5913-5914.

19. Letter J. Howard McGrath to the Secretary of the Treasury, November 27, 1950. Memos SAC New York to Director, March 27, 1951; SAC New York to Director, April 2, 1951. Calomiris File. *Dennis v. US,* vol. 6, April 25, 1949, pp. 4946, 4953.

20. Memo D. M. Ladd to Director, October 25, 1950. Calomiris file.

21. Memo D. M. Ladd to Director, October 25, 1950. Calomiris file.

22. Memos L. B. Nichols to Tolson, March-April 1951, March 1952, quoted in Veronica A. Wilson, "Red Masquerades: Gender and Political Subversion During the Cold War, 1945-1963," p. 170, note 63. See pp. 144-185, for a chapter dedicated to contrasting the careers of Calomiris and Philbrick. Letter (blacked out known to be Ogden Reid) to Hoover, February 5, 1952, enclosing an autographed copy of *I Led Three Lives*. "Herb, as you perhaps know, has just joined our retail advertising staff." Philbrick file.

23. Memo H. B. Fletcher to D. M. Ladd, November 7, 1949. Calomiris file.

CHAPTER 5

1. Memo H. B. Fletcher to D. M. Ladd, November 7, 1949. Calomiris file. Hoover is quoted in Anthony Summers, *Official and Confidential: The Secret Life of J. Edgar Hoover*, p. 191.

2. Memo H. B. Fletcher to D. M. Ladd, November 7, 1949. Calomiris file.

3. "Janny, Crones, Commies, & Co's," in Marcy Adelman, ed., *Long Time Passing: Lives of Older Lesbians* (Boston: Alyson, 1986), pp. 192-195.

4. Memo H. B. Fletcher to D. M. Ladd, November 7, 1949. Calomiris file. *Red Masquerade*, pp. 222-225.

5. *Red Masquerade*, pp. 239-240, 255. The defense of the National Board threatened bankruptcy for the Party. $250,000 in 1948 = $2,470,248.96 in 2016. http://www.bls.gov/data/inflation_calculator.htm

6. *Long Time Passing: Lives of Older Lesbians*, p. 193.

7. See Ellen Kay Trimberger, "Women in the Old and New Left: The Evolution of a Politics of Personal Life," *Feminist Studies*, vol. 5, no. 3 (Fall 1979), pp. 431-450, quoting Dorothy DeLacy, wife of Hugh DeLacy, New Deal Democratic Congressman and closet Communist; and Bettina Aptheker, "Keeping the Communist Party Straight, 1940s-1980s," *New Politics*, vol. 12, no. 1 (Summer 2008), pp.22-27.

8. Interview, Dr. Annette Rubinstein, April 15, 2005, New York City. Interview, Sol Libsohn, with Gary Saretzky, January 28, 2000, in "Remembering the 20th Century: An Oral History of Monmouth County," Monmouth County Library, http://www.visitmonmouth.com/oralhistory/bios/LibsohnSol.htm

9. Howard Fast, *Being Red* (Boston: Houghton Mifflin Company, 1990), p. 168. Chuck Rowland is quoted in Stuart Timmons, *The Trouble with Harry Hay, Founder of the Modern Gay Movement* (Boston: Alyson, 1990), p. 144.

10. The ONE National Gay and Lesbian Archives are part of the University of Southern California Libraries. Kepner is quoted in Timmons, p. 185. For Kepner as "ex-CP member," see Timmons, p. 204. See Millard in Kate Weigand, *Red Feminism: American Communism and the Making of Women's Liberation* (Baltimore: The Johns Hopkins University Press, 2001) and Millard's obit (1911-2010) in http://www.peoplesworld.org/feminist-pioneer-betty-millard-dies-at-98/

11. See Rosalyn Fraad Baxandall, *Words on Fire: The Life and Writing of Elizabeth Gurley Flynn* (New Brunswick, New Jersey: Rutgers University Press, 1987), and Bettina Aptheker, "Keeping the Communist Party Straight," for suspicions about Flynn's relationship with Dr. Equi. Also see Michael Helquist, *Marie Equi. Radical Politics and Outlaw Passions* (Corvallis, Oregon: Oregon State University Press, 2015).

12. See Janet Lee, *Comrades and Partners: The Shared Lives of Grace Hutchins and Anna Rochester* (Lanham, Maryland: Bowman & Littlefield Publishers, Inc., 2000), and Julia M. Allen, *Passionate Commitments: The Lives of Anna Rochester and Grace Hutchins* (Albany, New York: State University of New York Press, 2013). See Sam Tanenhaus, *Whittaker Chambers*, pp. 66, 342. Chambers and his bride shared a small apartment with another male/female couple. For the suspicion that all four were homosexual, see Tanenhaus, pp. 65, 343.

13. Hay was in San Francisco with his lover in 1934, actor Will Geer, who later played Grandpa Zebulon Tyler Walton in the 1970s TV series *The Waltons*. Quoted in John D'Emilio, *Sexual Politics, Sexual Communities: The Making of a Homosexual Minority in the United States, 1940-1970* (Chicago: The University of Chicago Press, 1983), p. 59.

14. Timmons, p. 159, and Will Roscoe, ed. *Radically Gay. Gay Liberation in the Words of Its Founder* (Boston: Beacon Press, 1996) for many of Hay's writings. See Roscoe, p. 55, note 6, for Article 10, section 5, of the 1938 *Constitution and By-Laws of the Communist Party of the United States of America*. In the years immediately following the Russian Revolution, homosexual acts were legalized by the Bolshevik government, but re-criminalized (with a penalty of five years hard labor) during the 1930s. The law, Article 121, was not repealed until 1993. See Dan Healey, *Homosexual Desire in Revolutionary Russia: The Regulation of Sexual and Gender Dissent* (Chicago: University of Chicago Press, 2001). It is said that Joseph Stalin feared homosexuals because he believed them to be in cahoots with the Fascists as part of a far Right homosexual conspiracy.

15. Timmons, p. 109, and Roscoe, p. 37. Mattachine's successful defense (1952) of one of its members, unjustly accused in such a sting, brought hundreds of gay people into the organization. See Timmons, pp. 163-168.

16. See Timmons, pp. 92, 159-161, for Hay's farewell to the Party, and 132, note, for Miriam Sherman's firing. For a history of local police Red Squads and their FBI allies, see civil rights lawyer Frank Donner, *Protectors of Privilege: Red Squads and Police Repression in Urban America* (Berkeley: University of California Press, 1990). For a detailed historical analysis of gay and leftist issues, see Leslie Feinberg, author of *Stone Butch Blues* (Ithaca, New York: Firebrand Books, 1993), "Lavender & Red: Lesbian, Gay, Bi, and Trans Pride Series," nos. 1-120, in *Workers World*, 2004-2008, and especially no. 40, "Harry Hay: Painful partings," June 28, 2005. http://www.workers.org/lavender-red/

17. Timmons, p. 185. Interview, Dr. Annette Rubinstein, April 15, 2005, New York City. Interview, Miriam Grossman Cohen, July 22, 2010, New York City.

18. Herbert Brownell Jr., Eisenhower's Attorney General, quoted in David K. Johnson, *The Lavender Scare*, p. 123.

19. For the story of "Andrew" and the firings at the State Department, see David K. Johnson, pp. 169-170, and Will Roscoe, p. 60. Memo H. B. Fletcher to D. M. Ladd, November 7, 1949. Calomiris file.

20. Senator Wherry is quoted in David K. Johnson, *The Lavender Scare*, pp. 37-38. Nicholas Von Hoffman is quoted in Timmons, p. 186.

21. Timmons, p. 69. Jack Lait and Lee Mortimer, *Washington Confidential* (Dell paperback edition, 1951; originally published in hardcover by Crown), p. 123. The book sold millions of copies in paperback. "…enticing them into a life of Lesbianism" is quoted in David K. Johnson, p. 80.

22. See Timmons, pp. 135 and 302, for Harry Hay's "Preliminary Concepts" which went into the organization of Mattachine. Hay's comments are collected in *A Homosexual Emancipation Miscellany, 1835-1952*, ed. Jonathan Ned Katz (New York: Arno Press, 1975). Harry and his wife Anita, of thirteen years, were divorced in September of 1951.

23. See Leslie Feinberg, "Lavender & Red: Lesbian, Gay, Bi, and Trans Pride Series," nos. 31-39 on Hay's early career. http://www.workers.org/lavender-red/ Hay had observed during a stay in New York City (1939-1942) Party tolerance for African-American and white gay men in the performing arts, especially for celebrities (Timmons, p. 109). He mentions Marc Blitzstein, composer of *The Cradle Will Rock*, which served as the basis for Tim Robbins' film *Cradle Will Rock* (1999)—where Cherry Jones as Hallie Flanagan, head of the short-lived Federal Theatre Project, explains to HUAC that Christopher Marlowe (1564-1593) was not a Communist.

24. For the whole story and the commitment of Mattachine to "accommodation and consensus" (p. 91), see John D'Emilio, *Sexual Politics, Sexual Communities*, pp. 75-91, and especially p. 85 for the threat, by David

"Nellie" Finn, to turn in names to the FBI. Harry Hay, who was summoned to a Los Angeles HUAC hearing in 1955, would make a comeback after Stonewall.

25. D'Emilio, pp. 87, 86. Rowland quoted in Timmons, p. 179.

26. *Red Masquerade*, p. 222

27. *Red Masquerade*, pp. 219-221. Interview, Nora E. North, May 5, 2006, New York City, who, as a child and daughter of journalist Joseph North, overheard conversations about the unreliability of gay and lesbian Communists.

28. *Red Masquerade*, pp. 208, 215. For the unnamed informant and "Klein, Rena—3/10/47," who lived at 47 Morton Street, Greenwich Village, see American Business Consultants/*Counterattack* Research Files, 1930-1968, Box 27, Tamiment Library, New York University. A review in the *New Leader* (November 27, 1950) of *Red Masquerade*, "An FBI Girl Inside the CP," called Ms. Klein "the little Ana Pauker of the West Side." Ana Pauker, a Jewish Romanian Communist, held a high position in her country's Party.

29. *Red Masquerade*, pp. 223-257.

30. *Daily Worker*, January 17, 1950. Lautner had numerous Hungarian Communist contacts. For that reason, he was suspected of involvement with Hungarian Laszlo Rajk, accused of being sympathetic to Tito in Yugoslavia, which in those harrowing postwar years resulted in Rajk's execution by Hungarian hardliners.

31. See Lautner in Herbert L. Packer, *Ex-Communist Witnesses: Four Studies in Fact Finding* (Stanford, California: Stanford University Press, 1962). "Sauce for the Commies, National Affairs," *Newsweek*, January 30, 1950, p. 22.

32. *Red Masquerade*, p. 262.

CHAPTER 6

1. The original title was *Undercover Girl*. Memos SAC Edward Scheidt, New York, to Director, October 19, 1949, p. 1; D. M. Ladd to Director, October 19, 1949, p. 5. Calomiris file. For Lippincott, see "Books: Philadelphia Renaissance," in *Time*, June 2, 1941. http://www.time.com/time/magazine/article/0,9171,790145,00.html

2. *Newsweek*, January 30, 1950, pp. 20-22. George Marion, *The Communist Trial: An American Crossroads* (New York: Fairplay Publishers, 1950), p. 119. Another measure of the fear abroad in the land was President Harry Truman giving the go-ahead to the Atomic Energy Commission, on January 31st, for the development of a hydrogen bomb. For a new history

of Judith Coplon's travails, see Marcia and Thomas Mitchell, *The Spy Who Seduced America. Lies and Betrayal in the Heat of the Cold War. The Judith Coplon Story* (Montpelier, Vermont: Invisible Cities Press, 2002).

3. "Sauce for the Commies, National Affairs," *Newsweek,* January 30, 1950, p. 22.

4. Memo, SAC Edward Scheidt to Director, February 1, 1950. Calomiris file.

5. Memo, SAC Edward Scheidt to Director, February 1, 1950. Calomiris file. According to an FBI internal memo, November 23, 1953, Angela was paid the total sum of $19,704.17 ($175,737.58 in 2016) for her Bureau services. http://www.bls.gov/data/inflation_calculator.htm/

6. Interview, Morry Baer, October 1, 2002, Whiting, New Jersey. Morry also told the story of being called, when she worked the Youth Division in Midtown, to a hotel in Times Square where there had been a report of young girls meeting older women for sex. On her way to the elevator, the desk clerk threatened her with "Hey, Miss, we don't allow dykes in here." She silenced him by showing her police badge. She called the FBI the "Fuller Brush Institute," and said they blew your cover all the time, would take your information for themselves, and louse you up any way they could. Whenever you started something, she continued, they'd take over because they wanted all the glory. Interview, Ruth Parish, French Jacky's lover of 40 years, October 2, 2003, Hallandale, Florida.

7. This story was told in my original interview with Morry, October 1, 2002, repeated with more detail in a phone interview, August 9, 2004, and confirmed by e-mail, July 6, 2009.

8. Interview, Ruth Parish, October 2, 2003, Hallandale, Florida. *Red Masquerade,* p. 82.

9. *Red Masquerade,* p. 257.

10. *Dennis v. US,* vol. 7, April 29, 1949, pp. 5216, 5220.

11. *Dennis v. US,* vol. 7, April 29, 1949, pp. 5220-5221, 5225, 5221. Italics mine.

12. *Dennis v. US,* vol. 7, April 29, 1949, pp. 5221, 5225.

13. *Dennis v. US,* vol. 7, May 2, 1949, p. 5278.

14. *Dennis v. US,* vol. 7, April 26, 1949, p. 5060. Harry Sacher was disbarred as a result of the trial. In 1954, the Supreme Court under Chief Justice Earl Warren overturned the New York disbarment order on the grounds that it was "unnecessarily severe." See Stanley I. Kutler, *The American Inquisition: Justice and Injustice in the Cold War* (New York: Hill and Wang, 1982), pp. 164-68. Earl Warren had been appointed by Eisenhower (1953) but proved unexpectedly liberal, presiding over the landmark *Brown v. Board of Education* (1954) ending segregation in public schools. Conservatives

called for his impeachment throughout the 1960s. For the Furriers Union, see Philip S. Foner, *The Fur and Leather Workers Union: A Story of Dramatic Struggles and Achievements* (Newark, NJ: Nordan Press, 1950).

15. See *Dennis v. US*, vol. 15, September 20, 1949, pp. 11680-11687, for Robeson. "...Communism to tales of sabotage and plots to bring the Red Army down through Canada to Detroit," in George Marion, *The Communist Trial*, p. 125.

16. See Introduction for Nicodemus in *Dennis v. US*, vol. 6, April 19, 1949, pp. 4804-4805. See Russell Porter, *New York Times*, April 23, 1949, pp. 1, 3; and *New York Sun*, April 22, 1949, pp. 1, 17. As we now know, the decline of Detroit would come later, and not at the hands of the Russians.

17. "Armed forays...," in George Marion, *The Communist Trial*, p. 125. Herbert Aptheker (1915-2003) was the author of *American Negro Slave Revolts* (1943) and the 7-volume *Documentary History of the Negro People*. In the 1950s, he was blacklisted and unable to work as a university lecturer, despite a Columbia University PhD and numerous publications. See *Dennis v. US*, vol. 14, August 22, 1949, pp. 10542-10545, for Aptheker; vol. 5, March 29, 1949, pp. 3639, 3646-47, for Budenz, who, in several days of testimony, divulged Communist plans to infiltrate heavy industry, plus news of secret training schools, and the "Aesopian language."

18. *Dennis v. US*, vol. 14, August 30, 1949, p. 10914; vol. 14, August 22, 1949, p. 10545.

19. *Dennis v. US*, vol. 7, April 29, p. 5256; April 27, p. 5071; May 2, 5315, 5316. Vol. 6, April 13, p. 4537; May 2, p. 5344; May 3, p. 5408. Medina took care of himself. Immediately after the 1949 trial, he left for a three-month vacation in Bermuda, and lived to be 102 (1888-1990). Also, years later, he explained to people at a social gathering that whenever he had looked at the spectators at the Communist trial, he had consciously forced himself to keep his eyes moving so that he wouldn't let himself be placed in a trance by the hypnotists that the Party might have placed in the courtroom. For his delusions, see Ellen Schrecker, *Many Are the Crimes*, p. 198, *author's note.

20. *Dennis v. US*, vol. 14, August 24, pp. 10653-10656. Harold R. Medina Papers, Seeley G. Mudd Manuscript Library, Princeton University, Carol E. Nathanson Affidavit, p. 38. My sincere thanks to Prof. Barbara J. Falk, Canadian Forces College and University of Toronto, for the Nathanson Affidavit, and many pages shared of Angela's trial testimony on cross-examination. Also see David Caute, *The Great Fear: The Anti-Communist Purge Under Truman and Eisenhower* (New York: Simon and Schuster, 1978), p. 189 for Janney.

21. *Dennis v. US*, vol. 6, April 19, 1949, p. 4695. See Russell Porter, "Jury Is Completed at Trial of 11 Reds," *New York Times*, March 19, 1949, pp. 1, 6. Carol E. Nathanson Affidavit, p. 23.

22. Carol E. Nathanson Affidavit, pp. 69, 84, 39. *The Miracle of the Bells*, from RKO, starred Fred MacMurray, Italian actress Alida Valli, Lee J. Cobb, and Frank Sinatra as the local priest.

23. Carol E. Nathanson Affidavit, p. 49.

24. Russell Porter, "Girl Aide of FBI Testifies of 7 Years as 'Communist'," *New York Times*, April 27, 1949, pp. 1, 11. *Herald Tribune*, April 26, 1949. Malcolm Logan, "Medina Slaps Down 'Insinuating' Queries," *New York Post*, May 2, 1949. Interview, Jonathan Ned Katz, speaking about his late mother, Phyllis Katz, December 28, 2009, New York City.

25. *Dennis v. US*, vol. 7, April 29, 1949, pp. 5254, 5219.

26. *Dennis v. US*, vol. 7, May 2, p. 5263.

27. *Dennis v. US*, vol. 7, May 2, p. 5258.

28. *Dennis v. US*, vol. 7, May 2, p. 5259.

29. *Dennis v. US*, vol. 7, May 2, p. 5260; May 3, p. 5439.

30. *Dennis v. US*, vol. 7, May 4, pp. 5453, 5455. Younglove testified at Foley Square that a Midwestern Party leader (not one of the defendants) had taught "that the ballot box was not the answer to bring about socialism, that it would have to come about by violent action" (p. 5471). See Peter L. Steinberg, *The Great "Red Menace: United States Prosecution of American Communists, 1947-1952* (Westport, CT: Greenwood Press, 1984) and David Caute, *The Great Fear*.

31. *Red Masquerade*, pp. 257, 258. Russell Porter, "Girl Aide of FBI Testifies of 7 Years as 'Communist'," April 27, 1949, p. 11.

32. See Kutler, *The American Inquisition*, and especially Chapter 6, "Kill the Lawyers" for the contempt citations and aftermath. Ruark, *Washington Daily News*, October 18, 1949. For other opinions, see Kutler, who quotes Supreme Court Justice Felix Frankfurter's recollection of Medina as "the most insufferable egotist by long odds who had appeared before us" (p. 267, note 21).

33. Memos SAC New York to Director, February 21, 1951; SAC New York to Director, September 8, 1958. Also D. M. Ladd to Director, February 17, 1951; SAC New York to Director, December 27, 1955. Calomiris file.

34. Teletype (Urgent), SAC Edward Scheidt, New York, to Director, August 31, 1950, pp. 1-2. Calomiris file. The Teachers Union (TU) should not be confused with the later American Federation of Teachers (AFT) and United Federation of Teachers (UFT). See Celia L. Zitron, *The New York City Teachers Union, 1916-1964: A Story of Educational and Social Commitment* (New York: Humanities Press, 1968); Clarence Taylor, *Reds at the Blackboard: Communism, Civil Rights, and the New York City Teachers Union* (New York: Columbia University Press, 2011); and Marjorie Heins, *Priests of Our Democracy: The Supreme Court, Academic Freedom, and the*

Anti-Communist Purge (New York: New York University Press, 2013). Louis Budenz obligingly testified against the eight teachers. Irving H. Saypol was appointed in 1952 to the New York State Supreme Court where he served until 1968.

35. The subpoenas are preserved in the Calomiris Papers, LHA. Regarding HUAC, see Teletype (Urgent), SAC Edward Scheidt, New York, to Director, April 26, 1951. Calomiris file. The Subversive Activities Control Board (SACB) was created by the Internal Security Act of 1950, or the McCarran Act, for the Senator from Nevada. For more on his career, see Michael J. Ybarra, *Washington Gone Crazy: Senator Pat McCarran and the Great American Communist Hunt.*

36. Memos SAC New York to Director, July 3, 1950; SAC Edward Scheidt, New York, to Director, February 21, 1951. Teletype (Urgent) SAC Edward Scheidt to Director, February 14, 1951, p. 4. Calomiris file. *Red Masquerade,* p. 80.

37. For IWO friends and members, see Arthur J. Sabin, *Red Scare in Court: New York versus the International Workers Order* (Philadelphia: University of Pennsylvania Press, 1993), p. 18. Sabin, Professor Emeritus of Law at the John Marshall Law School (Chicago) defined the IWO as, "with the exception of certain labor unions, the largest, most successful left-wing organization in modern American history" (p. 351).

38. Interview, Melva Wade, August 8, 2003, Accord, New York. Since Angela was given to exaggeration, it is well to remember that, according to *Red Masquerade,* she had diphtheria as a child and lost all her hair (p. 21), which could account for a bald spot. Teletype (Urgent) SAC Edward Scheidt, New York, to Director, February 14, 1951, p. 5. Calomiris file.

39. See Ellen Schrecker, *Many Are the Crimes,* p. 196, for witnesses the government wanted for the Foley Square trial who refused to testify, fearing the consequences of public exposure and the threat of retaliation. By 1955, Angela, too, wanted her former FBI handlers to protect her identity "in spite of past public testimony." Memo SAC Albany to Director, June 3, 1955, p. 3. Calomiris file.

CHAPTER 7

1. Michal R. Belknap, *Cold War Political Justice: The Smith Act, the Communist Party, and American Civil Liberties* (Westport, Connecticut: Greenwood Press, 1977) for the mental strain of undercover work, the drop-out rate, and why some stuck with the job (p. 36).

2. *Dennis v. US,* vol. 7, April 27, 1949, p. 5079; April 26, p. 5023. Letter SAC E. E. Conroy, New York, to Director, June 13, 1944, p. 1. Calomiris file. Membership lists were very dangerous. Years later, information provided by Angela on the West Mid-Town CP Club was used as proof that "Sarah Rose Plotkin" had been a Communist, and therefore "deportable on subversive grounds." Memo SAC, New York, to Director, December 27, 1957. Calomiris file. *Red Masquerade,* pp. 225, 161.

3. *Dennis v. US,* vol.7, April 26, pp. 5027-5028. Angela tells the story of Green dusting off his jacket in *Red Masquerade,* p. 255.

4. *Dennis v. US,* vol. 8, May 18, 1949, p. 6151

5. Green is quoted in Victor Navasky, *Naming Names,* p. 32.

6. For the Lautner scandal, as reported in *Newsweek,* January 30, 1950, see Chapter 6. *Red Masquerade,* p. 225.

7. *Dennis v. US,* vol. 7, April 27, 1949, pp. 5074-5075. Harry Raymond, "Mme. Jekyll and Miss Hyde," *Daily Worker,* April 29, 1949, p. 3.

8. Quoted in *Dennis v. US,* April 27, 1949, vol. 7, pp. 5074, 5064-5066. McGohey was appointed a judge to the federal bench by Harry Truman immediately after the trial (October 21, 1949). He served as a judge on the US District Court for the Southern District of New York from early 1950 until his death in July of 1972.

9. Nelson Frank, "Browder Rebuked By French Reds," *New York World-Telegram,* May 22, 1945, pp. 1, 5. Frank would later write a series of articles on informant/witness Elizabeth Bentley. The *Daily Worker* published Duclos a couple of days later, on May 24, 1945. This sequence caused Peggy Dennis, wife of the CP General Secretary Eugene Dennis, to ponder years later: "It was published by the commercial press here in our country while it was still being translated from the French for our leadership." See *The Autobiography of an American Communist* (Westport/Berkeley: Lawrence Hill & Co./Creative Arts Book Co., 1977), p. 162. For the complete Duclos text see http://permanentred.blogspot.com/2009/11/history-re-visited-on-dissolution-of.html

10. *Dennis v. US,* April 26, 1949, vol. 7, pp. 5054-5055. See Hoover's March 1947 speech before HUAC in Fred Jerome, *The Einstein File: J. Edgar Hoover's Secret War Against the World's Most Famous Scientist,* p. 100.

11. Dimitroff, Secretary General of the Comintern (1934-43), was a Bulgarian Communist found not guilty of setting the Berlin Reichstag fire of 1933. In Europe and the USA during the 1930s, the term "Popular Front" defined the alliance of leftist political groups (especially Communists) and liberals in the fight against Fascism.

12. *Dennis v. US,* vol. 7, April 26, 1949, p. 5055; April 27, 1949, p. 5079.

13. *Dennis v. US,* vol. 8, May 10, 1949, p. 5776; vol, 7, May 9, 1949,

p. 5685. The "Battle of Toledo" had resulted in injuries and loss of life. See Philip A. Korth and Margaret R. Beegle, *I Remember Like Today: the Auto-Lite Strike of 1934* (East Lansing, MI: Michigan State University Press, 1988).

14. *Dennis v. US*, vol. 7, April 27, 1949, pp. 5113, 5119, 5111. This was not the first time that books had been placed on trial to secure convictions against American radicals. The texts cited here had been used at the trial of Communists who ran a bookstore in Oklahoma City, charged in 1940 under the state's 1919 criminal syndicalism law. See Shirley and Wayne Wiegand, *Books on Trial: Red Scare in the Heartland* (Norman, OK: University. of Oklahoma Press, 2007). The IWW trials during World War I—also conspiracy trials with a number of defendants, in one case 101—were also based on the organization's literature. See *Many Are the Crimes*, p. 54, and Robert Justin Goldstein, *Political Repression in Modern America: From 1870 to 1976* (Urbana, IL: University of Illinois Press, 2001), especially pp. 115-121.

15. *Red Masquerade*, p. 11. After her husband's death, Joan Hall was interviewed for the PBS series *Nova*, February 5, 2002, on a show called "Secrets, Lies and Atomic Spies." For the entire transcript, see www.pbs.org/wgbh/nova/venona For Blanc's testimony, see *Dennis v. US*, vol. 8, May 17, 1949, pp. 6105, 6111. On the other hand, the late Joe Gelders, an American Communist, Professor of Physics at the University of Alabama in the 1930s, a supporter of the Southern Conference for Human Welfare and the National Committee for the Defense of Political Prisoners, had his life transformed by reading Stalin's *Foundations of Leninism*, according to his daughter, Marge Frantz, Professor Emeritus, University of California, Santa Cruz. Interview, February 26, 2006, Santa Cruz, California.

16. *Dennis v. US*, vol. 7, April 27, 1949, pp. 5082, 5114, 5117.

17. *Dennis v. US*, vol. 13, August 15, 1949, pp. 10138, 10145-10148, 10139; August 17, 1949, p. 10175. Ms. "Gretche" is spelled into the record by the prosecution (vol. 7, p. 5138) and by the defense as "Gretch" (vol. 13, p. 10138). Angela recalled her quoting Stalin on Communists who "are dedicated to the overthrow of capitalism and to the establishment of socialism" (p. 5138). See Martha Biondi, *To Stand and Fight: the Struggle for Civil Rights in Postwar New York City* (Cambridge, Massachusetts: Harvard University Press, 2003) on "Stretch" Johnson, who was "drawn to the Party's thesis that Black Americans constituted a nation" (p. 5).

18. *Dennis v. US*, vol. 7, April 27, 1949, pp. 5123, 5129.

19. *Dennis v. US*, vol. 7, April 27, 1949, p. 5049; April 28, 1949, p. 5174. Norma Abrams and Harry Schlegel, "Angela Unveils Big Red Plot to Run Transport," *New York Daily News*, April 29, 1949, pp. 3, 25.

20. *Red Masquerade*, p. 19, for Angela's gift for making people laugh. On the increasing numbers of women in the Communist Party and their promotion to fill gaps in the secondary leadership, see Maurice Isserman, *Which Side Were You On?The American Communist Party during the Second World War* (Urbana, Illinois: University of Illinois Press, 1993), p. 148, where he states: "By 1944 nearly half of all party members were women (compared to less than 10 percent in 1930, and just over 25 percent in 1936)."

21. *Dennis v. US*, vol. 7, April 26, 1949, p. 5024, where Angela methodically misspells "S-e-r-o-n" into the record, raising questions about how well they really knew each other. *Red Masquerade*, p. 48.

22. See *The Spy Who Seduced America*, pp. 101-114, and p. 58 for Judge Reeves. *Dennis v. US*, vol. 7, May 2, 1949, p. 5270; April 27, 1949, p. 5067.

23. See Mona Z. Smith, *Becoming Something: The Story of Canada Lee* (New York: Farrar, Straus & Giroux, 2004). Bernard DeVoto (1897-1955), a historian of the American West, wrote a column "The Easy Chair" for *Harper's* from 1935 until his death. DeVoto is quoted in *Official and Confidential. The Secret Life of J. Edgar Hoover*, pp. 172-173, which also provides the names of those under surveillance. For the FBI's war on DeVoto see Tom Knudson, "FBI Was Out to Get Freethinking DeVoto," *High Country News*, August 8, 1994 www.hcn.org/issues/13/407

24. *Chicago Tribune*, June 10, 1949. Saron is not named in *The Spy Who Seduced America*, but she is the "embassy employment applicant" referred to on p. 110. On May 25, 1956, Saron replies in a letter, on behalf of *The National Guardian*, to a request from Dr. Martin Luther King, Jr., in Montgomery, AL, for several issues of the publication with stories about Montgomery (Dr. Martin Luther King, Jr. Archive, Howard Gotlieb Archival Research Center, Boston University).

25. *The New York Daily News*, February 19, 1951, p. 3. See Memo, SAC E. E. Conroy, New York, to Director, December 14, 1944, p. 2, for Angela's good work in providing photos of local CP functionaries. Calomiris file.

26. *Red Masquerade*, pp. 59, 60-61. *Dennis v. US*, vol. 7, April 26, 1949, pp. 5029-5030, 5050; April 27, 1949, pp. 5099, 5105. See Marvin E. Gettleman, "Defending Left Pedagogy: U.S. Communist Schools Fight Back against the SACB and Lose (1953-1957)," *Reconstruction: Studies in Contemporary Culture*, vol. 8, no.1 (2008).

27. *Dennis v. US*, vol. 7, April 27, 1949, p. 5102.

28. Quoted in Fariello, *Red Scare*, p. 222.

29. "My Day," October 7, 1946.

30. *Dennis v. US*, vol. 6, April 22, 1949, pp. 4868-4869, for "Outline of Marxist-Leninist Fundamentals for Class Use and Self Study," State Education Commission Illinois District Committee, CPUSA, and April 25, p. 4946, for "$60 a month," previously cited in Chapter 4.

31. Harry Raymond, "Stoolie Swipes a Marxist Outline," *The Daily Worker*, April 26, 1949, pp. 2, 11. *Dennis v. US*, vol. 6, April 25, 1949, pp. 4888-4906; April 22, 1949, pp. 4875-4876, 4873.

CHAPTER 8

1. *Union Maid*'s classic refrain is "*Oh, you can't scare me, I'm sticking to the union, I'm sticking to the union 'til the day I die.*" http://www.woodyguthrie. org/Lyrics/Union_Maid.htm Copyright TRO-Ludlow Music, Inc. copyright@songways.com

2. *Red Masquerade*, p. 25.

3. The Wagner Act for its sponsor Senator Robert F. Wagner (D-NY). For a dramatic history of those times, see Philip Dray, *There Is Power in a Union. The Epic Story of Labor in America* (New York: Doubleday, 2010); and Robert J. Goldstein, *Political Repression in Modern America: From 1870 to 1976*. Also see Walter Linder, "The Great Flint Sit-Down Strike Against General Motors 1936-37," http://www-rohan.sdsu.edu/~rgibson/ flintstrike.html For a closer look at opposition to unions, see Robert Michael Smith, *From Blackjacks to Briefcases: A History of Commercialized Strikebreaking and Unionbusting in the United States* (Athens, OH: Ohio University Press, 2003).

4. *Red Masquerade*, p. 25. See Chapter 2 for Mrs. Roosevelt's close friendship with Esther Lape and her life partner Elizabeth Read.

5. *Red Masquerade*, pp. 49-50.

6. *Dennis v. US*, vol. 7, April 29, 1949, p. 5222. She jokingly recounted in *Red Masquerade* how she had spoken out of turn when asked to join the union. "What's in it for me?" she wanted to know from comrades who had expected a commitment to "the cause of the toiling workers" (p. 73). Papers of the United Office and Professional Workers of America (UOPWA), 1929-1957, are held at the Tamiment Library, New York University; the Walter P. Reuther Library, Wayne State University, Detroit; and the Charles E. Young Research Library, UCLA.

7. *I Led Three Lives*, pp. 279-280. Philbrick worked as a minor advertising executive for a New England movie theater chain. UOPWA Papers, Tamiment Library.

8. See Martha Biondi, *To Stand and Fight: The Struggle for Civil Rights in Postwar New York City*, p. 32. A motion for acquittal was granted when Albert Einstein offered to appear at the trial as a character witness for Dr. Du Bois. See Fred Jerome and Rodger Taylor, *Einstein on Race and Racism* (New Brunswick, NJ: Rutgers University Press, 2005), pp. 119-120. Also see Bert

Cochran, *Labor and Communism. The Conflict that Shaped American Unions* (Princeton, NJ: Princeton University Press, 1977) and especially Chapters 10-12, for Communists and the CIO. Of the 11 unions that were expelled or resigned, only UE and the ILWU remain in existence today.

9. For 300,000 Michigan war workers who lost their jobs, see Bill Goode, *Infighting in the UAW. The 1946 Election and the Ascendancy of Walter Reuther.* Contributions in Labor Studies, No. 44 (Westport, CT: Greenwood Press, 1994), p. 73.

10. *Dennis v. US,* vol. 7, May 4, 1949, p. 5465, for Younglove, who would later testify for the prosecution at the second New York trial (1951) of the CP leadership; and for Yolanda Hall, vol. 12, July 28, 1949, p. 9268. Bendix Aviation dated from 1929, when it went from manufacturing brake systems for cars and trucks to hydraulic systems and other products for aircraft. World War II was a boom time for Bendix.

11. See Goldstein, *Political Repression in Modern America,* and especially Chapter 9, "Truman-McCarthyism, 1946-1954."

12. The reading (*Dennis v. US,* vol. 7, April 28, 1949, pp. 5155-5171) is from *History of the Communist Party of the Soviet Union (Bolsheviks).* The 1954 film *On the Waterfront* (Columbia Pictures), shot across the river in Hoboken, NJ, would immortalize that time and place. A series of newspaper articles—"Crime on the Waterfront" (November, 1948-February, 1949)— had won *New York Sun* reporter Malcolm Johnson the 1949 Pulitzer Prize for Local Reporting, and served Budd Schulberg as the basis for his screenplay. The film's director, Elia Kazan, had been a friendly witness before HUAC (1952) and named names, as had Budd Schulberg. See a recent re-edition of Johnson's articles in *On the Waterfront: The Pulitzer Prize-Winning Articles That Inspired the Classic Movie and Transformed the New York Harbor,* ed. Haynes Johnson (New York: Chamberlain Bros., 2005). *Dennis v. US,* vol. 7, April 26, 1949, p. 5023.

13. *Red Masquerade,* p. 178.

14. The ILA, under its president Joe Ryan, is not to be confused with the leftist West Coast ILWU, whose leader was Harry Bridges. For "The 1948 New York Strike," see Colin J. Davis, *Waterfront Revolts. New York and London Dockworkers, 1946-61* (Urbana, IL: University of Illinois Press, 2003), Chapter 4, pp. 84-108.

15. *Red Masquerade,* pp. 182-183.

16. For Red Scare propaganda based on the use of "loaded language" to describe "commonplace political behavior," see Roger Keeran, *The Communist Party and the Auto Workers Unions* (Bloomington: Indiana University Press, 1980). For example, "non-Communists join unions; Communists 'infiltrate' or 'invade' them" (p. 11). *Dennis v. US,* vol. 7, April 28, 1949, p. 5177.

17. *Dennis v. US*, vol. 7, April 28, 1949, p. 5178.

18. *Red Masquerade*, pp. 179, 201. Despite the postwar tensions between Stalin and Josip Broz Tito (1892-1980), one of the prime movers behind the Non-Aligned Movement, and Yugoslavia's independent stand on important issues, it is portrayed here as part of an international conspiracy threatening the US. Those present in the courtroom would also have recalled that the French liner *Normandie* had caught fire and capsized (1942) at Pier 88, one of Angela's recruiting assignments, a luxury liner passenger ship terminal.

19. *Red Masquerade*, p. 178.

20. *Dennis v. US*, vol. 8, May 18, 1949, pp. 6123. The American contingent, the Abraham Lincoln Brigade, fought in several major battles against Francisco Franco's Nationalist/Fascist forces. The Brigade made the US Attorney General's List of Subversive Organizations, and survives today in the Abraham Lincoln Brigade Archives (ALBA) and Friends and Family of the Abraham Lincoln Brigade (FFALB). Lawrence (Larry) Cane authored a memoir, *Fighting Fascism in Europe: The World War II Letters of an American Veteran of the Spanish Civil War* (New York: Fordham University Press, 2003). Defendants Robert Thompson and John Gates also fought in Spain for the Republic

21. *Dennis v. US*, vol. 8, May 18, 1949, pp. 6135-6136, 6144.

22. For Julie Katz, aka O'Donnell, see *Dennis v. US* vol. 8, May 18, 1949, p. 6136; and for Angela Calomiris as "Angela Cole," vol. 7, April 26, 1949, pp. 5025-5026, 5038. A copy of the certificate she received on completion of the course under that name is in her FBI file. Calomiris file. For Cummings, *Dennis v. US*, vol. 7, May 9, 1949, pp. 5708-5709. In her autobiography *Close to My Heart* (New York: Quantuck Lane Press, 2005), pp. 64-65, long-time activist Dorothy Sterling made clear that "Party membership was hardly a plus on a job application." Ms. Sterling's section organizer, in the 1930s, advised her to choose a pseudonym "so that if the FBI penetrated the files at 12th Street [Party headquarters] (they did), the agents would not be able to identify us." After a couple of years, she added, her pseudonym "was dropped" in Party circles, and her "real name used instead." Ms. Sterling authored *Freedom Train: The Story of Harriet Tubman* (New York: Scholastic, 1954) and other histories of African-American women. She and her husband were active members of the Port Chester-Rye branch of the NAACP.

23. *Dennis v. US*, vol. 7, May 9, 1949, pp. 5697-5698.

24. *Dennis v US*, vol. 12, July 28, 1949, p. 9277; August 1, 1949, pp. 9396, 9403.

25. *Dennis v. US*, vol. 13, August 15, p. 10218, for Johnson; and vol. 7, April 29, 1949, p. 5329, for Angela.

26. *Dennis v. US*, vol. 13, August 17, 1949, pp. 10270, 10331, 10328.

27. *Red Masquerade*, p. 174. According to Martin Broms, son of Wilbur Broms, his father was pursued by the FBI for years after. Phone interview, Martin Broms, October 3, 2011, New York City. See "1934 Campus Red Testifies at NY Trial," *The Minnesota Daily* (The University of Minnesota), August 19, 1949, p. 1, and Carl Ross, *Radicalism in Minnesota, 1900-1960: A Survey of Selected Sources* (Minneapolis: Minnesota Historical Society Press, 1994). Also see Colette A. Hyman, *Staging Strikes: Workers' Theatre and the American Labor Movement* (Philadelphia: Temple University Press, 1997) and "Culture as Strategy: Popular Front Politics and the Minneapolis Theatre Union, 1935-39." http://collections.mnhs.org/MNHistoryMagazine/articles/52/v52i08p294-306.pdf

28. *Dennis v. US*, vol. 8, May 13, 1949, pp. 5961-5962, 5964. Park Drop Forge originally made engine parts, crankshafts, camshafts, and other components used in large diesel locomotives, trucks, and buses. The present company, Park-Ohio, was created through the 1967 merger of Park Drop Forge Co. and Ohio Crankshaft Co. Following a 1983 strike by UAW workers, one Cleveland plant was moved to Alabama, and another hired "replacement workers." See http://www.answers.com/topic/park-ohio-industries-inc#ixzz1XreGwt7C

29. *Dennis v. US*, vol. 8, May 13, 1949, p. 5974, 5977. R. J. Thomas was described as "bumbling, good-natured," while George Addes was the one to watch out for. See "Labor: Who's George For?" *Time*, March 18, 1946 http://www.time.com/time/printout/0,8816,934440,00.html Addes was quoted as saying that he would back Communists or Republicans if it would help the union.

30. *Dennis v. US*, vol. 8, May 13, 1949, p. 5978; May 16, 1949, p. 5982. A socialist in his youth, Walter Reuther spent considerable time in the Soviet Union. He purged American Communists from the UAW, which he headed until his death (1970), and in the 1950s forged a more moderate labor movement. See Keeran, *The Communist Party and the Auto Workers Unions*, for a detailed history, and Bert Cochran, *Labor and Communism*. Nat Ganley (né Nathan Kaplan in New York City), a life-long union organizer, was one of six individuals brought to trial and convicted under the Smith Act in Michigan (1954). His papers are in the Archives of Labor History and Urban Affairs, Walter P. Reuther Library, Wayne State University, Detroit.

31. Ellen Schrecker, in *Many Are the Crimes*, p. 228, remarks the number of African Americans engaged by the FBI for surveillance. See David Caute, *The Great Fear: the Anti-Communist Purge Under Truman and Eisenhower*, "Appendix A," pp. 547-550, for a list of "Undercover Agents," including some well-paid African Americans: Lola Bella Holmes in Chicago, Timothy Evans, Jr. in Oakland, and Berry Cody in Detroit, among others. *Dennis v. US*, vol. 6, April 22, 1949, p. 4805, for Nicodemus.

CHAPTER 9

1. From McKay's speech at the Fourth Congress (1922) of the Communist International (Comintern) in Moscow, as quoted in Wayne F. Cooper, *Claude McKay. Rebel Sojourner in the Harlem Renaissance* (Baton Rouge, Louisiana: Louisiana State University Press, 1987), Chapter 6, "The Journey to Russia, 1922-1923," p. 178. Also see William J. Maxwell, *New Negro, Old Left: African-American Writing and Communism Between the Wars* (New York: Columbia University Press, 1999) for McKay in Moscow. The Fourth Congress (1922) also marked the formation of a "Negro Commission," some of whose papers are housed in the Schomburg Center for Research in Black Culture, the New York Public Library, as "Documents from the Comintern Archives on African Americans, 1919-1929."

2. *Dennis v. US,* vol. 6, May 3, 1949, pp. 5408-5409, for Angela's testimony, and vol. 14, August 22, 1949, p. 10570, for George Crockett examining defense witness Abner Berry, Harlem editor of the *Daily Worker.*

3. See Ovid Demaris, *The Director: an Oral Biography of J. Edgar Hoover,* for interviews with a variety of people soon after Hoover's death (1972), most of whom affirm that "Hoover was opposed to civil rights" (p. 210). The interview with his chauffeur, James E. Crawford, "The First Black Special Agent," is revealing (pp. 32-39). The identification of King with Communism is quoted from an internal FBI memo (1963) in "The FBI's War on King" http://americanradioworks.publicradio.org/features/king/d4.html

4. During the war, the slogan "Double V," for victory against fascism abroad and racism at home, had raised many hopes in the African-American community. See Biondi, *To Stand and Fight: the Struggle for Civil Rights in Postwar New York City,* pp. 11, 19. Letter SAC Edward Scheidt, New York, to Director, September 17, 1946, p. 2. Calomiris file. $180.00 in 1946 = $2,217.56 in 2016. http://www.bls.gov/data/inflation_calculator.htm The same letter (p. 1) confirmed that Angela ("informant") had been contacted by agents of the New York Field Division 11 times during the three-month period, and had submitted 29 typewritten reports, a total of 34 pages.

5. *Red Masquerade,* pp. 122, 127, 119.

6. *Red Masquerade,* pp. 119, 19, 126, 127.

7. See Biondi, *To Stand and Fight: the Struggle for Civil Rights in Postwar New York City,* for a civil rights struggle that predates Martin Luther King by a generation. *Red Masquerade,* p. 17. Regarding the ethnic composition of the Lower East Side when Angela was a child (1920s), "Negro and Spanish children" would have been so rare as to be non-existent.

8. *Red Masquerade,* pp. 199-200, 189, 240-241. The poll tax, money that

African Americans had to pay at election time for the right to vote, was only eliminated by the ratification of the 24th Amendment to the Constitution (1964). Proposed restrictions on voting eligibility, by demanding picture and signed IDs, are attempts to revive discriminatory practices. See John Lewis, "A Poll Tax by Another Name," *New York Times*, Op-Ed, August 26, 2011.

The Civil Rights Congress (1946-1956) grew out of the merger of groups with ties to the CPUSA, including the International Labor Defense (ILD), which had defended the Scottsboro Boys, the nine young African-American men accused of raping two white women on an Alabama freight train, in 1931, whose convictions were later overturned by the US Supreme Court. The CRC, under William Patterson, became a victim of Cold War anti-communism and government repression. See Gerald Horne, *Communist Front? The Civil Rights Congress, 1946-1956* (Rutherford, New Jersey: Fairleigh Dickinson University Press, 1987).

9. *Red Masquerade*, pp. 189, 121, 118, 119. See Mark Naison, *Communists in Harlem during the Depression* (Urbana: Univ. of Illinois Press, 1983), p. xvi, and Chapter 1, "The Roots of Party Growth in Harlem." "White chauvinism" was taken very seriously by the CPUSA. See Hassan Mahamdallie, "To Fight Chauvinism Everywhere," *Socialist Review* (July 2005) for a recent interview with Naison on the re-publication of his book. http://www.socialistreview. org.uk/article.php?articlenumber=9471

10. See, for the 1946 murders in Georgia, Laura Wexler, *Fire in a Canebrake: the Last Mass Lynching in America* (New York: Scribner, 2003). *Red Masquerade*, p. 189. The lynching of African-Americans continued into the 1960s. See "The Lynching Calendar: African-Americans Who Died in Racial Violence in the United States during 1865-1965." www.autopsis.org/ foot/lynch/html Also see Carol Anderson, *Eyes Off the Prize: the United Nations and the African-American Struggle for Human Rights, 1944-1955* (New York: Cambridge University Press, 2003). Federal anti-lynching legislation, proposed several times during the first half of the 20th century, was never passed by the US Congress.

11. *Dennis v. US*, vol. 15, September. 20, pp. 11707-11708. Henry Winston (1911-1986) was born in Hattiesburg, Mississippi, grew up there and in Kansas City, Missouri, and left school early to help support his family. He remained an active force in the American Communist Party until his death. Convicted along with the other defendants, Henry Winston served his time in the Federal Prison at Danbury, Connecticut, where failure to diagnose a brain tumor caused him to lose his sight.

12. From a discussion around the testimony of Arthur Schusterman, former organizer for the Textile Workers Union (TWU, CIO), on the

witness stand to refute Nicodemus' statement about the Red Army attack on Detroit, in *Dennis v. US*, vol. 14, August 30, 1949, p. 10914. Angela is vol. 7, May 3, 1949, p. 5409. Medina to Henry Winston is vol. 15, September 20, 1949, p. 11708.

13. Born in Dawson, Georgia, Ben Davis (1903-1964) spent his youth in Atlanta, where his father was founder and editor of the *Atlanta Independent*. He graduated from Morehouse College Academy, Amherst College (Massachusetts), and Harvard Law. He served his time in the Federal Prison at Terre Haute, Indiana, and filed suits in US District Court to stop the segregation of African-American inmates in federal penitentiaries. Upon his release, he was charged with failing to register as a Communist in violation of the Internal Security Act of 1950 (the McCarran Act) but died before the case against him came to court. *Red Masquerade*, p. 52.

14. The integrated Georgia protest led by Herndon had marched to the county courthouse to demand relief and unemployment insurance. See the Angelo Herndon indictment, 1932, p. 2, Mary Cornelia Barker papers, Manuscript, Archives, and Rare Book Library, Robert W. Woodruff Library, Emory University, Atlanta, Georgia. http://larson.library.emory.edu/marbl/DigProjects/swh/imges/Barker%20528/0528-055.html Also see Herndon's prison autobiography *Let Me Live* (Ann Arbor: University of Michigan Press, 2006; orig. ed., 1937). Benjamin J. Davis, *Communist Councilman from Harlem. Autobiographical Notes Written in a Federal Penitentiary* (New York: International Publishers, 1969), p. 75.

15. See http://en.wikipedia.org/wiki/Angelo_Herndon for Herndon going to Atlanta to organize UCs, and http://en.wikipedia.org/wiki/Henry_Winston, for a young Winston (age nineteen) in the UC in 1930. Also see Manning Marable and Leith Mullings, *Let Nobody Turn Us Around: Voices of Resistance, Reform, and Renewal*. (Lanham, Maryland: Rowman & Littlefield, 2003) and Danny Lucia, "Bringing Misery Out of Hiding. The Unemployed Movement of the 1930s," *International Socialist Review (ISR)*, Issue 71, May-June 2010 www.isreview.org/issues/71/feat-unemployed.shtml#top

The first UC demonstration (March 6, 1930) drew 500,000 people in twenty-five cities across the country. For Nowell and Detroit UCs, see August Meier and Elliott Rudwick, *Black Detroit and the Rise of the UAW* (New York: Oxford University Press, 1979), p. 46. In 1932, the UC and the Auto Workers Union (a forerunner of the UAW) led the Ford Hunger March, which marked the beginning of the unionization of American auto companies that took place later in the decade.

16. See Philip Dray, *There Is Power in a Union: The Epic Story of Labor in America*, p. 477, for Bennett, and *Black Detroit and the Rise of the UAW*,

p. 32 note, for Nowell before HUAC, and throughout for his allegiance to the UAW's Homer Martin, who joined the American faction of Jay Lovestone (Communist Party [Opposition]), which had taken its cue from Soviet power struggles that led to the Great Purges (1936-38). Stalin emerged victorious from the disaster, including the execution (1938) of the Lovestoneite favorite Nikolai Bukharin.

17. *Dennis v. US*, vol. 6, April 22, 1949, p. 4863; vol. 6, April 25, pp. 4918, 4921. *Red Masquerade*, p. 11. "Just watching Communists," from Henry Raymond, "Stoolie Swipes a Marxist Outline," *The Daily Worker*, April 26, 1949, p. 2. In *Red Masquerade*, Angela was given time to think over the FBI's offer, and came to the conclusion that it was a request that, in wartime, no one could refuse (pp. 16, 30).

18. *Dennis v. US*, vol. 8, May 12, 1949, pp. 5890, 5893-5894. As a member of Food and Tobacco Workers, Cummings worked for Archer Daniels Midland Company (ADMC), makers of food and animal feed products. *Dennis v. US*, May 9, 1949, vol. 7, pp. 5686; May 12, 1949, vol. 8, pp. 5896, 5945, 5879. See David Caute, *The Great Fear*, p. 119, for Cummings, described as "unscrupulous and mendacious," who earned a total of $11,023.25 (by 1951) for his FBI service. $11,023.25 = $101,853.13 in 2016. http://www.bls.gov/data/inflation_calculator.htm

19. *Dennis v. US*, vol. 7, April 27, p. 5066; vol. 7, April 29, 1949, pp. 5222, 5226. *Red Masquerade*, p. 257. Herbert Philbrick also said the Party told him to join the union (UOPWA) but denied any anti-labor bias in his reports to the FBI. See Walter Arm, "Philbrick Tells of Spying on Union for F.B.I.," *New York Herald Tribune*, April 12, 1949, pp. 1, 28; and "Philbrick Kept Eye on Reds in Wallace Party. Tells Trial He Also Joined Civil Rights Congress. Denies He Spied on Labor," *New York Herald Tribune*, April 13, 1949, pp. 1.

20. See Philip Dray, *There Is Power in a Union: The Epic Story of Labor in America*, and especially pp. 480-481, for the La Follette Committee. *Dennis v. US*, vol. 6, April 19, p. 4699. Robert M. La Follette, Jr., a Republican and Progressive Party Senator (1925-1947), was a champion of organized labor. Had his 1946 reelection bid been successful, the country would have been spared Joseph McCarthy, who beat La Follette in the Wisconsin Republican primary by a narrow margin, spent 10 years in the US Senate, and died of acute hepatitis exacerbated by alcoholism at age 48. For a closer look at the business community and unions, see Robert Michael Smith, *From Blackjacks to Briefcases: A History of Commercialized Strikebreaking and Unionbusting in the United States*.

21. *Dennis v. US*, vol. 6, April 18, p. 4678; April 19, pp. 4706, 4693, 4710, 4694-4695. Also see "Witness Says Reds Dropped Things at Him," *New York*

Sun, April 19, 1949. See Dray, *There Is Power In a Union*, p. 477, for "private army and extensive spy network." Richard Gladstein's papers, chronicling his legal career (1930-1969), are in The Southern California Library for Social Studies and Research, Los Angeles, CA.

22. *Dennis v. US*, vol. 6, April 25, 1949, pp. 4902-4904, for that section in Herron's "Outline of Marxist-Leninist Fundamentals for Class Use and Self Study"; April 18, 1949, pp. 4619, 4629.

23. *Dennis v. US*, vol. 6, April 18, 1949, pp. 4629, 4631. A resolution was passed in 1928 at the Sixth Congress of the Comintern recognizing a "Black Belt Nation" in the American South, based on majority population. American Communists accepted the commitment to African-American liberation and full racial equality alongside working-class organizing. See Biondi, *To Stand and Fight*, and Thomas D. Musgrave, *Self-Determination and National Minorities* (Oxford: Clarendon Press, 1997), and especially "Self-Determination and the Bolsheviks," pp. 17-22.

24. *Sun*, April 20, 1949, pp. 1, 8. Russell Porter, "Plan for Negro Nation in U.S. Is Told by Red Trial Witness," as part of a "Plot for Rebellion and New Regime in Southern States," *New York Times*, April 19, 1, 14. Walter Arm, "U.S. Reds' Plan For Negro State In South Is Told," *New York Herald Tribune*, April 19, 1949, p. 1. *Dennis v. US*, vol. 8, May 10, 1949, p. 5777.

25. *Communist Councilman from Harlem*, p. 79. Biondi, *To Stand and Fight*, pp. 46-47. The Black Belt Nation is an idea that refuses to die. 1960s Black Nationalists, comparing African-American ghettos to third world colonies, embraced the concept, and the 21st century continues to grapple with the problem of self-determination. See the Malcolm X Grassroots Movement, Kamau Franklin, "The New Southern Strategy—The Politics of Self-Determination in the South—A Discrete Public Journal—Entry 1," September 11, 2011 http://mxgm.org/grassroots-thinking-the-new-southern-strategy/htm

26. Nowell died May 24, 1955. See List of "Individuals Previously in the Program. Espionage and International Security Investigations," June 3, 1955. Calomiris File. Caute, *The Great Fear*, pp. 129, 207. Nowell testified at the Baltimore Smith Act trial (March, 1952).

27. *Red Masquerade*, p. 252.

28. The Farm Security Administration (originally the Resettlement Administration) was instituted in 1937 as part of the New Deal to combat American rural poverty during the Great Depression. Some of its photographers were connected with the Photo League.

29. Caute, p. 129, for Nowell's new job.

CHAPTER 10

1. "I Spied on the U.S. Communists," p. 26. This rehearsal for *Red Masquerade*, which contained much of the same material, was billed as "A *True* Book-Length Feature" (pp. 25-27, 120-132). *True* paid $2,250 ($22,428.67 in 2016) for the article, of which Angela's agents, Russell & Volkening, gave her $1,012.50 ($10,092.90 in 2016). See note about check for $1,012.50, January 6, 1950. Calomiris Papers, LHA. Part of the Fawcett media empire, *True* (1937-1976), the first men's magazine with over one million in circulation, published Angela because hers was a "true" story. The theory was that men preferred factual material to fiction. From the 1930s on, Fawcett published at various times *True Confessions*, *Daring* Detective, and *Woman's Day*. Memo SAC P. E. Foxworth, New York, to Director, March 10, 1942.

2. *Dennis v. US*, vol. 7, April 26, 1949, p. 5023. "RESUME," undated, known to be mid-1950s. Calomiris Papers, LHA. Berenice Abbott (1898-1991) was a lesbian who spent the 1920s in Paris. In New York, she became the long-time companion of art critic Elizabeth McCausland (1899-1965), who authored the text for *Changing New York*. There is a new edition (New York, Dover Publications, 1973) under the title *New York in the Thirties*. Both Abbott and McCausland were on the Photo League's Advisory Board from the late 1930s.

3. For Hal Phyfe (1892-1968), see biographical notes in "Broadway Photographs. Art Photography and the American Stage 1900-1930," by David S. Shields at http://broadway.cas.sc.edu.

4. E-mail from Walter Rosenblum (1919-2006), long-time President of the Photo League, to author, December 20, 2004, New York, where he also stated that Sid Grossman had been at the heart of his own teaching philosophy, in a long career at Brooklyn College, CUNY. See Jane Livingston, *The New York School. Photographs 1936-1963* (New York: Stewart, Tabori & Chang, Inc. and Professional Imaging, Eastman Kodak Company, 1992). See *Photo Notes*, the League's publication, February 1939 and May 1940. Rare extant issues of *Photo Notes* were compiled into one volume by the Visual Studies Workshop (Rochester, NY, 1977). All references are to that volume.

5. For Peggy Vaughn, see *Photo Notes*, June 1942, p. 1, and Interview, Ruth Parish, October 2, 2003, Hallandale, Florida. Her address appeared in a new batch of Angela Calomiris' Unprocessed Papers, LHA. The description of the Photo League school, 31 East 21st Street, is quoted in the League's publication *Photo Notes*, May 1942, p. 3, from an April article in *PM (Picture Magazine)*, a leftist New York City newspaper, 1940-1948, bankrolled by the Chicago millionaire Marshall Field III.

Information about costs comes from the Photo League's fairly extensive FBI file (Headquarters File #100-114718), "General Report on the Photo League" (June 2, 1942), probably written by Angela herself. Most reports in the Photo League surveillance file bear the New York File #100-79069, and there was also an early New York Investigative File #100-392. E-mail from Sonia Handelman Meyer, July 7, 2009, Charlotte, North Carolina, whose book *Into the Light* (Raleigh, NC: Boson Books, 2009) collects work from her Photo League period.

6. *Red Masquerade,* pp. 23-24. *True: The Man's Magazine,* April 1950, p. 26. Note from Eleanore La Grotta, Bronx, NY. Calomiris Papers, LHA. Angela was sent out of the city as a poor child to fresh air camps, and, according to her FBI file (March 10, 1942, and December 11, 1947), subsequently found employment there.

7. See *Photo Notes,* May 1942, p. 5; June 1942, p. 1; and December 1943, pp. 3, for Marian Hille back in the job of Executive Secretary, around the same time the Museum of Modern Art in New York City opened its new Photographic Center, at 9 W. 54th Street (pp. 1-2). Also see long-time Photo Leaguer George Gilbert's photo of Angela, at a party in 1946, posed with an arm around Jacob Deschin, at that time photo page editor for the *New York Times,* in *The Radical Camera: New York's Photo League, 1936-1951,* eds. Mason Klein and Catherine Evans (New Haven: Yale University Press, 2011), Fig. 56, p. 76. Several former Photo Leaguers insisted that Angela was never around the League after the war. Phone interview, Miriam Cohen, April 13, 2010. New York City. Interviews, Sonia Handelman Meyer and Ida Wyman, April 27, 2012, Columbus, Ohio.

8. See *Photo Notes,* February 1943, pp. 2-3, for the "War Production Group." Also see Michael Denning, *The Cultural Front. The Laboring of American Culture in the Twentieth Century* (London, New York: Verso, 1996), p. 147, for the CCYCW.

9. *Red Masquerade,* p. 134.

10. A "photography of social betterment" was what the Photo League's spiritual predecessor Lewis W. Hine (1874-1940)—who photographed tenements and sweatshops, children working in factories, and Ellis Island immigrants—called it. Now recognized as one of America's greatest pioneering photographers, Hine left his photograph collection to the League because no one else wanted it. With the demise of the Photo League, the collection went to the George Eastman House in Rochester, New York. The Museum of Modern Art had turned it down. *Red Masquerade,* pp. 76, 77. See Chapter 7 for a published photo of Leona Saron, and Chapter 6 for portraits of IWO members. Memos SAC P. E. Foxworth, New York, to Director, September 19, 1942; SAC E. E. Conroy, New York, to Director, December14, 1944. Calomiris file.

11. *Red Masquerade,* p. 94. Calomiris Papers, LHA. John Reed, author of *Ten Days that Shook the World* (1919), lived in Croton with Louise Bryant. Joe North, "a leading writer for *The New Masses,*" was the first Party member Angela named in *Red Masquerade* (p. 47). Indictments in the second New York Smith Act trial were issued immediately after the Supreme Court rejected the appeal of those convicted in the 1949 trial, where Angela testified. Bittelman was among the Party leaders indicted, tried, and convicted, and served a three-year federal prison term.

12. Adolf Elwyn was a professor of neuroanatomy at Columbia University, who sent his children to the progressive Hessian Hills School in Croton. Albert Eugene Kahn (1912-79) was a journalist, author, and the publisher of former Communist and paid government witness Harvey Matusow's confessional *False Witness* (1955). Richard Boyer (1903-73) wrote for *The New Yorker* and authored a biography of John Brown. He was called before the Senate Internal Security Subcommittee (McCarran Committee) during a 1956 inquiry into the New York City press. See Michael J. Ybarra, *Washington Gone Crazy: Senator Pat McCarran and the Great American Communist Hunt.*

13. *Red Masquerade,* pp. 13, 55. FBI report (NY File #100-79069) on the Photo League, August 30, 1945, probably written by Angela. Her FBI file acknowledged the submission of "two very good reports regarding the activities and identities of all the present officers of the Photo League," presumably one from June 1942, and this one. Letter SAC E. E. Conroy to Director, September 18, 1945, p. 3. Calomiris file. See Walter Rosenblum in *Photo Notes,* December 1941.

14. *Dennis v. US,* vol. 7, April 26, 1949, pp. 5023-5025, 5035. See Chapter 8 for Angela naming names. Her testimony runs from pp. 5022-5440, April 26-May 3.

15. *Dennis v. US,* vol. 7, April 26, 1949, p. 5024. See a previous reference, Chapter 7, to Leona's name as "S-e-r-o-n" and her naming at the Judith Coplon trial. In *Photo Notes,* Grossman's wife is always "Marian." Memo SAC E. E. Conroy, New York, to Director, July 10, 1943, p. 1, has "Emma Marion Hill Grossman, alias Emma Marion Hille, Emma Marion Hillie, Pete Hille, Mrs. Sid Grossman." Sidney Grossman FBI file, Headquarters File #100-6866 (New York File #100-3921), referred to throughout as Sid Grossman file. In *Red Masquerade,* filmmaker Leo Hurwitz's name was consistently misspelled as "Leo Herowitz" (p. 75). Word was, according to former Leaguers, that Marian Hille was supposedly living with another man by the time Sid got out of the Army. Phone interview, Arthur Leipzig, April 5, 2010, Sea Cliff, New York.

16. Phone interview, Miriam Cohen, April 13, 2010, New York City.

Memo SAC, New York, to Director, April 29, 1949. Sid Grossman file. The quote is from J. Edgar Hoover. The Custodial Detention Index (CDI), or Custodial Detention List was formed in 1939-1941, as part of the "Custodial Detention Program" or "Alien Enemy Control."

Because she had been to the Soviet Union, Margaret Bourke-White (1904-1971), one of the period's most distinguished photographers, also had a custodial detention card, as revealed in her extensive FBI file (Headquarters File #100-3518), April 24, 1943. She was "the subject of a security-type investigation" from 1941 to 1951, and the last entry in her file is dated 1965. Also see Robert E. Snyder, "Margaret Bourke-White and the Communist Witch Hunt," *Journal of American Studies*, 19 (1985), I, 5-25.

17. Phone interview, Miriam Cohen, April 13, 2010, New York City. Memo SAC, New York, to Director, May 13, 1955, p. 2. In 1954, Sid had also been "tabbed" for Custodial Detention (Detcom) and Communist Sabotage (Comsab). Memo SAC, New York, to Director, November 29, 1954. Sid Grossman file.

18. Interview, Sol Libsohn, by Gary Saretzky, January 21, 2001, p. 12: "But what she did to Sid was really horrible." Walter Rosenblum, e-mail to author, December 20, 2004: "That Angela ruined his life was a terrible crime."

19. Romana Javitz was in charge of the Picture Collection from 1929 until her retirement in 1968. For a catalog of the Public Library exhibit, see http://www.nypl.org/research/chss/spe/art/photo/league/index.html *The Women of the Photo League* had two untitled photos—one of a political demonstration, another of a sidewalk table for collecting petition signatures. These, together with *The Radical Camera* catalog photo *Father and Son* (p. 57, fig. 47) of an African American with a toddler on his shoulder, were possibly shot for identification purposes. Also see the essay by Catherine Evans, "As Good as the Guys: The Women of the Photo League," in *The Radical Camera* catalog, which exposes Angela's betrayal, pp. 46-59.

20. *Red Masquerade*, pp. 28, 110, 174, 50, 29. "Gruesome Grossman" is from *Photo Notes*, April 1943, p. 2. Rosenblum's e-mail to author, December 20, 2004. *True*, p. 120. Phone interview, Miriam Cohen, April 13, 2010, New York City.

21. *Red Masquerade*, pp. 48, 52. Memo Assistant Director P. E. Foxworth, New York, to Director, June 23, 1942. Calomiris file.

22. Memo SAC P. E. Foxworth, New York, to Director, April 22, 1942. Attached is the Informant's "report dated April 16, 1942 [...] which contains information concerning Sidney Grossman, and the Photo League." Sid Grossman file. Memo SAC New York to Director, May 13, 1955, p. 1. Calomiris file.

23. Memo for the Officer in Charge, May 13, 1943, p. 2. It was the second "Interview with Subject under subterfuge" included in the file. Sid Grossman's Army Intelligence file. *Red Masquerade*, p. 36.

24. E-mail to author, December 20, 2004. Photo Leaguer Suzy Harris, who lived from 1940 until her death in 2004 on Grove Street in Greenwich Village, could easily have known Angela, who lived on Jane Street, a few blocks away. See "Suzy Harris, 91, Always Had Her Camera With Her," Obit in *The Villager*, vol. 74, no. 9 (June 30-July 6, 2004). Millard Lampell, of the Almanac Singers and the People's Songs movement, later wrote the text for Grossman's last photographs, *Journey to the Cape* (1959).

25. New York report, March 25, 1943, p. 2. Sid Grossman file. See Waldemar Hille's obit in the *Los Angeles Times*, December 20, 1995, where he is identified as the musical director of First Unitarian Church in LA, Paul Robeson's accompanist, and the one who brought the song "We Shall Overcome" from the Highlander Folk School in Tennessee to national attention.

26. See the Wikipedia article on Commonwealth College, and especially in connection with Lee Hays. See www.encyclopediaofarkansas. net for more articles on Commonwealth College, Lee Hays, and the Southern Tenant Farmers' Union (STFU). *Educational Commune: the Story of Commonwealth College* (New York: Schocken Books, 1972) is a firsthand account by longtime participants Raymond and Charlotte Koch.

27. Sid Grossman, Oklahoma City FBI File #100-173, December 18, 1940, "determined that Subjects [Mr. and Mrs. Grossman] had been in Commonwealth, Mo., and Mena, Arkansas, before arriving in Oklahoma City [August 22, 1940] (p. 3)." A slight confusion; Commonwealth College was near Mena, Arkansas. Also see Sid Grossman, Little Rock, Arkansas, File #100-243, pp. 1-2, for the Grossman's "connected with the Peoples Theater, Inc." at Commonwealth College in the summer of 1940. For background, arrests in Oklahoma City, trials and aftermath, see Shirley A. Wiegand and Wayne A. Wiegand, *Books on Trial: Red Scare in the Heartland*, and especially p. 6 for warrants, pp. 10-11 for criminal syndicalism.

28. See *The Radical Camera* catalog, p. 22, Fig. 10; p. 23, Fig. 11. Sid Grossman, Oklahoma City File #100-173, December 18, 1940, pp. 1-3; and March 3, 1941, p. 1.

29. Sidney Grossman, US Army Intelligence and Security Command, Freedom of Information/Privacy Office, Fort George G. Meade, Maryland, "Interview with Subject under subterfuge," May 8, 1943, and May 13, 1943. Sworn statement, May 12, 1943.

30. Angela probably had a network of well-to-do women who welcomed her into their homes, to judge by a note from 515 Park Avenue,

that congratulated her and recalled that "in '46 you came to our apartment to photograph my first grandchild at the recommendation of Dorothy Dolan" (March 19, 1951, signed "Dorothy [illegible] Mrs. C. R. D."). Calomiris Papers, LHA. Russell Porter, "Girl Aide of FBI Testified Of 7 Years as 'Communist'," April 27, 1949, pp. 1, 11.

CHAPTER 11

1. Quoted in "Reds Plow Under FBI's Plant," *New York World-Telegram* (April 7, 1949), p. 1, referring to Herbert Philbrick of Boston.

2. Memos SAC Edward Scheidt, New York, to Director, March 25, 1949, and June 26, 1950. Calomiris file. See Chapter 9, for William Nowell, and for Budenz, Robert P. Newman, *Owen Lattimore and the 'Loss' of China*, p. 270, and throughout Chapter 18, "Agony at the FBI: Louis Budenz," pp. 266-286. It was a commonplace appointment for former informant/witnesses. See George Marion, *The Communist Trial. An American Crossroads*, pp. 116-117, for Charles Baxter, clerk in the Cleveland Immigration Service.

The Economic Cooperation Administration (ECA) was a United States government agency set up in 1948 to administer the Marshall Plan in postwar Europe. It was succeeded in 1961 by the United States Agency for International Development (USAID).

3. *Limelight: A Greenwich Village Photography Gallery and Coffeehouse in the Fifties. A Memoir* by Helen Gee (Albuquerque: University of New Mexico Press, 1997), p. 14. Helen Gee's Limelight Coffeehouse (1954-60) on Seventh Avenue South in Greenwich Village was the first US gallery dedicated exclusively to photography. Memos SAC Edward Scheidt, New York, to Director, October 27, 1948, p. 5; September 9, 1949; and March 25, 1949. Calomiris file.

4. Memos SAC Edward Scheidt, New York, to Director, March 25, 1949; and June 27, 1949, p. 2, where Stryker's name is spelled "Striker." Calomiris file. Several former FSA photographers—like Arthur Rothstein, John Vachon, and Edwin Rosskam—had also been active in or sympathetic to the Photo League.

5. Memo SAC Edward Scheidt, New York, to Director, June 27, 1949, p. 2, where the secretary's name is given as "Carol Leeds." Victor Riesel (1913-1995), "the main journalistic point man on labor matters for the anticommunist network" (Schrecker, p. 332), also campaigned against organized crime's infiltration of labor unions. He was blinded in 1956 by acid, thrown at him by a petty gangster in the mob's employ.

6. Memo D. M. Ladd to Director, October 19, 1949. Calomiris file. See

Chapter 4 for Woltman's articles "Girl Photog Cut Career to Expose Reds' Plot" (October 17, 1949) and "Leading Double Life No Picnic, FBI Girl Found" (October 18, 1949). See Chapter 1 for Lasky and Angela on the same radio program, talking about "the mental poisons of Communism." Memo L. B. Nichols to Mr. Tolson, January 30, 1951, about Lasky's review of *Red Masquerade*, from which the citation is taken, in *The Freeman* (January 22, 1951). Calomiris file.

7. Memo Director to D. M. Ladd, October 4, 1950, p. 5. Memos SAC Edward Scheidt, New York, to Director, October 20, p. 6; October 28, 1950, p. 1; and October 31, p. 2. The US Attorney had reminded the "unpredictable" Angela that "the fact of her compensation from the Bureau for her informant service might come to light, and that the Communist Party defense attorneys might seize upon this as new evidence upon which to base a motion." Memo SAC, New York, to Director, September 8, 1950. Calomiris file.

8. Memos SAC Edward Scheidt, New York, to Director, October 31, 1950, p. 2; June 27, 1949, p. 4; and August 11, 1949. Calomiris file.

9. Memo D. M. Ladd to Director, October 19, 1949, pp. 4-5. This is a seven-page brief prepared by D. Milton Ladd, one-time Head of the FBI's Domestic Intelligence Division, after Woltman's articles on Angela hit the newsstand.

10. *Red Masquerade*, p. 12. See David Everitt, *A Shadow of Red. Communism and the Blacklist in Radio and Television* (Chicago: Ivan R. Dee, 2007), especially pp. 6-9, where Angela is named as Bierly's "most notorious spy [...] a young photographer" (p. 9).

11. Interview, Melva Wade, August 8, 2003, Accord, New York. Letter Ken to "Angelus," n.d. (late February-early March, 1954). Calomiris Papers, LHA. *Red Masquerade*, pp. 32, 260. Phone Interview, Mr. & Mrs. Richard D. Bierly (brother and sister-in-law of Ken), April 9, 2004, Peoria, Illinois.

12. See Schrecker, *Many Are the Crimes*, for the development of the anti-Communist network, the players and their impact. *Counterattack* Headquarters File # 100-HQ-350512, 1947-1971. *Counterattack*, Newsletter No. 157, May 26, 1950. Memo SAC Edward Scheidt to Director, June 2, 1950. Calomiris file.

13. Letter Angela Calomiris to Pennsylvania State Board of Law Examiners, March 3, 1954. Calomiris Papers, LHA.

14. Everitt, *A Shadow of Red*, p. 10.

15. See Deborah C. Peterson, *Fredric March: Craftsman First, Star Second* (Westport, Connecticut: Greenwood Press, 1996), pp. 161, 169. See Chapter 2 for the Polish ham affair in Mary Margaret McBride's autobiographical *Out of the Air* (pp. 145-147).

16. See the memo mentioning Gene Kelly (February 9, 1948) in American Business Consultants/*Counterattack* Research Files, Tamiment Library, New York University, Box 27, Folder 14-65. These files were a gift to Tamiment from Jerry Falwell's Liberty University, Lynchburg, Virginia, and contain folders, for example, on a variety of entertainers (Gypsy Rose Lee, Pearl Primus), New Deal Democrats (Claude Pepper, Florida), labor union leaders (Mike Quill), labor lawyers (Leonard Boudin), and writers (Garson Kanin of *Born Yesterday*).

17. For Mary Margaret McBride, see Memo "Re: Counterattack," SAC Edward Scheidt, New York, March 21, 1950, p. 1, in an early FBI file # 62-9189. The blacklisted who were sincere penitents could purportedly get help about how to re-establish their reputations from Hedda Hopper, Walter Winchell, and Victor Riesel, of Hearst's *New York Daily Mirror*.

18. Memo L. R. Pennington to Mr. Ladd, September 13, 1951, Kenby Associates FBI file #62-95474. Bierly, in *Sponsor*, a magazine "For Buyers of Broadcast Advertising," claimed to disagree with the sloppy investigation and classification techniques that had gone into *Red Channels*, and promised factual research into accusations of Communist affiliations (October 8, 1951, p. 19). Phone interview, Melva Wade, August 21, 2010, Rhinebeck, New York, on Angela talking about any connection she ever had to a prominent person.

19. For "Judy Holliday's Sworn Statement," see The Judy Holliday Resource Center www.judyhollidayrc.com, retrieved January 8, 2004. For the draft statement, see American Business Consultants/*Counterattack* Research Files, Box 28, Folder 14-202, pp. 1-4.

20. For "The Bierly Report" to Columbia Pictures Corp., 729 Seventh Avenue, New York 19, N.Y., June 8, 1951, p. 1, see The Judy Holliday Resource Center www.judyhollidayrc.com, retrieved January 8, 2004.

21. For "Transcript of Judy Holliday's Testimony," p. 9, The Judy Holliday Resource Center www.judyhollidayrc.com, retrieved June 3, 2003. Also, see Holtzman, pp. 9-24 for the testimony. Concerning Yetta's name—C-o-h-n—Holtzman commented that "something about Jewish names seems to require spelling" (p. 17), and on Arens' reputation for anti-Semitism (p. 164). Arens later became staff director of HUAC, and served as a paid consultant on research grants trying to prove that "Negroes" were genetically inferior. Interview, Morry Baer, October 1, 2002, Whiting, New Jersey, who had worked during the war on NYPD counterespionage Special Squads 1 and 2. She added that Yetta was not a very good cop, and later ran "a computerized horoscope thing." Morry implied that Judy had more to hide about her leftist affiliations than was ever brought to light, and claimed Yetta "took the heat" for her.

22. *Original Story By*, p. 96. Laurents was also included in *Red Channels*. For "Chronology" and a letter written on or around November 28, 1952, see The Judy Holliday Resource Center www.judyhollidayrc.com, retrieved April 4, 2010. The letter also includes a reference to José Ferrer as another of Angela's "victims."

23. For Angela and Myrtis in the courtroom together, see Memo D. M. Ladd to Director, October 19, 1949, p. 5. Calomiris file. "Marta Robinet" (1906-1983) published short stories in *McCall's* and less distinguished women's pulp magazines of the 1940s. By the 1950s, she wrote for a Hearst Sunday newspaper supplement called *The American Weekly*, and still got newspaper work when she lived in Philadelphia, in the 1960s and 1970s, with the Women's News Service. Mr. and Mrs. Richard D. Bierly remembered her as a writer of children's books and romance novels. Phone Interview, April 9, 2004, Peoria, Illinois. Phone interview, Melva Wade, September 28, 2004, Accord, New York.

24. Angela and Myrtis had a two-week vacation in London, March, 14-29, 1950. Memos SAC Edward Scheidt, New York, to Director, March 9 and 14, 1950. Calomiris file. Letters Ellen Wiley, Real Estate Agent, Westport, Connecticut, to Angela, mentioning "Mrs. Johnson," March 5, 1951; and Dottie Hayman (née Thawley), Doylestown Pennsylvania, to Angela, asking how the "farm" was coming along, June 18, 1951. Calomiris Papers, LHA.

25. Letter to "Miss Coggans," Myrtis Johnson, April 8, 1951, describing the Bierlys' home situation and suggesting that "Angela and I look forward to seeing you again." Calomiris Papers, LHA. Interview, Ruth Parish, October 2, 2003, Hallandale, Florida. From Gruman Hill Road, Wilton, Connecticut, March 3, 1954, Angela wrote to the Pennsylvania State Board of Law Examiners, Philadelphia. Calomiris Papers, LHA.

26. Interview, Melva Wade, July 15, 2004, Accord, New York, about how she helped Angela with papers for courses at NYU, because "she couldn't write anything." Russell, who founded the agency in 1940, was a former editor at Putnam's. For the story of his relationship with one client see Michael Kreyling, *Author and Agent: Eudora Welty and Diarmuid Russell* (New York: Farrar, Straus and Giroux, 1991).

His father, George William Russell (1867–1935), was an Irish nationalist and Renaissance man who excelled as writer, editor, critic, poet, and artistic painter. His pseudonym was written Æ, sometimes AE or A.E. Letter, Angela to "Mr. Russell," March 25, 1954. Calomiris Papers, LHA. Contract/"Agreement" in Caroline Bird Papers, Box 61 (1943-1956), Vassar College Libraries. Thanks to Gretchen Lieb, Research Services, Vassar. "Books—Authors," *New York Times*, October 18, 1949, and FBI reaction, Memo SAC Edward Scheidt to Director, October 19, 1949, p. 1, also cited at the beginning of Chapter 6.

27. See the Caroline Bird Papers, in the Vassar College Libraries. Besides writing several books, Ms. Bird (1915-2011) was a Consultant to the National Commission on the Observance of International Women's Year in 1977, and the author of its report. Phone interview, Carol Barath (daughter of Caroline Bird), June 19, 2006, Nashville, Tennessee.

Dorothy Sterling, in *Close to My Heart,* describes the same female researcher-male writer duo when she worked for *Life* in the 1940s, pp. 129-134. Caroline Bird undoubtedly wrote the lengthy feature article "I Spied on the U.S. Communists," published over Angela's name in *True* magazine, April 1950, but I find no reference to her getting paid. See Chapter 10 for more on the *True* article.

28. Letter from Diarmuid Russell to George Stevens, Lippincott, August 22, 1950, regarding the libel clause, "this agreement should also apply to Mrs. Menuez." Letter from George Stevens to Kenneth M. Bierly, August 15, 1950, recalling that, since the contract was signed both by Angela and "by Miss Caroline Bird Menuez [...] the new provision should apply to both." George E. Sokolsky, "Urges All to Read 'Red Masquerade,'" *New York Journal-American,* November 2, 1950. Calomiris Papers, LHA.

29. Letter Kenneth M. Bierly to Mr. Lynn Carrick, Lippincott, February 13, 1950, about the libel clause. Calomiris Papers, LHA. Memos SAC Edward Scheidt, New York, to Director, May 8, 1950; SAC New York to Director, March 13, 1950. Calomiris file.

30. Letter to Mr. [Richard H.] Dana [Promotion Manager] from Eugene Lyons, "Roving Editor of the *Reader's Digest,*" October 20, 1950. Letter to Mr. Richard H. Dana, Promotion Manager, J. B. Lippincott Co., Philadelphia, Pennsylvania, from Irene Corbally Kuhn, journalist, author and radio personality, on staff at NBC, October 22, 1950. Calomiris Papers, LHA. Letter SAC Edward Scheidt, New York, to Director, August 10, 1950, quoted Angela, who never made the *Reader's Digest* Condensed Books list. Calomiris file.

CHAPTER 12

1. Quoted in Albert E. Kahn, *The Matusow Affair,* p. 34. See Chapter 2 for more on Angela as Mary Margaret McBride's guest, and the October 25 interview. The New York FBI office was concerned about Angela's radio premiere, and acquired a transcript of the entire program to send to Headquarters in Washington. Memo SAC Edward Scheidt to Director, with enclosure, November 10, 1950. Quoted in Memo SAC Edward Scheidt, New York, to Director, October 26, 1950. "Extract from Broadcast of

Walter Winchell on Sunday, October 29, 1950." Calomiris file. Regarding the reliability of *Red Masquerade*, Interview, Ruth Parish, October 2, 2003, Hallandale, Florida.

2. Memos SAC Edward Scheidt, New York, to Director, October 12, 1950, and October 30, 1950, passing on Angela's news that she had gone to a party sponsored by J. B. Matthews, and a couple of weeks later (October 28), he had thrown a party in her honor. Calomiris file. Victor Riesel's regular column "Inside Labor," *New York Mirror*, May 28, 1950.

3. "These Days," Thursday, November 2, 1950. See Warren I. Cohen, *The Chinese Connection: Roger S. Greene, Thomas W. Lamont, George E. Sokolsky and American-East Asian Relations* (New York, Columbia University Press, 1978). Not surprisingly, Angela kept up her contact with Sokolsky as long as she could, sending him photographs for which he thanked her, praising her "remarkable work." Note George E. Sokolsky to Angela, January 9, 1951. Calomiris Papers, LHA.

4. "Remember Angela Calomiris?" *New York Daily News*, Sunday, November 12, 1950, p. 55. John Hutchens, "Books and Things." Review of *Red Masquerade*, *New York Herald Tribune*, November 11, 1950, p. 12. Arthur Schlesinger, Jr., "Inside Reports." Review of *Red Masquerade*, *The Nation*, January 27, 1951, pp. 91-92. In 1947, Schlesinger organized, with Eleanor Roosevelt and others, the liberal Americans for Democratic Action (ADA). A. H. Raskin, "The F.B.I. Planted Her There." Review of *Red Masquerade*, *New York Times*, November 19, 1950. John K. Hutchens, "On the Books. On an Author." Interview with Angela Calomiris, *New York Herald Tribune Book Review*, November 26, 1950. Calomiris Papers, LHA. Budenz had published *This Is My Story* in 1947 (McGraw-Hill).

5. "Cruising Car Best for FBI Contacts, Woman Spying on Commies Found," *New York World-Telegram and Sun*, November 13, 1950, p. 4. Calomiris Papers, LHA. A copy of the article was forwarded to FBI Headquarters in Washington by SAC, New York, November 16, 1950. Calomiris file. *Red Masquerade*, pp. 234, 237, 130, 78.

6. Memo SAC New York to Director, September 8, 1950, announcing the $300 *Catholic Digest* deal. ($3,000.47 in 2016) http://www.bls.gov/data/inflation_calculator.htm. Calomiris file. Lippincott Press Release, n.d., featuring the book's appearance "in part" in the *Digest*. Letter Daniel A. Poling, *Christian Herald*, to Angela, November 22, 1950, enclosing a copy of his review. Calomiris Papers, LHA.

7. "Remember Angela Calomiris?" *New York Daily News*, November 12, 1950. John K. Hutchens, "On the Books. On an Author." Interview with Angela Calomiris, *New York Herald Tribune Book Review*, November 26, 1950. Calomiris Papers, LHA.

8. Memo SAC Edward Scheidt, New York, to Director, October 30, 1950. Calomiris file. Harvey Breit, *New York Times Book Review Section*, November 26, 1950. Calomiris Papers, LHA. Among other literary efforts, Breit co-wrote the play *The Disenchanted* (1958) with Budd Schulberg, adapted from Schulberg's novel about the life of F. Scott Fitzgerald.

9. Memo SAC Edward Scheidt, New York, to Director, December 1, 1950. Calomiris file. Ad for *Red Masquerade, New York Times,* November 29, 1950, 5th printing "On Press." *New York Daily News,* February 18-25, 1951. Letter Dottie Hayman (née Thawley), Doylestown, PA. to "Angela," December 4, 1950. Calomiris Papers, LHA.

10. Letter SAC Edward Scheidt, New York, to Director, November 16, 1950, 6 pp. FBI Memo Mr. [Louis B.] Nichols to Mr. [Clyde] Tolson, "Angela Jean Calomiris," July 6, 1950. Letter, November 16, pp. 2, 3. Letter SAC Edward Scheidt, New York, to Director, November 28, 1950, pp. 1-2. Calomiris file.

11. Anonymous (known to be Jonathan Tichenor, husband of surrealist artist Bridget Bate Tichenor), *U.S. Camera,* vol. 13, no. 3, pp. 32-35. Letter SAC Edward Scheidt, New York, to Director, announcing the *Modern Photography* article for March 1950, and the appointment at MOMA, November 28, 1949, p. 2. Edward Steichen, it turns out, had done a lot of work for J. Walter Thompson. In a Letter, SAC Edward Scheidt, New York, to Director, December 27, 1949, p. 2, the appointment at MOMA with (name blacked out) is set for "the near future." Calomiris file.

12. *Resumé,* undated (known to be 1956). Calomiris Papers, LHA. Memos SAC Edward Scheidt, New York, to Director, October 30, 1950; Director to SAC, New York, April 2, 1951. Calomiris file. $8,000-$10,000 in 1945 = $107,128.00-$133,910.00 in 2016. http://www.bls.gov/data/inflation_calculator.htm/ Woltman, *New York World-Telegram,* October 17, 1949. See Chapter 4 for evidence that Angela paid nothing to the IRS, 1940-1944, and not much 1945-1949, which prompted Hoover to admonish informants that their salaries must be declared as income to the IRS.

13. Maxwell Fox, The Advertising Council, Inc., April 27, 1949. Calomiris Papers, LHA. *Photo Notes,* June 1943, p. 3; and February 1943, pp. 2-3.

14. "Honorably Discharged," *Parade,* September 3, 1944. Photography by Black Star. Interview, October 2, 2003, Hallandale, Florida.

15. Phone Interview, Miriam Cohen, April 13, 2010, New York City. Referring to Angela's photography career, Miriam said that "anything else [besides nightclub photography] is laughable."

16. Letter SAC Edward Scheidt, New York, to Director, November 16, 1949, p. 2. Calomiris file. *Red Masquerade,* p. 94.

17. Letters SAC Edward Scheidt, New York, to Director, November 16, p. 2, and November 28, p. 1, 1949. Calomiris file. Of course, Angela could not have known that Margaret Bourke-White (1904-1971) had her own extensive FBI file, Headquarters File #100-3518, a custodial detention card, and had been "the subject of a security-type investigation" from 1941 to 1951. The last entry in her file is dated 1965. See Robert E. Snyder, "Margaret Bourke-White and the Communist Witch Hunt," *Journal of American Studies*, 19 (1985), I, 5-25.

18. In daily column "As Pegler Sees It," "Margaret Bourke-White Versus Angela Calomiris," September 18, 1951.

19. Pegler, "As Pegler Sees It," *New York Journal-American*, September 19, 1951, p. 3. Letter SAC Edward Scheidt, New York, to Director, November 16, 1949, p. 3. Memo SAC, New York, to Director, January 15, 1951. Calomiris file. Riesel, "Inside Labor," *New York Daily Mirror*, May 28, 1950.

20. Note Walter Winchell to Director, June 19, 1950. Photo League file. After covering the war in the Pacific, W. Eugene Smith went on to create major photo essays on topics as diverse as Albert Schweitzer and victims of Minamata (Japan) disease, triggered by industrial pollution of the local bay with mercury. Actress and photographer Elizabeth Timberman, originally from Ohio, retreated to Mexico during the Red Scare. Robert Capa, killed (1954) by a landmine while photographing the French campaign to secure their colonial empire in Vietnam, had photographed the Spanish Civil War and World War II, including the American landing at Omaha Beach. His brother, Cornell Capa, founded New York's International Center of Photography (1974).

21. Letter SAC Edward Scheidt, New York, to Director, November 16, 1949, p. 5. "As Pegler Sees It," "Girl Spy for FBI Recounts Insult by a Picture Editor," September 19, 1951, p. 3.

22. Several drafts of a letter about Morris are dated December 2, 1949. Calomiris Papers, LHA. Letter SAC Edward Scheidt, New York, to Director, December 27, 1949, 3 pp. Memos, SAC New York to Director, February 1 and November 21, 1950, January 15, 1951. Calomiris file. *Counterattack*, May 26, 1950. See John Morris, "Red-Baited," in *Get the Picture: A Personal History of Photojournalism* (New York: Random House, 1998), pp. 129-132. Angela's note (ca. July 19, 1993) to the editors of M. H. Mahoney, *Women in Espionage: A Biographical Dictionary* (Santa Barbara, CA: ABC-CLIO, 1993), which included her (pp. 37-39). In the same note she answered a question about her date of birth by knocking some ten years off her age, "8/1/26."

23. Letter SAC Edward Scheidt, New York, to Director, November 16,

1949, pp. 5-6. Memo SAC, New York, to Director, April 10, 1953. Teletypes, Urgent, SAC New York to Director, December 1 and December 8, 1950.

24. Memo SAC, New York, to Director, February 27, 1951. Calomiris file. Letters Diarmuid Russell to Angela, January 6 and November 22, 1950; March 9, 1951. Memorandum of Agreement, A.-B. Skoglunde Bokforlag, Stockholm, January 29, 1951. "Angela Calomiris To [Lee] Keedick [booking agent], in *Program. The Magazine of the American Platform*, November-December, 1950, p. 13. Calomiris Papers, LHA. $1700 in 1950 = $17,002.68 in 2016. http://www.bls.gov/data/inflation_calculator.htm/

25. Letter SAC Edward Scheidt, New York, to Director, quoting Angela, August 10, 1950, p. 1. Calomiris file. Cvetic's story appeared in the *Post* on July 15, 22, and 29, 1950. Frank Lovejoy headed an undistinguished cast in the movie role of Cvetic.

26. Letters Richard Sokolove, Famous Artists Corporation, Beverly Hills, California, to Angela, October 24 and November 10, 1949. Calomiris Papers, LHA. *Counterattack*, "Communication No. 164," October 31, 1949. From The Desk of T. C. Kirkpatrick, "Here is the report from West Coast. If you need any more on it, let me know. Ted," November 4, 1949. Counterattack file 100-HQ-350512. Memo SAC, Los Angeles to Director, December 2, 1950. The handwriting is not Hoover's; the signature could be "Lou" for propaganda chief Louis B. Nichols. Calomiris file.

27. The Freedoms Foundation award was scheduled, re-scheduled and finally presented on May 3, 1951, at the Casa Italiana of Columbia University. Letter W. C. "Tom" Sawyer, Freedoms Foundation, to Angela, April 20, 1951. The heavy bronze medallion, with an image of George Washington at Valley Forge, is preserved in the Lesbian Herstory Archives.

Hear "Big Joe" Rosenfeld on http://musicradio.computer.net/bigjoe/html. He wrote a book *The Happiest Man In the World*, and had Eleanor Roosevelt on his board. Letter from William G. O'Connor, 123 Palmetto Street, Brooklyn 21, New York, October 28, 1950. Postcard from Mrs. R. Bardach, 355 Avon Ave., Newark, New Jersey, November 8, 1950. Note from Dottie Hayman (née Thawley, Myrtis' relative), Doylestown, Pennsylvania, June 18, 1951. Angela's radio appearance on *We, the People* was December 7, 1950, according to a memo from Barbara Frost of Lippincott, November 15, 1950. Calomiris Papers, LHA.

28. *You and Communism*, with Angela as guest, aired December 11, 1950; her *David Harding, Counterspy* on December 24, 1950. *Inside Communism* aired in April, 1951, after Lasky's review of *Red Masquerade*, January 22, 1951, in the "libertarian" journal *The Freeman*. See FBI Memo L. B. Nichols, to Mr. [Clyde] Tolson, January 30, 1951. See Chapter 1 for Lasky's book *Seeds of Treason: The True Story of the Hiss-Chambers Tragedy*

(1950). He later authored derogatory biographies of Jimmy Carter, John and Robert Kennedy, and in praise (not surprisingly) of Richard Nixon. See "Transcribed Radio Broadcast," pp. 8, 2. Calomiris Papers, LHA.

29. Eric Bentley, *Thirty Years of Treason* (New York: Thunder's Mouth Press/Nation Books, 2002, 2nd ed.), p. 194, for Berkeley. Internal correspondence Milton E. Pickman (Hollywood) to J. Raymond Ball (New York), Columbia Pictures Corporation, January 19, 1954. Calomiris Papers, LHA. The full title was *I Led Three Lives: Citizen, "Communist," Counterspy* (New York: McGraw-Hill) which became *I Led Three Lives*, in 117 episodes narrated by Philbrick himself. Cvetic's show ran for 78 episodes.

30. Letter Robert W. Friedheim, ZIV Television, to Angela, acknowledging receipt of a copy of *Red Masquerade*, December 18, 1953. Note Victor Lasky ("Vic") to Angela, February 8, 1954. Note Martin Berkeley to Angela, February 19, 1954. Contract from Berkeley to Angela and Lasky, February 19, 1954. Letters Berkeley to Angela, March 22 and February 20, 1954. Hand-written letter, Angela to Berkeley, n.d. Calomiris Papers, LHA.

31. Angela to Hoover, February 26, 1954, and SAC New York to Director, March 4, 1954. Assistant Director D. M. Ladd to Director. October 25, 1950, with Hoover notation. Calomiris file. Letter (blacked out known to be Ogden Reid) to Hoover, February 5, 1952, announcing that Philbrick had joined their "retail advertising staff." Philbrick file.

32. Hand-written note appended to letter, Berkeley to Angela, March 22, 1954. Letter Berkeley to Angela, May 8, 1954, the last correspondence between the two. Calomiris Papers, LHA.

33. Memo Mr. [Lee N.] Steiner, of Weil, Gotshal & Manges, to Angela, March 12, 1954. Letter Angela to Mr. [Diarmuid] Russell, of Russell & Volkening Inc, March 25, 1954. Letter Angela to Motion Picture Assn of America Inc, March 26, 1954. Letter Lee N. Steiner to Angela, May 12, 1954. Calomiris Papers, LHA.

34. See George Marion, *The Communist Trial: An American Crossroads*, who wrote that the prosecution informant/witnesses were "of such low grade that no real sacrifice was entailed" by putting them on the stand and revealing their identity in that "reckless and irresponsible case." They were of no "real value to the FBI [...] in short, expendables" (p. 126).

EPILOGUE

1. Teletype "Angela Calomiris," New York to Bureau Headquarters, February 21, 1956. Memo SAC New York to Director, February 21, 1956,

letter enclosed from Bayles Employment Service, Inc. 140 West 42nd St., New York 36, NY, February 21, 1956. Memo A. H. Belmont to L. V. Boardman, February 28, 1956. Calomiris file.

2. Memo SAC New York to Director, May 28, 1957. Calomiris file.

3. Simon Gerson's "Record of Smith Act Cases," typescript with charts, October 1, 1956, 11 pp., in Gil Green Papers, Box 7, 1st folder, Tamiment Library, New York University, remains the best source. See Introduction.

4. Khrushchev spoke on February 25, 1956, but the text of his speech became widely known, even among the Party faithful, only after a version of it appeared in the *New York Times*, June 5, 1956. The exchange between Robert Kennedy and Hoover is quoted in Arthur M. Schlesinger, Jr., *Robert Kennedy and His Times* (New York: Houghton Mifflin, 1978) pp. 261-262.

5. "Communist Party U.S.A. Who's Who in the Red Hierarchy Here," *American Legion Magazine*, January 1962, pp. 10-11, 13, 45. Memos SAC New York to Director, Assistant Director Cartha D. DeLoach, December 12, 1961; M. A. Jones to Mr. DeLoach, December 15, 1961; SAC New York to Director, October 22, 1965. Calomiris file.

6. Angela Calomiris' Unprocessed Papers, LHA. Kenneth M. Bierly, 1916-1958. See Brad Hamm, Dean of the Northwestern University Medill School of Journalism, "From College Expulsion to Pulitzer Prize: How the *New York World-Telegram*'s Fred Woltman Became the 'No. 1 Newspaper Specialist' on Communists." Also see Fred Woltman's FBI file, Headquarters File #62-85195.

7. Interview, Melva Wade, August 8, 2003, Accord, New York, for the 12th St. property. The Barnstable County Registry of Deeds lists, on Commercial, #420, #353, #348A, #111, #1; 6 Nickerson (between Cottage and Soper); the cottages on Route 6; and in Wellfleet, 2 Ridge Street Extension, and 21 West Street. See Angela's original loan statement from the Sandwich Co-operative Bank, Sandwich, Massachusetts, July 5, 1961. The price for 353 Commercial St., paid to Frank Diego, was $14,500.00 in 1961. Calomiris Papers, LHA. For "wash-ashore" see Karen Christel Krahulik, *Provincetown: From Pilgrim Landing to Gay Resort* (New York: New York University Press, 2005), p. 14.

8. Interview, Willa Levitt, December 29, 2005, Atlantic City, New Jersey. Phone interview, Irma Ruckstuhl, May 15, 2011, Provincetown, Massachusetts.

9. Quoted in Larry Collins, "Sid Grossman's Escape to Provincetown," *Provincetown Arts*, vol. 18 (2004/05), pp. 79-81.

10. Phone interview, Miriam Cohen, January 6, 2011, New York City.

11. Phone interview, Roslyn Garfield, May 15, 2011, Provincetown, Massachusetts.

12. Interview, Melva Wade, August 8, 2003, Accord, New York. For Provincetown real estate values, see Karen Christel Krahulik, *Provincetown: From Pilgrim Landing to Gay Resort*, pp. 190, 198-200. Last Will and Testament, Angela Calomiris, January 12, 1995, Surrogate's Court of the State of New York, County of New York.

13. The Venona cables, decrypted Soviet diplomatic cables collected during the war by the US Army's Intelligence Service, the forerunner of the National Security Agency, together with the opening of Soviet records of the Communist International (Comintern), have created a large body of critical literature. John Earl Haynes and Harvey Klehr, *Venona: Decoding Soviet Espionage in America* (New Haven: Yale University Press, 1999) is a good start. See opposing views in Ellen Schrecker and Maurice Isserman, "The Right's Cold War Revision," *The Nation*, July 24/31, 2000; and Walter and Miriam Schneir, "Cables Coming in From the Cold," *The Nation*, August 21, 1995. Also see Walter and Miriam Schneir's last word from a lifetime of research, *Final Verdict: What Really Happened in the Rosenberg Case* (Brooklyn: Melville House, 2010). Interview, Ruth Parish, October 2, 2003, Hallandale, Florida. *Naming Names*, p. 329.

Selected Bibliography

ARCHIVAL COLLECTIONS

American Business Consultants/*Counterattack* Research Files, 1930-1968, Tamiment Library & Robert F. Wagner Labor Archives, New York University.

Bird, Caroline. Papers. Vassar College Libraries.

Calomiris, Angela. Special Collections #99-02 and Unprocessed Papers, Lesbian Herstory Archives. Brooklyn, New York.

(Eugene) Dennis v. United States. Criminal Docket 128, Boxes 1320-1342. US Court of Appeals, Second Circuit. National Archives and Records Administration, Northeast Region, New York, NY.

Documents from the Comintern Archives on African Americans, 1919-1929. Papers of the "Negro Commission" of the Fourth Congress (1922) of the Communist International, Schomburg Center for Research in Black Culture, New York Public Library.

Green, Gil. Papers. Tamiment Library & Robert F. Wagner Labor Archives, New York University.

Holliday, Judy. The Judy Holliday Resource Center. www.judyhollidayrc.com

Roosevelt, Eleanor. Papers Project. George Washington University. http://www.gwu.edu/~erpapers/myday

United Office and Professional Workers of America (UOPWA), 1929-1957. Papers. Tamiment Library & Robert F. Wagner Labor Archives, New York University.

FILM, RADIO SCRIPTS AND SOUND RECORDINGS

Cooke, Dwight, with Angela Calomiris. Broadcast Script. *You and Communism*, CBS, December 11, 1950. Calomiris Papers, Lesbian Herstory Archives, Brooklyn, NY.

Harding, David, with Angela Calomiris. Broadcast Script, *Counterspy*, NBC, December 24, 1950. Calomiris Papers, Lesbian Herstory Archives, Brooklyn, NY.

McBride, Mary Margaret, with Angela Calomiris. Recording LWO 15577 107B, October 25, 1950, Motion Picture, Broadcasting and Recorded Sound Division, Library of Congress. Recording, LWO 15577 14B, November 8, 1950 (almost identical but expanded for Chicago).

————————————————————————————. Radio Broadcast Transcript, ABC, October 25, 1950. Calomiris FBI File.

Nestle, Joan, with Buddy/Bubbles Kent. Audio tape, January 27 and February 8, 1983, Lesbian Herstory Archives, Brooklyn, NY.

Ordinary Miracles: The Photo League's New York. Produced and directed by Daniel Allentuck and Nina Rosenblum. Contributing Producer Mary Engel. Written by Daniel Allentuck. Narrated by Campbell Scott. Daedalus Productions, Inc. 2012. Film. http://www.thephotoleaguefilm.com

Roosevelt, Eleanor, with Angela Calomiris. Recording RWC 5544 A1-3, December 1, 1950, Motion Picture, Broadcasting and Recorded Sound Division, Library of Congress.

Slater, Bill, with Angela Calomiris and Victor Lasky. Broadcast Transcript, *Inside Communism* (America's Future, Inc.), April 8-14, 1951. Calomiris Papers, Lesbian Herstory Archives, Brooklyn, NY.

NEWSPAPER AND JOURNAL ARTICLES

Abrams, Norma, and Harry Schlegel. "Angela Unveils Big Red Plot to Run Transport." *New York Daily News* (April 29, 1949), pp. 3, 25.

Aptheker Bettina. "Keeping the Communist Party Straight, 1940s-1980s." *New Politics*, vol. 12, no. 1 (Summer 2008), pp.22-27.

Arm, Walter. "U.S. Reds' Plan For Negro State In South Is Told." *New York Herald Tribune* (April 19, 1949), p. 1.

_____."F.B.I. Agent Tells How She Posed as Red." *New York Herald Tribune* (April 27, 1949).

_____. "Pay Is Doubled For 16 Jurors at Reds' Trial." *New York Herald Tribune* (April 28, 1949).

Breit, Harvey. "Talk With Miss Calomiris." *New York Times* (November 26, 1950).

Brown, Robbie. "Civil Rights Photographer Unmasked as Informant." *New York Times* (September 13, 2010).

Calomiris, Angela. "I Spied on the U.S. Communists, A *True* book-length feature." *True: The Man's Magazine* (April 1950), pp. 25-27, 120-132.

Collins, Larry. "Sid Grossman's Escape to Provincetown." *Provincetown Arts*, vol. 18 (2004/05), pp. 79-81.

Gerson, Simon. "Record of Smith Act Cases." Typescript with charts, 11 pp., October 1, 1956, in Gil Green Papers, Tamiment Library, New York University.

Gettleman, Marvin E. "Defending Left Pedagogy: U.S. Communist Schools Fight Back against the SACB and Lose (1953-1957)." *Reconstruction: Studies in Contemporary Culture*, vol. 8, no.1 (2008).

Hutchens, John K. "Books and Things." Review of *Red Masquerade*. *New York Herald Tribune* (November 11, 1950), p. 12.

_____. "On the Books. On an Author." Interview with Angela Calomiris. *New York Herald Tribune Book Review* (November 26, 1950).

Life Magazine. "Communist Trial Ends With 11 Guilty." (October 24, 1949), pp. 21-25.

Logan, Malcolm. "Girl Tells of Red Grab for City's Transport." *New York Post Home News* (April 28, 1949), p. 4.

McNulty, Joy. "Angela Calomiris, 79," Obit. *Provincetown Advocate-News* (February 17, 1995).

Millard, Betty. Obit. http://www.peoplesworld.org/feminist-pioneer-betty-millard-dies-at-98/

Nathanson, Carol E. Affidavit, in Harold R. Medina Papers. Seeley G. Mudd Manuscript Library, Princeton University.

New York Daily News. Red Masquerade, in eight installments. (February 18-25, 1951).

New York Sun. "Reds Crammed on Revolution." (April 27, 1949).

New York Times. "FBI Aide Says Reds Taught Treason." (April 13, 1949).

Newsweek. "Sauce for the Commies, National Affairs." (January 30, 1950), pp. 21-22.

Pegler, Westbrook. "As Pegler Sees It. Margaret Bourke-White Versus Angela Calomiris." *New York Journal-American* (September 18, 1951), p. 3.

_____. "As Pegler Sees It. Girl Spy for FBI Recounts Insult by a Picture Editor." *New York Journal-American* (September 19, 1951), p. 3.

Porter, Russell. "Plan for Negro Nation in U.S. Is Told by Red Trial Witness. Plot for Rebellion and New Regime in Southern States." *New York Times* (April 19, 1949), pp. 1, 14.

_____. "Girl Aide of FBI Testifies of 7 Years as 'Communist.'" *New York Times* (April 27, 1949), p. 1, 11.

Raskin, A. H. "The F.B.I. Planted Her There." Review of *Red Masquerade. New York Times* (November 19, 1950).

Raymond, Harry. "Stoolie Swipes a Marxist Outline." *Daily Worker* (April 26, 1949), pp. 2, 11.

_____. "Mme. Jekyll and Miss Hyde." *Daily Worker* (April 29, 1949), p. 3.

Roosevelt, Eleanor. "Story of Girl FBI Undercover Agent Is Odd." *Washington Daily News* (October 19, 1949), p. 32.

Rosenblum, Walter. E-mail to author (December 20, 2004).

Rushmore, Howard. "Girl Tells of 7-Year Role as FBI's Red 'Mata Hari,'" *New York Journal-American* (April 26, 1949), p. 1.

Santora, Philip. "Girl Counterspy Accuses 11 Reds." *New York Mirror* (April 27, 1949).

Saretzky, Gary. "Remembering the 20th Century: An Oral History of Monmouth County." Monmouth County Library. Interview with Sol Libsohn, Roosevelt, NJ (January 28, 2000) http://www.visitmonmouth.com/oralhistory/bios/LibsohnSol.htm

Schrecker, Ellen, and Maurice Isserman. "The Right's Cold War Revision," *The Nation* (July 24/31, 2000).

Snyder, Robert E. "Margaret Bourke-White and the Communist Witch Hunt," *Journal of American Studies,* vol. 19, no. 1 (1985), pp. 5-25.

Sokolsky, George E. "Urges All to Read 'Red Masquerade.'" *New York Journal-American* (November 2, 1950).

Schlesinger, Arthur, Jr. "Inside Reports." Review of *Red Masquerade. The Nation* (January 27, 1951), pp. 91-92.

Steinbeck, John. "The Death of a Racket." *The Saturday Review* (April 2, 1955).

"Surprise Witness in Red Trial," *New York Herald Tribune* (April 26, 1949).

Trimberger, Ellen Kay. "Women in the Old and New Left: The Evolution of a Politics of Personal Life." *Feminist Studies,* vol. 5, no. 3 (Fall 1979), pp. 431-450.

Winchell, Walter. "In New York. The Press Box." *New York Daily Mirror* (October 23, 1949), p. 10.

――――――――. "In New York. The Orchid Garden." *New York Daily Mirror* (October 26, 1950), p. 10.

Woltman, Frederick. "Girl Photog Cut Career to Expose Reds' Plot." *New York World-Telegram* (October 17, 1949), pp. 1, 10.

――――――――. "Leading Double Life No Picnic." *New York World-Telegram* (October 18, 1949), p. 8.

――――――――. "Cruising Car Best for FBI Contacts, Woman Spying on Commies Found: 7-Yr. Assignment Related in Book." *New York World-Telegram* (November 13, 1950), p. 4.

THESIS

Dejardin, Fiona. "The Photo League: Aesthetics, Politics and the Cold War." PhD Dissertation, University of Delaware, 1993.

Grant, Jimmy Randall. "Louis Francis Budenz: The Origins of a Professional Ex-Communist." PhD Dissertation, University of South Carolina, 2006.

Wilson, Veronica A. "Red Masquerades: Gender and Political Subversion During the Cold War, 1945-1963." PhD Dissertation, Rutgers University, 2002.

BOOKS

Allen, Julia M. *Passionate Commitments: The Lives of Anna Rochester and Grace Hutchins.* Albany, NY: State University of New York Press, 2013.

Aronson, James. *The Press and the Cold War.* New York: Monthly Review Press, 1970.

Baxandall, Rosalyn Fraad. *Words on Fire: The Life and Writing of Elizabeth Gurley Flynn.* New Brunswick, NJ: Rutgers University Press, 1987.

Belknap, Michal R. *Cold War Political Justice: The Smith Act, the Communist Party, and American Civil Liberties.* Westport, CT: Greenwood Press, 1977.

Bérubé, Allan. *Coming Out Under Fire: The History of Gay Men and Women in World War Two.* New York: The Free Press, 1990.

Bezner, Lili Corbus. *Photography and Politics in America: From the New Deal into the Cold War.* Baltimore: Johns Hopkins University Press, 1999.

Biondi, Martha. *To Stand and Fight: The Struggle for Civil Rights in Postwar New York City.* Cambridge, MA: Harvard University Press, 2003.

Black, Allida M., ed. *Courage in a Dangerous World: The Political Writings of Eleanor Roosevelt.* New York: Columbia University Press, 1999.

Campbell, Russell. *Cinema Strikes Back: Radical Filmmaking in the United States, 1930-1942.* Ann Arbor: University of Michigan Research Press, 1982.

Carey, Gary. *Judy Holliday: An Intimate Life Story.* New York: Seaview Books [PEI], 1982.

Carter, David. *Stonewall: The Riots that Sparked the Gay Revolution.* New York: St. Martin's Press, 2004.

Caute, David. *The Great Fear: The Anti-Communist Purge Under Truman and Eisenhower.* New York: Simon and Schuster, 1978.

Cochran, Bert. *Labor and Communism. The Conflict that Shaped American Unions.* Princeton, NJ: Princeton University Press, 1977.

Cook, Blanche Wiesen. *Eleanor Roosevelt, Volume I 1884-1933.* New York: Penguin, 1992.

Cook, Fred. *The FBI Nobody Knows.* New York: MacMillan, 1964.

_____. *Maverick: Fifty Years of Investigative Reporting.* New York: G. P. Putnam's Son, 1984.

Cooper, Wayne F. *Claude McKay: Rebel Sojourner in the Harlem Renaissance.* Baton Rouge, LA: Louisiana State University Press, 1987.

Davis, Colin J. *Waterfront Revolts. New York and London Dockworkers, 1946-61.* Urbana, IL: University of Illinois Press, 2003.

Demaris, Ovid. *The Director: An Oral Biography of J. Edgar Hoover.* New York: Harper's Magazine Press, 1975.

D'Emilio, John. *Sexual Politics, Sexual Communities: The Making of a Homosexual Minority in the United States, 1940-1970.* Chicago: The University of Chicago Press, 1983.

Dennis, Peggy. *The Autobiography of an American Communist.* Westport/Berkeley: Lawrence Hill & Co./Creative Arts Book Co., 1977.

Dew, Rosemary. *No Backup: My Life as a Female Special Agent.* New York: Carrol & Graf, 2004.

Dray, Philip. *There Is Power in a Union: The Epic Story of Labor in America.* New York: Doubleday, 2010.

Duberman, Martin. *Paul Robeson: A Biography.* New York: New Press, 1989.

Ehrenstein, David. *Open Secret: Gay Hollywood 1928-1998.* New York: William Morrow and Company, 1998.

Everitt, David. *A Shadow of Red: Communism and the Blacklist in Radio and Television.* Chicago: Ivan R. Dee, 2007.

Fariello, Griffin. *Red Scare: Memories of the American Inquisition, An Oral History.* New York: W.W. Norton, 1995.

Fast, Howard. *Being Red.* Boston: Houghton Mifflin Company, 1990.

Gee, Helen. *Limelight: A Greenwich Village Photography Gallery and Coffeehouse in the Fifties.* Albuquerque: University of New Mexico Press, 1997.

Gentry, Curt. *J. Edgar Hoover: The Man and the Secrets.* New York: W.W. Norton, 1991.

Goldstein, Robert Justin. *Political Repression in Modern America: From 1870 to 1976.* Urbana, IL: University of Illinois Press, 2001.

Hadleigh, Boze. *Hollywood Lesbians.* New York: Barricade Books, 1994.

Haynes, John Earl, and Harvey Klehr. *Venona: Decoding Soviet Espionage in America.* New Haven: Yale University Press, 1999.

Helquist, Michael. *Marie Equi: Radical Politics and Outlaw Passions.* Corvallis, OR: Oregon State University Press, 2015.

Hiss, Alger. *Recollections of a Life.* New York: Henry Holt and Company, 1988.

Holtzman, Will. *Judy Holliday.* New York: G. P. Putnam's Sons, 1982.

Horne, Gerald. *Communist Front? The Civil Rights Congress, 1946-1956.* Rutherford, NJ: Fairleigh Dickinson University Press, 1987.

Hortis, C. Alexander. *The Mob and the City.* Amherst, NY: Prometheus Books, 2014.

Hyman, Colette A. *Staging Strikes: Workers' Theatre and the American Labor Movement.* Philadelphia: Temple University Press, 1997.

Isserman, Maurice. *Which Side Were You On? The American Communist Party during the Second World War.* Urbana, IL: University of Illinois Press, 1993.

Jacoby, Susan. *Alger Hiss and the Battle for History.* New Haven: Yale University Press, 2009.

Jerome, Fred. *The Einstein File: J. Edgar Hoover's Secret War Against the World's Most Famous Scientist.* New York: St. Martin's Press, 2002.

_____, and Rodger Taylor. *Einstein on Race and Racism.* New Brunswick, NJ: Rutgers University Press, 2005.

Johnson, David K. *The Lavender Scare: The Cold War Persecution of Gays and Lesbians in the Federal Government.* Chicago: The University of Chicago Press, 2004.

Kahn, Albert E. *The Matusow Affair: Memoir of a National Scandal.* Mt. Kisco, NY: Moyer Bell Ltd, 1987.

Kashner, Sam, and Jennifer MacNair. *The Bad and The Beautiful: Hollywood in the Fifties.* New York: W.W. Norton, 2002.

Keeran, Roger. *The Communist Party and the Auto Workers Unions.* Bloomington: Indiana University Press, 1980.

Kessler, Lauren. *Clever Girl: Elizabeth Bentley, the Spy Who Ushered in the McCarthy Era.* New York: HarperCollins, 2003.

Klein, Mason, and Catherine Evans, eds. *The Radical Camera: New York's Photo League, 1936-1951.* New Haven: Yale University Press, 2011.

Korth, Philip A., and Margaret R. Beegle. *I Remember Like Today: The Auto-Lite Strike of 1934.* East Lansing, MI: Michigan State University Press, 1988.

Krahulik, Karen Christel. *Provincetown: From Pilgrim Landing to Gay Resort.* New York: New York University Press, 2005.

Kutler, Stanley I. *The American Inquisition: Justice and Injustice in the Cold War.* New York: Hill and Wang, 1982.

Lait, Jack, and Lee Mortimer. *Washington Confidential.* New York: Dell Publishing Company, 1951.

Lasky, Victor, and Rafael de Toledano. *Seeds of Treason: The True Story of the Hiss-Chambers Tragedy.* New York: Funk & Wagnalls, 1950.

Laurents, Arthur. *Original Story By: A Memoir of Broadway and Hollywood.* New York: Knopf, 2000.

Leab, Daniel J. *I Was a Communist for the FBI: The Unhappy Life and Times of Matt Cvetic.* University Park, PA: Penn State University Press, 2000.

Lee, Janet. *Comrades and Partners: The Shared Lives of Grace Hutchins and Anna Rochester.* Lanham, MD: Bowman & Littlefield Publishers, Inc., 2000.

Lichtman, Robert M., and Ronald D. Cohen. *Deadly Farce: Harvey Matusow and the Informer System in the McCarthy Era.* Urbana and Chicago: University of Illinois Press, 2004.

Mahoney, M. H., ed. *Women in Espionage: A Biographical Dictionary.* Santa Barbara, CA: ABC-CLIO, 1993.

Marion, George. *The Communist Trial: An American Crossroads.* New York: Fairplay Publishers, 1950.

Matusow, Harvey. *False Witness*. New York: Cameron & Kahn, Publishers, 1955.

Maxwell, William J. *New Negro, Old Left: African-American Writing and Communism Between the Wars*. New York: Columbia University Press, 1999.

McBride, Mary Margaret. *Out of the Air*. Garden City, NY: Doubleday, 1960.

————————. *A Long Way from Missouri*. New York: Putnam, 1959.

Mitchell, Marcia and Thomas. *The Spy Who Seduced America: Lies and Betrayal in the Heat of the Cold War. The Judith Coplon Story*. Montpelier, VT: Invisible Cities Press, 2002.

Morris, John. *Get the Picture: A Personal History of Photojournalism*. New York: Random House, 1998.

Naison, Mark. *Communists in Harlem during the Depression*. Urbana: Univ. of Illinois Press, 1983.

Navasky, Victor. *Naming Names*. New York: Hill and Wang, 2003.

Newman, Robert P. *Owen Lattimore and the "Loss" of China*. Berkeley: University of California Press, 1992.

Olmsted, Kathryn S. *Red Spy Queen: A Biography of Elizabeth Bentley*. Chapel Hill: The University of North Carolina Press, 2002.

Packer, Herbert L. *Ex-Communist Witnesses: Four Studies in Fact Finding*. Stanford, CA: Stanford University Press, 1962.

Philbrick, Herbert. *I Led Three Lives: Citizen, "Communist," Counterspy*. New York: Grosset & Dunlap, 1952.

Photo Notes, February 1938-Spring 1950 (Reprint, with 5 issues of *Filmfront*, December 1934-March 1935). Rochester, NY: Visual Studies Workshop, 1977.

Pratt, David, ed. *Celluloid Power: Social Film Criticism from "The Birth of a Nation" to "Judgment at Nuremberg."* Metuchen, NJ: Scarecrow Press, 1992.

Red Channels: The Report of Communist Influence in Radio and Television. New York: American Business Consultants/Counterattack, June 1950.

Roscoe, Will, ed. *Radically Gay: Gay Liberation in the Words of Its Founder*. Boston: Beacon Press, 1996.

Sabin, Arthur J. *Red Scare in Court: New York versus the International Workers Order*. Philadelphia: University of Pennsylvania Press, 1993.

Schrecker, Ellen. *Many Are the Crimes: McCarthyism in America*. New York: Little, Brown, 1998.

Schwarz, Judith. *Radical Feminists of "Heterodoxy": Greenwich Village 1912-1940*. Norwich, VT: New Victoria Publishers, 1986.

Smith, Mona Z. *Becoming Something: The Story of Canada Lee*. New York: Farrar, Straus & Giroux, 2004.

Smith, Robert Michael. *From Blackjacks to Briefcases: A History of Commercialized Strikebreaking and Unionbusting in the United States*. Athens, OH: Ohio University Press, 2003.

Steinberg, Peter L. *The Great "Red Menace": United States Prosecution of American Communists, 1947-1952*. Westport, CT: Greenwood Press, 1984.

Sterling, Dorothy. *Close to My Heart: An Autobiography*. New York: Quantuck Lane Press, 2005.

Streitmatter, Rodger, ed. *Empty Without You: The Intimate Letters of Eleanor Roosevelt and Lorena Hickok*. New York: Free Press, 1998.

Sullivan, William C. *The Bureau: My Thirty Years in Hoover's FBI*. New York: W.W. Norton, 1979.

Summers, Anthony. *Official and Confidential: The Secret Life of J. Edgar Hoover*. New York: G. P. Putnam's Sons, 1993.

Swearingen, M. Wesley. *FBI Secrets: An Agent's Exposé*. Boston: South End Press, 1995.

Tanenhaus, Sam. *Whittaker Chambers, A Biography*. New York: Random House, 1997.

Taylor, Clarence. *Reds at the Blackboard: Communism, Civil Rights, and the New York City Teachers Union*. New York: Columbia University Press, 2011.

Theoharis, Athan. *J. Edgar Hoover, Sex, and Crime: A Historical Antidote*. Chicago: Ivan R. Dee, 1995.

Timmons, Stuart. *The Trouble with Harry Hay, Founder of the Modern Gay Movement*. Boston: Alyson, 1990.

Von Hoffman, Nicholas. *Citizen Cohn*. New York: Doubleday, 1988.

Ware, Susan. *Partner and I: Molly Dewson, Feminism, and New Deal Politics*. New Haven: Yale University Press, 1987.

_____. *It's One O'Clock and Here Is Mary Margaret McBride: A Radio Biography*. New York: New York University Press, 2005.

Weigand, Kate. *Red Feminism: American Communism and the Making of Women's Liberation*. Baltimore: The Johns Hopkins University Press, 2001.

Weinstein, Allen. *Perjury: The Hiss-Chambers Case*. New York: Random House, 1997.

Wetzsteon, Ross. *Republic of Dreams: Greenwich Village: The American Bohemia, 1910-1960*. New York: Simon & Schuster, 2002.

Wexler, Laura. *Fire in a Canebrake: The Last Mass Lynching in America*. New York: Scribner, 2003.

Wiegand, Shirley and Wayne. *Books on Trial: Red Scare in the Heartland*. Norman, OK: University of Oklahoma Press, 2007.

Ybarra, Michael J. *Washington Gone Crazy: Senator Pat McCarran and the Great American Communist Hunt*. Hanover, NH: Steerforth Press, 2004.

Zitron, Celia L. *The New York City Teachers Union, 1916-1964: A Story of Educational and Social Commitment*. New York: Humanities Press, 1968.

INTERVIEWS

Morry Baer

Carol Barath

Mr. & Mrs. Richard D. Bierly

Martin Broms

Miriam (Grossman) Cohen

Marge Frantz

Roslyn Garfield

Mary Johnston

Emma ("Jerre") Kalbas

Jonathan Ned Katz

Arthur Leipzig

Willa Levitt

Sonia Handelman Meyer

Nora E. North

Ruth Parish

Annette Rubenstein

Irma Ruckstuhl

Melva Wade

Miriam Wolfson

Ida Wyman

FBI FILES

American Business Consultants/*Counterattack*

Margaret Bourke-White

Sid Grossman (also War Department, Military Intelligence Division file)

Kenby (Ken Bierly) Associates

Herbert Philbrick

The Photo League

Smith Act Prosecutions Gov't/Angela Calomiris

Frederick Woltman

Lisa E. Davis has lived in Greenwich Village for many years and loves to write about it. With a PhD in Comparative Literature, Davis taught for years in SUNY and CUNY, published numerous essays, and lectured widely on New World and European literary topics. Her novel *Under the Mink* (Alyson, 2001), a film noir tale of gay and lesbian entertainers in mob-owned Village nightclubs of the 1940s, was re-issued in 2015 to considerable acclaim, and has been optioned for a TV series/film. Her LGBTQ-themed short fiction and nonfiction have appeared in various anthologies and periodicals domestic and foreign. High points in her life include meeting Fidel Castro and almost drowning in the Colorado River. Visit Lisa online at http://lisaedavis.wix.com/fbilesbian.